ViRaL

How Friends and Family
Make Us Sick, Stupid and Sad

Prof. Dr. Michael J. Capone

authorHOUSE®

AuthorHouse™
1663 Liberty Drive
Bloomington, IN 47403
www.authorhouse.com
Phone: 1 (800) 839-8640

Published by AuthorHouse 12/12/2017

ISBN: 978-1-5462-1121-1 (sc)
ISBN: 978-1-5462-1119-8 (hc)
ISBN: 978-1-5462-1120-4 (e)

Library of Congress Control Number: 2017915119

Print information available on the last page.

Dedication

To my teenage son, Milo. Being smart is not uncool.

Table of Contents

Introduction

Dissatisfaction, sadness, anger, frustration, stress, and depression are not sudden occurrences. These are conditions that develop over time. There is a clear process and pattern, and there are obvious early warning signs that something is not right and can get worse. When we recognize the symptoms and understand the underlying factors for dissatisfaction, we can address the root causes before sadness and anger manifest into something negative or serious.

In June 2013, I published an article titled *Predictive Monitoring* in the German magazine *Transfers-Advertising Research*.[1] I had spent the previous decade studying consumer behavior at the point-of-sale, because I wanted to understand why consumers abandoned their shopping carts or why they left a store empty handed. I interviewed hundreds of shoppers and learned that the reason for their actions was dissatisfaction. Dissatisfaction exists when there is a gap between expectations and reality. The reality they experienced did not match their expectations. They couldn't find what they were looking for, the store was not tidy, the price was higher than expected, products were in the wrong place, the shelves were in disarray, or they couldn't find assistance. These shoppers reported that they rarely complained to a sales associate. Often they couldn't even find a sales person. Instead, they expressed their dissatisfaction by abandoning their baskets or carts, posting poor reviews online, spreading negative word-of-mouth, and not spending their money.

While shadowing some shoppers, I began to pick up on some nonverbal signals that they were growing frustrated. For example, I observed that shoppers who paced up and down an aisle apparently looking for something had almost always given up their search after the third lap. I also noticed that shoppers who picked a product from a shelf and then grimaced always put the product back. Apparently, something was wrong with the packaging or price. On the other hand, consumers who picked a product from a shelf and nodded slightly almost always placed the product in their shopping baskets. Shadowing shoppers provided some interesting insights, but it was tedious, creepy, and this method didn't provide the data sufficient to produce statistically relevant insights.

I shared the insights of my shadowing exercise with a giant retailer and asked for funding to develop a system to monitor thousands of shoppers simultaneously. My pitch was simple, "On any given Saturday afternoon there are thousands of shoppers in your store, but you only have 60 employees on the floor. Who should your employees help? The happy shoppers or the disgruntled shoppers who will leave empty-handed and complain to their friends? I will tell you which shoppers are frustrated and need assistance so you can prevent dissatisfaction, optimize your customer service and grow your sales." I immediately received the funding I needed to develop a system for monitoring the gestures, movement, actions and even the biometrics of thousands of shoppers simultaneously. Infrared and motion cameras installed on the ceilings made it possible to track a shopper's navigation through the store. Motion sensors and RFID readers, and cameras installed in shelves and point-of-sale displays tracked how shoppers interacted with products. Pulse sensors embedded in shopping cart handles could constantly track a shopper's stress level.

After designing and setting up the system, I began to collect enormous volumes of data. Fortunately, new technologies made it possible to analyze this amount of data and identify meaningful relationships between gestures, movement, and biometrics and shopping outcomes. For example, I identified that an elevated pulse, repetitious movement such as pacing, and frequent blinking were signs that the customer was growing anxious and would return a product to the shelf or abandon a shopping cart entirely. The hard work was identifying the difference between normal behavior and frustration. How much does a shopper's pulse change when they become anxious? How many times will a customer pace up and down an aisle before they give up their search? How much faster does a customer's eyes blink when they are anxious?

The results showed conclusively that there are obvious measurable early indicators of dissatisfaction. The indicators fell into four groups: biometric, interactive, navigation, and gestures. Therefore, I called them *BING Indicators*. Individually, an indicator such as a quickened pulse or a gesture like a stiff lip does not provide an accurate measurement of a customer's emotion, but when these indicators are combined they are a very accurate sign of an individual's unexpressed frustration during the shopping experience.

By secretly monitoring BING Indicators, retailers effectively have an early warning system for abandoned shopping carts, lost sales and customer complaints. Instead of reacting to complaints from customers, retailers can now predict dissatisfaction and proactively address it. This practice is called *prescriptive monitoring*, because we monitor behavior and prescribe a preventive action. As soon as a shopper is flagged in the system, an intervention can be automatically triggered, for example, a sales associate can receive a text message that shows the shopper's location and instructs the associate to offer assistance or a tutorial video can be played on a point-of-sale monitor. Prescriptive monitoring is a disruptive approach to managing customer dissatisfaction, because it prevents it before it is expressed in terms of a complaint or an abandoned shopping cart. For this reason, my research was later recognized by the DWG, a German advertising science society, as one of the most important contributions to customer relationship management (CRM) in the past 20 years.

After creating the BING catalog, I discovered that this approach had broad application. Today, prescriptive monitoring is used in casinos, retail stores, airports, hospitals and in prisons in the United States, France, Israel, and China to identify frustration and even violent tendencies even before they manifest. Predictive monitoring is also used by some automotive and consumer products companies to measure product usage to anticipate customer complaints and trigger proactive customer care interactions. In 2016, we started monitoring patients for signs of physical activity and symptoms of infections. The goal was to make sure that patients in physical therapy were adhering to their exercise regimes so they would get healthier quicker and return to work sooner. We also monitored patients post-operation to identify early signs of infection with the goal of treating an infection before the patient required readmission to a hospital.

The first prescriptive monitoring systems did not capture any personally identifiable information. At that time, facial recognition software was too expensive and not yet mature so the data we collected were assigned to anonymous persons. Personal privacy was not a concern, initially. Today, however, facial recognition software makes it possible to link such data to known persons. I admit that this practice is not only spooky, it is also illegal in some countries now.

At about the same time that I was finishing my research in customer dissatisfaction, I became aware of a growing frustration in my family and circle of friends. I don't think my friends and family had suddenly become more frustrated. I think I was probably tuned in to identifying negativity. I figured there had to also be early indicators of their dissatisfaction, so I started paying closer attention to their behaviors and I quickly uncovered some simple albeit troublesome patterns. I found that frustration was always linked to specific attitudes and decisions. By monitoring these, I could predict some life changing events for my closest friends and family. For example, I noticed a change in attitude and behavior of a friend which indicated to me that he would lose his job. I made this prediction two months before he was actually terminated. In another case, I saw the signs that the daughter of a friend would have an alcohol related incident three months before she was actually hospitalized for an accident she had following an episode of binge drinking.

I knew that hindsight is 20/20 so to eliminate observation bias, I started to document my predictions. I logged them in a spreadsheet and also printed them on index cards, placed the cards in envelopes and then mailed the sealed envelopes to myself. I never opened the sealed envelopes so that the post mark could serve as proof of the date of my prediction. Within 12 months, 24 of my 27 predictions came true, one prediction came true one month late, and two predictions were wrong.

This success freaked me out. I had accurately predicted life changing events like divorce, termination, and illness for my friends and family, but I had done nothing about it. I met with a good friend to confess my weird hobby and solicit his advice. He didn't believe that I had accurately predicted so many negative events until I handed him a sealed, postmarked envelope containing his prediction. I had correctly predicted that his wife would ask him for a divorce months before she actually did. He was perplexed and then very irate that I had not warned him. I explained to him my approach. Every person is motivated to satisfy some need, and friends and family play an important role in prioritizing these needs. I simply paid very close attention to what his wife's friends were saying and doing and how much of it she was repeating. Simply put, her friends were all divorced, single, or going through a divorce and they frequently repeated statements like, "Divorce is normal" and "Marriage is an old-fashioned concept." The first time his wife used one of these mantras away from her friends, I knew that she was no longer just listening to her friends, but she was now promoting their beliefs. Not only had her attitude about marriage changed, but she gradually changed her appearance and her behavior. She was never concerned or involved in managing their bills, so it was a an obvious sign that something was wrong when Markus came to me to get help building a spreadsheet, because his wife wanted an overview of their financial situation. These changes were gradual over months. I knew she was being influenced and I also knew that, with enough encouragement and coaching from her friends, she would act on her knew beliefs.

My friend was popular for his redneck prose and made dramatic pauses and made quotation marks gestures with his index and middle fingers when he spoke the words in quotation marks.

> Markus: I get it. In this case, Kate's friends and family were like farmers who planted seeds or "dumb ideas," fertilized them with manure or "bullshit" and sprayed

them with pesticides or "poison," until they bore fruit "divorce."

Markus urged me to intervene more frequently in the private affairs of friends and family. He insisted it was my "ethnic (sic!) duty." I began to intervene more frequently in the lives of my friends and family, and something curious happened. My prediction accuracy decreased drastically. By sharing my predictions with friends and family, my predictions had become self-defeating prophecies. My friends and family were keen on proving me wrong. For example, I predicted that the son of a friend would drop out of college a semester before graduating. On the day of his son's graduation from college, my friend called me during the ceremony to brag, "I told you my son wasn't a loser, Capone!" A couple weeks later, I happened to meet his son in a cafe. He told me he intended to drop out of college, just as I had predicted, but his father told him, "You're graduating. Please don't embarrass me!"

Just as I had cataloged behaviors that indicate a customer is growing frustrated and will take some action such as abandoning a shopping cart or complaining, I wanted to understand the attitudes and behaviors that preempted life-changing events like quitting school, getting divorce, or being terminated. Why did frustrated people believe and act the way they did?

Research Method

The remainder of this chapter describes my research methodology. You are welcome to skip to Part I if you are not interested in how I arrived at the conclusion, which is expressed in the title of my book.

I used a combination of *qualitative* and *quantitative* methods. I observed and interviewed participants to understand the meaning they gave their experiences and then used mathematical methods to develop statistical models. For the qualitative data, I relied on three sources: online surveys, support group observation, and face-to-face interviews.

From 2013 to 2016, I conducted an online survey involving 107 therapists, mentors, career and life coaches, psychiatrists, and psychologists in 11 countries. The contributors responded to an invitation to support a study titled "Decisions That Trigger Life Changing Events" and were screened in advance to ensure they had professional credentials and to ensure gender and cultural diversity. The contributors used a simple online form to record the answers to the five short questions. I purposely limited the study questions in order to make data entry quick and easy for the contributors.

1. What decision was made or what action was taken?
2. What belief or attitude influenced the decision?
3. Where did this belief or attitude come from?
4. What was the outcome of the decision?
5. How does subject feel about the outcome?

The contributors submitted answers for more than 4,000 patients and clients. No personally identifiable information was captured. My online form purposely did not have a name field. The system automatically assigned fictitious names for easy reference.

At the same time, my research team and I became support group enthusiasts. I still am, although I don't attend as frequently as I did during my study. Support groups are very educational and therapeutic, even for people who think they are mentally healthy. Over a period of three years, we attended 680 support group meetings for drug addiction, alcoholism, sex addiction, depression, anger management, eating disorders, divorce, homosexuality, internet addiction, veterans, self-esteem, burn-out, HIV, bullying, mobbing, single parents, and cancer to name a few. We also attended 92 meetings of friends-of groups and joined 47 different online support groups for many of the same topics listed above. The offline sessions were attended by four to ten persons, whereas the online groups had sometimes dozens of members. When documenting these cases, whether online or offline, we always used the same online form. Again, no real names were collected. When you read a story later about Kate or Tom, these people did not exist. These names were randomly assigned.

All together, we documented 6,850 cases and used several mathematical approaches to analyze the subject's stories. The Word in Context (WIC) method produced some of the most valuable insights. This method analyzes the words subjects used most in their narratives. For example:

> Sally: On my weekend retreat in Santa Barbara we had organic fruit, homemade pumpernickel bread and fair trade coffee with farm fresh milk for breakfast. For lunch, they served organic salad with hand-picked non-GMO vegetables and then for dinner we had wild organic baked salmon and free trade wine.

Using the WIC method to evaluate Sally's conversation reveals three things:

1. The significance of certain words is denoted by the frequency of usage. Sally uses the word "organic" and similar words multiple times in her story, so these words are deemed important to her in this context.
2. The frequent use of words does not denote positive meaning. Sally may have been excited that everything was organic or she may be someone who would have preferred a juicy hamburger and a greasy pepperoni pizza. In the latter case, she may have been disappointed that everything was healthy food. Her frequent use of words from the healthy food group indicates their importance in this context, but she may also have used these words sarcastically or derogatorily.
3. The omission of certain words from a narrative does not mean non-existent, it only denotes unimportant. Sally did not talk about greasy pizza or juicy hamburgers, but that does not mean she did not eat these foods on her weekend in Santa Barbara. Her omission of these words from her narrative only means that these foods played an insignificant role in her experience.

We can apply these learnings to an excerpt from a conversation with one of my study subjects:

Stephen: I love to draw and some of my buds even have tattoos drawn by me. I dropped out of college to pursue my dream of becoming an illustrator.

Therapist: How did that work out?

Stephen: Some friends hooked me up with some freelance corporate work, but I can't survive on it so I've been crashing at a friend's house. He's having a baby and I have to move out in a couple months. I have no real work experience, no formal training and no certifications. I can't find a job. I even got turned down for a job painting houses. I don't know what to do.

Therapist: Why did you believe being an illustrator would be a good career choice?

Stephen: My buddies told me I was really good and when I posted my drawings online, I got thousands of likes.

Therapist: How does your experience make you feel today?

Stephen: I feel like a loser. My friends are all married or getting married, they have careers, houses, and are taking vacations. I wish someone would have kicked me in the ass and told me to go to art college or graphic design school.

A WIC analysis of the conversation with Stephen reveals three major word groups: friend (buddies, buds, friends), work (job, career, gig, illustrator, profession), and art (draw, tattoo). Words belonging to the work group were used eight times, words belonging to the art group were used six times and words belonging to Stephen's friend group were used five times. This means that friends played an important role in Stephen's decision to work as an artist. We do not know if Stephen did any other homework before making his decision to become an illustrator.

Friend
Boyfriend
Girlfriend
Family
Relatives
Parents
Mother
Father
Sister
Brother
Aunt
Uncle
Grandmother
Grandfather
Wife
Husband
Colleague
Co-Worker
Boss
Buddies
Pals
Manager

Illustration 1: Friend Group Words

It's possible that he read articles, studied career reports, visited a college of graphic arts, spoke to a career counselor, and interviewed professional illustrators. But the fact that Stephen did not mention these other sources of information indicates that he either did not consult these other sources or he did not find this information important in his decision-making process. Aside from knowing that his friends played an influential role in his decision, we can also infer that work is now very important to Stephen, because words belonging to the work group are used more frequently than words belonging to the art group. Using the WIC method to analyze the conversations with 6,850 subjects that we documented showed that the top four word groups were friend, work, finance, and health. This means that these topics were top of mind for our subjects. Of the 8.2 million words used by subjects in their stories, the most frequently used noun was the word "friend." Words belonging to the friend group were used in 95 percent of the conversations and in 87 percent of the responses to the question, "Why did you think that was a good idea?" No other noun or word group was used more frequently to explain a decision that resulted in a negative outcome. Friends are obviously very important and also influential.

While the WIC analysis showed what topics were important to subjects and shed light on the source of information, it could not quantify the impact of those decisions. If friends played an important role in decisions that affected relationships, careers, finances and health, what were those decisions and their results? To measure this, we transcribed the conversations into new datasets. Illustration 2 is a sample dataset using Stephen's responses.

Field	Data
Content	verbal likes
Source	Friends
Attitude	follow dream
Action	quit college
Priority	realization > security
Outcome	security confidence
Event	change in residence, change in work
Indication	Developmental

Illustration 2: Dataset for Conversation with Stephen

The Content field refers to the type of information such as verbal, rumor, word-of-mouth, hear-say, social media post, social media like, professional news report, blog article, magazine article, government report, academic or scientific study.

The source field denotes how the content was obtained by the subject. Sources include friends, family, newspaper, new reports, etc. When the subject read the actual news report or government study then the content and the source are the same, but, in many cases, the information, report or post were passed on to the subject from a friend, family member, or co-worker.

Attitude refers to one of the dozens of different value statements described latter in this book. We found that certain attitudes have a significant relationship to frustration: go with the flow, follow your gut, follow your dreams, stick to your guns, winning isn't everything, everyone is beautiful, and money isn't important. These values were mentioned in more than half of the narratives.

The Action field is a short two to three word statement including a verb that summarizes the behavior. Actions include statements like quit job, quit school, rejected medication, got drunk, bought drugs, sold drugs, took drugs, had affair, divorced wife, divorced husband, purchased house, stole money, etc. Stephen quit college to become an artist.

Priority reflects Moslow's Hierarchy of Needs. An entire chapter is dedicated to this subject. Simply put, we have basic human needs including health, security, social, esteem, and self-realization. In this field, I identified the relative priority of the needs described by the person. In the example above, Stephen thought realizing his dream of becoming an illustrator was more important than getting an education and establishing financial security, therefore he prioritized self-actualization over financial security.

Outcome shows what needs were sacrificed or severely compromised through the subject's actions. Stephen's action resulted in his not finding a job, which negatively impacted his financial security and his self-esteem.

The Event field refers to the Holmes-Rahe list of life changing events. A section is dedicated to this topic. In short, Holmes and Rahe identified the impact that certain stressful events can have on psychological health. Many of these stressful events are avoidable, for example, getting terminated from a job is preventable by having the right skill set and attitude, while some of the Holmes-Rahe events are not avoidable, like the death of a family member. A person can control and improve their ability to handle both cases, but our subjects did not and they all sought counseling to deal with a life-changing event or a combination of events.

Indication describes the result or manifestation. These include developmental problems such as long-term unemployment or dependency, physiological issues like weight gain and hair loss, and psychological issues like anxiety and aggressiveness, as well as substance abuse and violence.

In Stephen's case, the information and encouragement he received from friends influenced him to quit college and become an artist. Now 27 years old, he has no formal education or training, he is unemployed and not self-sufficient. His decision halted his personal development. You may think that it was good that Stephen followed his dream, but, as you will read later, if a person can't even provide for themselves, a dream can be a nightmare. Stephen's friends and family promoted irrational priorities, which encouraged him to chase his dream, which adversely affected his financial stability, decreased his self-confidence, made it difficult for him to deal with life changing events, and caused stress.

By transcribing conversations in this manner, we could identify the leading sources of information linked to certain decisions and outcomes and we could answer some interesting questions. What attitudes are linked to stress? What sources of information are linked to decisions like dropping out of college, quitting a job, or divorce? What were the outcomes of getting fired, refusing medical treatment, or starting a family? We could track a negative outcome back to a specific action, the action to some decision, the decision to a belief, and the belief to some source of information.

All of the subjects in my study were in some form of therapy or counseling group. They were all unhappy and frustrated, unhealthy, unemployed or under-skilled, had financial problems, relationship issues, psychological or legal problems. They all suffered physically, developmentally or psychologically as a result of their decisions. Information passed on from family and friends played an important role in 95 percent of the subjects' actions, and more than 90 percent of the decisions were made without seriously considering information from professional sources such as news reports, scientific studies or government reports. These numerous alternative sources were readily available, the subjects may have read these sources, but they were apparently unimportant to the subject and, therefore, not mentioned in 6,100 of the 6,850 conversations we documented.

The results raised yet another question. Why do so many people make such important decisions about career, health, relationships, and financial matters based mostly on information from friends and family? Why, in the information age when we have unprecedented access to enormous volumes of information from many diverse sources and experts, do friends and family play such an unimportant role in our decision-making process?

In Part I-Fundamentals, I answer the question, "Why?" This section provides an overview of the prevailing knowledge about decision-making, motivation, social behavior, parenting, virtues, traits, values, attitudes, assimilation, attribution, stress, and depression. At the end of Part I, I marry several approaches to create a comprehensive view of the social process from birth to depression.

In Part II-Application, I address the question, "How?" Part II is essentially a catalog of stories we collected and then objectively analyzed to spotlight how friends and family established expectations and influenced certain behavior that produced stress and stifled the individual's development. All of the names in this book are fictive. No story in this book is completely true or accurate. All of the stories were altered slightly from the original story to make the subject unrecognizable. Stories were also edited for readability. None of the stories in this book were derived from my personal relationships. To the best of my knowledge, none of my friends, co-workers, neighbors and family members was a subject in my study. Of course, I cannot guarantee this, though. Thousands of reports were submitted by therapists online, and there is a slight chance that at least one of my friends or family members visited a therapist who just so happened to be contributing to my study. Furthermore, my research team and I joined dozens of support groups, so it is possible that a friend or family member was a member of the same support group that one of my research assistants attended.

That said, I wish I could assert that any coincidence to actual persons or events is coincidental, but this would not be mathematically correct. Humans are social beings and we tend to conform. If you recognize one of these stories, it's because these issues are actually quite common. We are not as unique as we think we are. Therefore, any similarity is not some weird coincidence, but rather a statistical surety.

Part III-Treatment answers the question "What?" What can we do? In this section, I describe the contemporary therapies and propose some new ideas for countering the negative influence of friends and family so we can achieve our full potential.

There are thousands of books written about parenting, behavior, depression, motivation, and therapy. I cannot do all of the theories and methods cited in this book justice. I define and briefly outline the significant points that are pertinent in this context.

A filter bubble exists when information supporting a position is made available and all other content is ignored or omitted. It's easy to create a filter bubble. When an author includes a reference section or a list of recommended reading material, they are essentially focusing the reader's attention on material that supports their position. The reference section at the end of this book is a list of the hundreds of sources that I used to support my findings. I couldn't find any material refuting my assertions, which is exactly what someone who intends to build a filter bubble would write. For this reason, I initially intended to omit endnotes and a reference section, but copyright laws require me to cite all sources. Therefore, I urge you to cross-reference, fact check and challenge my findings and I invite you to connect with me on LinkedIn to have a mature discussion.

Part I

Fundamentals

The first part outlines the prevailing theories for explaining social behavior with the goal of understanding why we think and behave the way we do. We look at the decision-making process, a brief background of social theory, the personality, behavior, motivation, social behavior, maturity, stress, depression, parenting styles, and the assimilation process.

At the end of this section, I unify several approaches to explain a contemporary phenomenon, which I call *Social Identity Disorder*.

Chapter 1

The Attention Economy

The internet and social media are the primary sources of information and news today. In the history of mankind, we have never had such ready access to so much content and expertise. Our ability to exchange information so quickly should be fueling incredible progress. But it is not. We have become lazy, stupid, and mediocre. We have democratized intelligence.

Around the turn of the 21st century, sociologists observed that more and more content and information was being exchanged for attention and visibility. They wrote that a growing competition for attention between corporations, politicians, business leaders, and entertainers had changed society. The Austrian sociologist, Georg Franck asserted that material capitalism was transforming into a *mental capitalism* "with bizarre and clownish traits."[2] Franck described a new economic system in which the traditional exchange of goods and services for money was being replaced. He called this new system the *attention economy*. In this bizarre world, attention was a new type of resource like land, oil, or water. And, like natural resources, attention is severely limited and, therefore, very valuable. In this new economy, companies can have enormous market capitalizations, even though they generate relative very little revenue and are sometimes hugely unprofitable. These companies' stock prices are not linked to traditional measures like sales, gross margin or profitability, but rather to other criteria like traffic, members, page views, and shares. For example, Snap, Inc. had, at one time, a market capitalization exceeding $28 billion on sales of just $405 million and losses of $514 million.[3]

Thomas Davenport and John Beck also wrote about this trend in their book titled *The Attention Economy: Understanding the New Currency of Business*. Davenport and Beck assert that a company's competitive advantage is based on its ability to capture and retain attention. Because the competition for attention is strong and humans tend to pay attention to unbelievable content, "a new economy has developed in which corporations and politicians benefit by creating and spreading misinformation."[4]

Artificial Stupidity

A *bot* is a computer program that automatically generates content. Bots play a big role in the new attention economy. Bots are not new. They've been around for at least a decade. There are productive and non-productive bots. The good bots are the worker bees of the internet. They were programmed to automate practical business tasks like collecting data, and many customer contact centers use bots to automate responses to common customer inquiries. Modern bots use *artificial intelligence* (AI), a computer program that automates learning and constantly improves the quality of the content it generates. The last time you chatted online with Brittany from your cable television provider, you were probably getting instructions from a bot powered by AI and posing as a human. This insight probably doesn't upset most consumers, because bots can give answers or instructions much faster than a real human agent in a customer service department.

Aside from the productive uses for bots, they can be used for unethical purposes. Bad bots are mischievous. Their creators are amateur or professional programmers, sometimes government agencies, who use bots to automate spam campaigns, spy on competitors, launch denial of service attacks, perform vulnerability scans, compromise corporate databases and even cause physical damage by hacking a machine or a power grid. Retailers have been using bots for several years to post fake positive comments about their products and services in order to draw your attention with artificially high rankings. More and more, public relations professionals are deploying bots to influence public opinion. They accomplish this by impersonating humans, building networks of friends and followers, and posting relevant content just like humans do, but at a scale and speed that no human can match.

The use of *social bots* became headline news during the 2016 U.S. presidential election. Social bots are software robots that were programmed to automatically create content on platforms like Facebook and Twitter. Identifying social bots today is difficult due to their level of sophistication and the strict data access policies imposed by social media platforms, but it is not impossible. A casual consumer may not recognize that a post was generated by a social bot, but investigative journalists like Patrick Ruffini spent the time to trace posts back to their source. In one case, Ruffini found 500 accounts that had posted identical messages simultaneously.[5] Another investigative journalist, Andrew McGill, used special bot-identifying software to analyze posts made by followers of Mr. Trump's and Mrs. Clinton's social media followers. He found that at least a third of the more than 50 million social media followers of Mr. Trump and Mrs. Clinton were "probably bots" and 25 percent were "definitely bots."[6]

The Post-Truth Era

The fact that millions of Mr. Trump's and Mrs. Clinton's social media followers were actually automated software programs that could even vote seems trivial during a democratic election, but there is much more to these bots. For one, they are incredibly productive. Imperva Incapsula's 2016 *Bot Traffic Report* showed that 24.9 percent of online traffic was created by impersonator bots. Douglas Guilbeault and Samuel Woolley found that one Trump follower created 1,200 posts during the final U.S presidential debate in October 2016.[7] The debate was only 90 minutes long. Posting a comment every 4 seconds is not humanly impossible, but highly improbable.

If humans still dominate the internet in number and the volume of content we create, why are we concerned about bots? Because bots distract from important issues by generating noise and spreading misinformation. Spearson and a team of graduate students randomly analyzed internet posts and found that 27 percent of the posts attributed to humans contained misinformation, whereas 53 percent of the posts traced back to bots contained false information. This is a concern, because misinformation and false information garner more attention than facts. A team of researchers lead by Walter Quattrociocchi at the IMT School for Advanced Studies compared social media accounts of humans and bots. One of the team's findings was that fantastic rumors that offer only a remote possibility of being true spark the most interest and the most shares. Due to the likes and shares made by users and social bots and compounded by search algorithms, misinformation spreads much faster than the objectively researched news published by professional news sources.[8] Another research team from Warwick University lead by Arkaitz Zubiaga found that fake or deliberately inaccurate information is shared 15 times more frequently than true information making the volume of misinformation on internet on any day 100 to 1,000 times greater than that of accurate information.[9]

Studies by Meeyoung Cha and colleagues on the interdependence of popularity and influence in social media showed that popularity does not imply influence and vice-versa.[10] Muhammad Ilyas and his team showed that influence depends on the poster's position on the social graph,[11] while Daniele Quercia showed that language plays a significant role in establishing trust.[12] These initial studies, however, were conducted when bots were less advanced than they are today. When those first studies were published, bot language and behavior was primitive. Today, bots are powered by AI. A more recent study on the relationship between popularity, influence and trust by Luca Maria Aiello and fellow colleagues at Turin University concluded that popularity does denote influence, because bots have become excellent human imposters.[13] They create and join groups, post relevant content, and even conduct meaningful dialogs. Emilio Farrara found that bot behavior is so similar to human behavior that it is humanly and also technically very difficult to detect social bots and that humans easily mistaken them for other humans.[14] Aeillo also found that when bots are popular, i.e. when they have many fans, followers, and friends who are often also bots, they are likely to be trusted. Furthermore, Aeillo learned that humans are likely to follow the suggestion of a bot over another human's advice when the bot has more followers or friends than the human independent of the quality of the information created by the bot. Simply put, popularity implies that the source is trusted and a trusted source denotes the information is correct and accurate. The misinformation created by bots and then shared by humans has more weight in our decision-making process and subsequent behavior than accurate information from a less popular, intelligent source.

Zubiaga also found that it takes on average 13 hours to refute false information, and another scientific study of the *cascading effect* of misinformation by Michela Del Vicario et al. showed that once misinformation is accepted as a belief, it is highly resistant to correction.[15] In other words, even when misinformation is debunked, it is often too late, because many social media users live in *filter bubbles* and tend to seek out and pay particular attention to information that reinforces an existing belief. They ignore information that does not match their beliefs. The British psychologist Peter Wason calls this *confirmation bias.*[16] During the British EU referendum campaign in 2016, the Vote Leave action committee made repeated use of a false claim that EU membership cost 350 million Euros a year. Even though this figure was proven incorrect by the UK Statistics Authority, the Institute for Fiscal Studies, by BBC News and other professional agencies, voters ignored the correct reports and continued to believe the fake news and lies.

Debunking a myth can even backfire and increase the likelihood of misinformation being accepted as true. To debunk a myth, it has to be mentioned. The more often information is repeated the more familiar people become with it and the more likely people are to accept it as true. Ian Skurnik showed subjects a flyer that refuted common myths that influenza vaccinations caused birth defects. Afterwards, the subjects were asked to separate the lies from the facts. When asked immediately after reading the flyer, the participants successfully identified the misinformation. However, when questioned 30 minutes after reading the flyer, most subjects scored worse. They recalled the misinformation as fact.

On November 9, 2016, the news channels announced that Donald Trump would be the 45th President of the United States. A majority of American voters were perplexed, and America's closest allies were flabbergasted.

The German Chancellor, Angela Merkel, stated sorrowfully in a press conference, "We have entered the 'post-truth' era," implying that the age of facts and logic was over. We now live in an age when decisions are made based largely on emotions and fully disconnected from the truth. The term *post-truth* is not new, but its importance became so profound following Brexit and the U.S. Presidential election that the Oxford Dictionaries selected it as "Word of the Year 2016."

Post-truth tactics do not simply include creating and disseminating misinformation or fake news. When confronted with a piece of information that directly contradicts a belief, *post-truthers* use what psychologist Geoffrey Munro from Towson University calls the *scientific impotence excuse*.[17] They argue that the topic is not amendable to scientific inquiry. For example, "Science can't prove that global warming is caused by humans" or "Medical professionals don't know if vaccines are really safe." These, of course, are completely ignorant arguments, because there is over-whelming scientific evidence and consensus that global warming is real and vaccines are effective. When a debate broke out about the number of persons attending President Trump's inauguration event, post-truthers ignored aerial photos and videos showing that President Obama's inauguration was attended by far more citizens than President Trump's swearing in. The White House Press Secretary, Sean Spicer, told reporters, "It was the largest audience to ever witness an inauguration. Period. Both in person and around the globe." When *Meet the Press* moderator Chuck Todd described Spicer's claim as a falsehood, Kellyanne Conway, a counselor for Mr. Trump, said, "Sean Spicer gave alternative facts," and "There's no way to really quantify crowds." Actually, there is a specialized field of study called *crowd science* and I found hundreds of scientific articles describing various approaches for measuring the formation, size, movement, and even the emotions of a crowd.

Post-truthers also make use of *conspiracism*. They attribute fact-based attacks to some enemy such as the establishment or the mainstream media. Mr. Trump used this tactic effectively. He proudly positioned himself as the anti-establishment candidate that hated the media. Clearly, this resonated with voters who desperately wanted drastic change and this meant electing an apparent outsider. Is Mr. Trump really an outsider? The author Rita Mae Brown (not Albert Einstein) wrote "Insanity is doing the same thing over and over again, but expecting different results." If you believe that, then voting for Donald Trump was not crazy, because voting for Mr. Trump, who had no prior experience in government, meant doing something different. He is an outsider in that he has no political experience. But there is an equally strong argument against voting for him, because he is a member of the establishment. The Man is a slang phrase that refers to someone in a position of power. Donald is not just a man, he is the embodiment of The Man. After all, he is a billionaire with a jumbo jet and a helicopter, he owns casinos, golf courses and a beauty pageant, and he's married to a fashion model wife.

An equally frail argument that change is only possible by voting for an outsider could have been made for making Mrs. Clinton the first female president. She is indeed a politician, but she is not a man and certainly not The Man. But facts and rationality played no role in this election. Carsten Luther wrote in the magazine the *Zeit* "The immune system failed, the one that has thus far protected healthy democracies from hollow populism."[18] It is, therefore, fully appropriate to refer to the social bot effect as *viral*. Social bots are indeed infectious and infections are not good.

Strength in Numbers

Bots are not really the problem, though. The bot story serves only to spotlight a human vulnerability that makes it possible for bot programmers to do significant harm. We are social beings driven by a strong primitive need to belong. Bots take advantage of this vulnerability. They are only a threat, because they create the false impression that an opinion is highly popular and endorsed by many. Bots have power, because people believe they have strength in numbers, and bots create an illusion of strength.

When an opinion or piece of information can be rendered fact by popular vote, then it means we have effectively *democratized intelligence*. This is a serious dilemma for the human condition and progress, because (a) true democracy does not allow non-humans to participate or influence outcomes, and (b) knowledge is not democratic. We cannot permit a majority to decide what is truth and fact. History teaches us that popular beliefs are often wrong. Until the 1700's most people were illiterate, and the popular consensus was that the earth was flat, even though scholars since the Ancient Greeks knew the earth was round. Ask any American, "Who invented the electric light bulb?" and most will tell you it was Thomas Edison, although the electric light bulb was actually invented by Warren de la Rue in 1840, when Edison was only 7 years old. There's no real harm in some popular beliefs. Believing the earth is flat and that Edison invented the light bulb do not cause any human suffering. But some popular beliefs are morally wrong and even dangerous. Up until the 1800's, slavery was widely accepted, it was regulated, taxed, and even condoned by canonical and secular law. Europeans and Americans believed that Africans were lower on the evolutionary ladder and this led to their abhorrent abuse. This belief was popular, but obviously wrong. The point is, when we accept negative, harmful ideas as fact or truth simply because they are popular, then we stifle our own and also human development. The following anecdote exemplifies this phenomenon.

A study subject told me his son had decided to drop out of college. When he, the father, asked his son why, his son showed him the following Facebook post:

COLLEGE GRADUATES EARN LESS TODAY
THAN THEIR PARENTS DID WITH A
HIGH SCHOOL DIPLOMA
LESS THAN 20% OF JOBS REQUIRE A COLLEGE DEGREE

The post was classic social media content featuring bold, capitalized text imposed over a picture of an image. It had garnered more than 70,000 likes and had been forwarded to his son by a friend. The son naively accepted social media content as accurate, because it was popular and sent to him by a friend. He shared it in his group and commented "It's not worth the debt. I quit!" In turn, many of his social media friends liked it and posted comments like, "You go, bro!" Misinformation shared by friends did not give this young man the idea to drop out of school.

He was already worried about his mountain of student loan debt, he was severely distracted from his studies by excessive partying and doing poorly. He was already contemplating quitting. The post and then the likes and comments from his friends validated his thinking and his decision. Supported by misinformation from his friends and family, this young man felt empowered and justified in making a bad decision.

Quitting school is not bad in the ethical or legal sense, but taking action based on wrong information is categorically a bad idea. A quick check on an official government website shows that, depending on degree level, college graduates earn 17 to 24 percent more than non-graduates, more than 33 percent of jobs today require a college degree, and roughly 40 percent of jobs in the future will require at least a Bachelor diploma.[19] When his father showed him the accurate data and tried to convince him to finish college, his son grew irate. "Thanks for your support, dad!" he retorted sarcastically. "All my friends are behind me." Dad's information was accurate albeit unpopular and, therefore, it was ignored. Knowledge, truth and wisdom lost to populism.

Chapter 2

The Decision-making Process

We make hundreds of decisions every day. Most are trivial, but some are important like choosing a vocation or profession, taking medication, getting married or divorced, and investing. Throughout the decision-making process we need information. Good decision-making outcomes are based on good information and to ensure good information, we should always consult multiple, diverse sources.

How we make decisions has been an area of scientific and academic study for many decades. Today, experts agree that there are six steps in this process:

Step		Description
1	Awareness	The person recognizes some need or want.
2	Education	The person identifies alternative solutions.
3	Evaluation	The person compares alternatives.
4	Commit	The person makes a decision.
5	Consume	The person uses or consumes a product or service
6	Feedback	The person assesses and shares results.

Illustration 3: The Decision-Making Process

Organizations and corporations have formal processes that usually include soliciting information and proposals from multiple vendors, conducting multiple reviews, and following a formal approval process to assure that the right decision is made. This makes complete sense, because, when we are committing a company's valuable resources, we want to make sure our decision is logical and defendable.

When we make personal decisions, we follow the same process, but we are usually not as formal, strict or thorough. The consumer decision-making process is more a less a natural one. Like many other processes outlined later in this book, the steps in this process are dependent. It feels unnatural to talk about price and terms before understanding features and alternatives. Likewise, it seems weird to recommend a product one has never used. The probability of making a good decision depends on completing all prior steps. Of course, when steps are skipped, the likelihood that a bad decision is made is high.

1. Awareness

During the awareness phase, a person recognizes some unmet need. There are five main need groups that can trigger the decision-making process. These are described in detail later. They include nutrition, safety, affection, respect, or fulfillment. We don't actually need a cheese burger, a job, friends, or an iPhone. We need nutrition, we need to pay rent, and we need love and self-esteem. Food, money, friends and a mobile phone are merely means for fulfilling some need.

The recognition of some unmet need is always triggered by physiological processes or emotions. We may recognize our hunger when our stomach growls, our need for sleep can be triggered by a yawn or itchy eyes, and the need for intimacy can be triggered by loneliness or arousal. It is a fallacy to believe that needs can be created by some external stimuli such as advertising. According to eMarketer, advertisers globally spend more than $600 billion annually to create awareness for their products and services. More than $170 billion is spent on digital advertising and $70 billion is spent on mobile advertising, and the growth rate for digital and mobile advertising is triple digit.[20] On a daily basis, we see more 4,000 to 10,000 commercials, billboards, and advertisements, but we remember and act on few, because most ads promote products or services that address a need which is already met. Ads cannot create a need. An advertisement for a perfume that promises to attract a mate cannot make someone feel lonely or aroused. You may remember the ad, but you won't take action unless your need for intimacy is indeed unmet. Likewise, an advertisement for a delicious pizza or juicy hamburger may capture your attention, but you won't run out and order a pizza or burger if you are not hungry or have some other unmet need that food can satisfy.

We never buy things we don't need. Behavior is always motivated by some unmet need. Admittedly, many of us have things we do not practically need, but we have psychological needs. No one practically needs a Ferrari, a Rolex watch or a Louis Vuitton handbag. Nevertheless, when we bought these things, we did so to satisfy specific emotional needs like intimacy, respect or esteem.

2. Education

Once we have recognized a need, the next natural step is to investigate the options. If we are hungry, we may look around for restaurants, we might ask a taxi driver or someone on the street what restaurants are in the neighborhood, we could search the internet for restaurants nearby, or we could respond to an advertisement that we remember. If we need a new mobile phone or alarm clock, we might visit an electronics store and ask a sales associate to show us the different options, we could visit the internet to see what is offered, and we can ask our friends and family for a recommendation.

3. Evaluate

After identifying the options, we evaluate them. We may compare product attributes like price and availability or consider service and quality. We may review the ratings on the internet, read consumer reports, ask a sales associate to explain the difference in features, or ask friends for their recommendations. The evaluation criteria we consider and the information we collect in this phase can be very disparate depending on the sources we consult. What criterion should we use to compare foods, neighborhoods, careers, partners, cars, colleges and cellular providers? There are no standards and it is completely subjective. It has a lot to do with attitudes and priorities, which are discussed later. Even when it comes to picking something simple like a mobile phone provider, one friend might tell us to compare price, another says to look at coverage area, and yet another tells us to compare download speeds.

During the evaluation phase, we may also attempt to determine value, which is calculated as the benefit minus the cost. This is often difficult to quantify. The value of an insurance policy or a college education can easily be calculated. The cost of an insurance policy is fixed, its face value is stated in the policy and, when insurance is needed, the benefit is measurable. Likewise, the value of a college education is also calculable. Studies by government agencies show that college graduates earn more than non-graduates. If this income difference over a lifetime of working is greater than the tuition, then the college education is a good value, because the benefit exceeds cost. There are dozens of websites that offer return-on-investment calculators to determine the value of a college education. The value of food, a vacation, a television, or a new necklace, however, are difficult to calculate. These things have price tags, but it is tricky to quantify the benefit of an emotion, experience, relaxation, or beauty. It is for this reason that many marketers and politicians use emotional messages to promote their products and themselves. They do not want us to think about the costs and benefits, because these are unclear.

It's rare that we find something perfect - the best quality for the lowest price available exactly when we need it. Because there are usually several options and many subjective criteria, we almost always have to make some compromise between quality, quantity, price, and time. Imagine we are downtown New York City with only two dollars in our pocket, our stomach is growling and we have less than five minutes to our next appointment. Do we attend the meeting hungry and not care if our stomach growls? Do we attend the meeting hungry, because we need the two dollars for the bus ride home and risk embarrassment when our stomach growls? Do we grab something quick to eat to prevent any embarrassment and figure out later how to get home? If we decide to eat something quick, are nutrition, sanitation, fair trade and environment important considerations? In other words, what need value has the highest priority - satisfying our hunger, getting home, preventing embarrassment, making a good impression, protecting the environment, or eating healthy? We may be able to satisfy a combination of needs, but rarely can we satisfy all these needs at the same time. Making a compromise is almost always necessary.

I purposely described a decision-making scenario that seems trivial to show that even the most simple situations can turn out to be quite complex. Surprisingly, we make this kind of decision many times every day. We just do not analyze every situation this thoroughly. We make most decisions subconsciously and quickly. We rely on what psychologists call *heuristics*, a short-cut for finding a satisfactory solution. This short-cut relies on emotions, memories and perceptions. We seldom spend the time to gather and assess enough information to make the most optimal decision and settle usually for the more expedient and acceptable solution. It is for this reason that advertisements for many products appeal to emotions. Marketers want us to act now without thinking.

4. Commitment

We make decisions based on some combination of criteria. Depending on what we are committing to, our decision can be to buy, rent, lease, join, subscribe, enroll, attend, participate, marry, divorce, apply, etc. This commitment creates an expectation. We join the gym with the expectation of getting fit and losing weight, we enroll in college with the expectation of launching a career and earning an income, and we buy a home with the expectation of being safe, sending our children to good schools, and building equity.

The commitment usually requires some transaction or exchange. When we join a fitness gym, subscribe to a magazine, enroll in college, buy a car, purchase a home, or get divorced, we fill out forms and pay money. Some of the commitments we make today are simple exchanges, i.e. we do not pay with money, but with our information and time. This is the case with many online services and the basis for the attention economy. The commitment involves giving the provider information about ourselves so we can receive services in exchange for our time and attention.

5. Consume

After making a commitment, we consume. We do something. We drink a beverage, eat a meal, go to work, train at the gym, read a magazine, meet friends, take a trip, attend college, get married, perform charity work, etc. At some time during this phase we may need instructions, help, assistance, or guidance. We need additional information in order to experience the full benefit. When the washing machine is not working properly, we call customer service, read the manual, or search online for tips and tricks. If we're not doing well in school, we hire a tutor, speak to a teacher or meet a guidance counselor. If we are in a difficult relationship, we can consult a therapist or a relationship expert. If we are not losing weight, we can consult a trainer, a dietician, or a physician.

6. Feedback

Also during the consumption phase we experience something which may or may not be aligned with our expectations. Our decision to study botany or history may have resulted in a good job, a bad job, or maybe no job. The decision to sign-up for a dating service may result in a date or disappointment. If we had a positive experience, then we are likely to rave or recommend the product or service to a friend. If our experience does not reflect our expectations, we may refuse payment, talk to a manager, call customer service, rant on social media, complain to friends, write letters, send an email, spread word-of-mouth, contact news agencies, seek legal action, picket or boycott the business.

The Decision-Making Journey

Throughout this process, we use information. What options exist? What criteria should I use to compare the options? What are the important features and price? What is the benefit? How do I use it? Whether we are deciding where to eat lunch, what career to pursue, what medication to take, or what neighborhood to live in, we cannot make the best decision if we do not have good information at every step in the process. Considering many different sources of information at each step in the process requires energy and time, but it improves the likelihood of having more good information than bad and making the best decision.

It is possible that a single source has all the right answers to our questions, but in most cases, a single source produces only limited or biased information. Ask any manufacturer's sales representative which criteria are important for making a decision about any product and he will inevitably suggest the criteria which favor his product.

The decision-making process is often referred to as a journey and it looks like a map when we plot the steps in sequence to the various types of content and sources of information. Illustration 4 shows how we travel through the process of making a decision, going from one source to another to get information. There are, in fact, hundreds probably thousands of different sources.

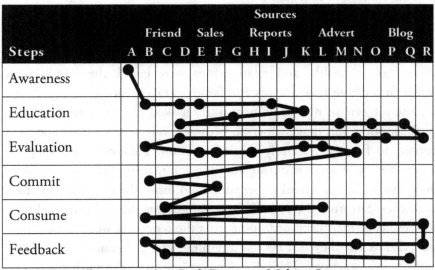

Illustration 4. A Rich Decision-Making Journey

I used column labels A through R to represent different sources when, in reality, they have names like Mark, Sally, CNN, Fox News, USA Today, Consumer Reports, the World Health Organization, the CDC, FHM, and

Vogue, etc. These sources would not fit in the header cells. By the way, Google is not a source of information, but a platform for finding sources.

In the journey shown in Illustration 4, the person consulted 17 different sources representing five different content types (friends, sales associates, professional reports, ecommerce websites and blogs) 35 times during the decision-making process. We can trace the journey step-by-step. First, the person became aware of a need and asked a friend, "How can I satisfy this need?" Then the person asked another friend and then a sales associate a related question, "What are my options?" This person consulted 11 different sources for information about the alternatives. Then, one after the other, they consulted 11 other sources to collect information about features, benefits, and costs. We can see that before they made their decision to commit, they consulted a friend and then the sales associate again. During the consumption phase, the person apparently had questions and consulted five sources for help. The person then shared their experience online and told three friends. This is a rich decision-making journey in that diverse sources were consulted multiple times. Such a journey is important when making important decisions.

This is not how our unhappy and frustrated subjects made their important decisions. My study showed that some of their most important decisions about career, health, and relationships were based almost solely on information from their friends and family. The decision-making process for the subjects in my study most likely looked like the journey shown in Illustration 5 in that the person became aware of some need and then turned to friends or family for information, guidance, and support. Consulting few sources during the decision-making process will likely yield incomplete or biased information and most likely produce negative outcomes. Surprisingly, even though our subjects were dissatisfied with the results of their decisions, sometimes the outcomes were serious, they nonetheless felt they did not do anything wrong, because their friends validated their actions. Their decision was "normal," a word that was used so frequently to justify terrible decisions that my team and I developed an abhorrence for it.

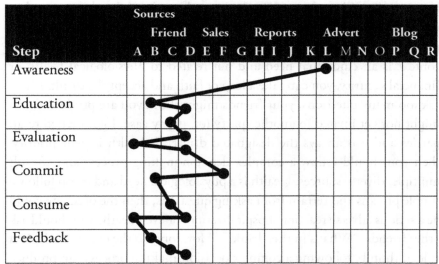

Step	Sources Friend A B C D E F	Sales G H I	Reports J K L	Advert M N O	Blog P Q R
Awareness					
Education					
Evaluation					
Commit					
Consume					
Feedback					

Illustration 5. An Abbreviated Decision-Making Process

The complexity of the journey has to reflect the significance of the decision. High priority decisions like health, security and social should follow a complex decision-making process, i.e. multiple different sources need to be consulted multiple times. As a rule of thumb, needs that we commonly associate with accepting responsibility trigger more complex processes. On the other hand, needs that are not directly linked to health or security usually trigger simple processes. Assume you are at a party, a friend offers you something exotic to drink, and you have no idea what it is. Here are some of the thoughts that might go through your head depending on your priority:

Priority	
Health	No. I need to stay healthy. I have to drive.
Security	No. I have to work tomorrow. I can't afford it
Social	Yes, I want to belong. I need friends.
Esteem	Yes, I want to be cool. I want to be respected.
Self-realization	Yes, I like to experience new things. I am curious.

Illustration 6. Party Priorities

If your priority is to be perceived as a cool person and to be accepted in the group, then you should not ask too many questions and your decision-making journey can be abbreviated and simple. Because belonging in this context is an emotional need and not related to physiological health or financial security, you can take a leap of faith and accept the drink. If you ask too many questions, your friends might think you are prude and you might not get invited to another party (or, in my case, I got invited to all parties and was always the designated driver). If health is your priority, then you should follow a complex decision-making process and consult multiple, diverse sources. Health is a physiological need and if you follow a simple process and refrain from asking questions, then the outcome could be a serious adverse reaction, hospitalization, or even death. You should ask other friends, "What's in this drink?" "How long do the effects last?" As a rule of thumb, following a complex decision-making process can produce some negative albeit seldom disastrous consequences. It's always better to err on the side of caution.

Earlier in this chapter, I mentioned that some marketers and politicians use emotional messages to trigger a reflexive decision-making process. Illustration 7 shows how an impulsive decision-making process might look.

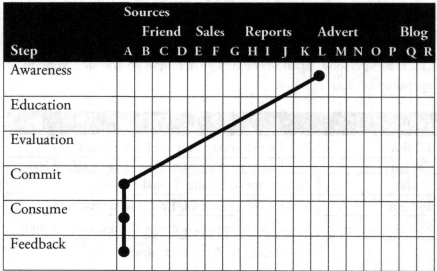

Illustration 7. The Reflexive Decision-Making Process

In this example, the person saw and advertisement and made a rash decision to purchase something without investigating the options. Such an abbreviated decision-making process is fully acceptable when making impulsive purchases for a pack of chewing gum that costs 99 cents, assuming it's not your last 99 cents and your stomach isn't growling. But such a truncated, reflexive or heuristic process will likely produce disastrous outcomes when used to make important decisions about health, career, finances, and relationships.

Coincidentally, my bank recently launched an advertising campaign with the motto, "I am conservative with my money most of the time so that I can afford to be frivolous sometimes." If you are smart and follow a complex decision-making journey most of the time, then you can afford to be stupid, silly, impulsive, and whimsical sometimes. But following your gut most of the time and making important decisions using a simple journey are not sustainable. You may derive short-term pleasures, but you will not achieve long-term stability. The goal of self-fulfillment is to realize our full potential so that we can contribute to society in a meaningful and lasting way. Making good decisions consistently is important for achieving sustainability and altruism.

Chapter 3

Social Behavior

Social behavior is an instinct remnant that grew out of our need for security, i.e. safety in numbers, but we still rely on it today and it can be beneficial. There are several forms for social interaction and these produce starkly different outcomes.

The Evolution of Social Behavior

The most sophisticated form of social behavior can be observed in *eusocial* animals. Eusocial species form and live in colonies. A small number of animals in the colony reproduce, while other colony members provide resources and defense. The list of eusocial animals includes ants, termites, wasps, bees, some aphids, several species of reef-dwelling shrimp, and some mammals, including humans. The colony protects and provides for its members.

For millions of years, belonging to a colony, clan or tribe was important to human survival. Our planet was a dangerous place and membership in a group provided safety and stability. A solitary human was an easy target for bandits or a large predator such as a bear or lion. When humans formed a group, then the individual risk was reduced. In the circumstance of an attack by a marauder or predator, the odds of one individual being injured are 100 percent for the solitary hunter, 1 percent in a group of 100, and 0.1 percent in a group of 1,000. Belonging to a group improved our chances of survival.

Today, we live in complex communities and societies, where people form groups for mutual protection and support. These groups include families, friends, tribes, gangs, cliques, clans, states, and nations. Since the group enhances the members' chances of survival, group survival means personal survival. The individual benefits by supporting the group, because the group reciprocates by supporting the individual. Living in groups involves a balance of conflict and cooperation, which is mediated by the benefits. When the benefits of social living exceed the costs and risks, social cooperation is favored.

Reciprocity is important for the survival and success of the group. In order to remain within the group, members choose to cooperate. This involves accepting responsibilities, sharing resources, and agreeing who will have what task and role in obtaining and distributing resources like food, water, and shelter. It also involves accepting rules, values and beliefs. Cooperation is, therefore, intentional.

Humans have the most sophisticated cooperative society of any eusocial creature on earth, because we extend self-preservation beyond personal survival to group survival and success. Humans are altruistic. An altruistic act is one that improves the condition of an individual at some cost to the members who perform the act. Evolutionary biologists and behaviorists call this the *problem of altruism*. Whereas natural selection operates against unfit members of the group, human social behavior operates on behalf of unfit individuals. In order to care for its unfit members, the group accepts certain costs or consequences such as fewer resources or exposure to dangers for the fitter members.

Cooperative Intelligence

The comparative psychologist, Michael Tomasello, asserted that the evolution of human cognition is based on *intentionality*, which refers to "the awareness of the thoughts, wishes and feelings of others and the extent to which we engage with others."[21] Chimps and other apes act at the level of *individual intentionality*. Chimps, for example, spend most of their days in small groups foraging for food.

While chimps are social creatures and recognize hierarchical and social relationships, their interactions are primarily self-serving. Moreover, when chimps do engage in collaborative hunting, their actions remain largely individualistic, rather than truly collaborative.[22]

For example, chimps sometimes partake in the group hunting of monkeys. In this situation, when a monkey is separated from its group, the chimps opportunistically surround and capture the monkey, a strategy that can only work through collaboration. One chimp initiates the chase, while others position themselves to block possible escape routes. Despite the collaborative effort, only one chimp actually captures the monkey and that is the chimp who consumes most of the meat.

Tomasello argues that chimps engage in *co-action,* meaning each individual is pursuing his own goal of capturing the monkey. The pursuit can only be successful by collaborating, but the fact that the meat is not shared, i.e. those that don't actually do the capturing are left with scraps, suggests that chimps are not quite operating beyond individual intentionality. The hunt is not fully cooperative. Chimps recognize the need for co-action, but not cooperation, which involves performing specific individual roles in the hunt, in exchange for the promise of a fair share of the spoils.

At stage two, humans achieved what Tomasello calls *joint intentionality.* This involves an understanding that the greatest spoils can be achieved by hunting in a truly collaborative manner. When individuals work as a team, there can still only be one captor, but working as a team and bringing down large game means individuals who are not actually involved in the kill are equally rewarded. Their role is, after all, crucial to the successful hunt, and it is the understanding that greater spoils result from pooling resources and subsequently sharing food that characterizes cooperative behavior. Our capacity for joint intentionality appears to be a defining feature of human social behavior. We make collective decisions that affect us and our group. This type of reciprocity is only possible through cooperative intelligence, meaning joint intentionality.

In the third and final evolutionary stage of cooperative intelligence, humans developed what Tomasello calls *collective intentionality*. This type of cooperation involves the extension of joint intentionality with rules, rituals and other social structures that support, sustain, and regulate the social way of life. For example, we pay taxes to build roads and schools, to fund police and military forces, and provide healthcare and other social programs. We make compromises to ensure our safety and also improve the survival and success of the entire group.

Teams

Teams are a form of co-operative intelligence in that (a) the members have a collaborative task, (b) they cooperate to maximize results, (c) the rewards are shared by all members, and (d) the team has roles, rules, and rituals. The goal of team building is to enhance the social relations within a group. Team building is one of the foundations of organizational development and is based on the knowledge that groups performed better when they experience fewer interpersonal conflicts. Team building methods can be applied to groups such as sports teams, school classes, business units, military, as well as, social groups. Salas et al. showed that there are four components of an effective team: an assignment, roles, rules, and communication.[23]

A sports team has the assignment to earn points and win games or contests. Members of the team have specific roles like coach, forward, defender, and captain. The team has to follow the rules of the game like what to wear, where to run, and when to pass and throw. Team members communicate with each other on the field or court using secret codes and body language to execute tactics from a playbook. Military units and business teams are no different. They have specific tasks and missions. Both have chains of command and hierarchal reporting structures with titles like officer and manager. Military and businesses teams follow rules pertaining to dress code, work hours, access to information, signature authority, and budgetary discretion. Both have special vocabulary, rituals, codes, and are famous for the extensive use of acronyms.

Our social group or *cohort*, which is made up of family and friends, also works like a team. A cohort has a mission or an agenda to provide for and protect its members and advance the group's agenda like being the most popular kids in school or being respected in the community. Like a sports team or workgroup, the members of a cohort have roles like leader and follower, which are not always official, but implicit. Some social groups like gangs and patriarchal families have formal hierarchies and roles. Every group has rules that govern what brands, styles and colors its members are encouraged to wear, what foods they are permitted to eat, what they believe, and who they may interact with. Our social groups also have a vocabulary. Although most social groups do not have a printed playbook or manual like sport teams and work groups, the rules and expectations are tacit, i.e. what we wear, say and do is influenced by our social cohort. Whether it is a military, sport, business team or social group, our membership is intentional and we comply in order to belong.

Another attribute of teams is competition. All teams compete against other teams and want the competitor to suffer, lose, or not win. When our team is successful, we celebrate. When we lose, we cry and complain. When the competitor loses or suffers, we are also thankful. The German language has a word for this emotion, *schadenfroh*. It literally translates as *harm happy*. You are schadenfroh if you feel joy when, for example, your friend gets fired or doesn't get promoted, even though you had nothing to lose or gain from the experience. Schadenfroh is sometimes understandable and acceptable, for example, when a member on the competing basketball team misses a shot, but feeling schadenfroh when a member of your own team misses a free throw shot is troubling.

Some experts point out that formal groups like military units differ from social groups in that formal groups are created by someone outside the group like a senior manager or official to complete a specific mission, whereas social groups are always formed by someone in the group. This is not always true. First, social groups can be created by persons outside the cohort. For example, paroled convicts are often forbidden from interacting with other felons, and parents often decide who their children are allowed to play with. Second, the trend to empower autonomous team building in military and business is growing. In some formal settings today, junior managers or officers may pick their own team members.

Humans intentionally form groups and have the capacity to act cooperatively and intelligently to compete against other groups and improve the status and security of their own group, but this capacity is not always fully leveraged. The success of a group is directly related to the level of diversity of its members.

Collective Intelligence

Collective intelligence (CI) refers to "anonymous multi-agent problem-solving."[24] The premise of CI is that the best decision is made when many individuals contribute to the conversation in an environment that allows free-thinking. According to CI, creativity and critiquing come easier when contributors are not motivated to protect some relationship. When the members or contributors are anonymous, they have nothing to lose by expressing their ideas or honest opinions. This does not mean the contributors do not have names like Mark or Sally, identities like SuperCool127 or ChocoDawg, or profiles showing their status and hobbies. In this context, anonymous means there is no membership criterion or formal selection process, and the members have no pre-existing relationship. If they do, it is merely a coincidence.

Crowd-sourcing is based on the CI concept and the making of the Oxford English Dictionary (OED) in the mid-19th century is one of the greatest crowd-sourcing successes, although it took more than 70 years to collect and edit the 6 million submissions sent by thousands of volunteers. It was possible for James Murray, the leader of the OED project, to collect hundreds of different definitions for the word duck, for example, because thousands of volunteers contributed and, by chance, the contributors were heterogeneous. Murray knew who is volunteers were by name, but he did not screen them to assure they had a diverse education, unique backgrounds or special expertise. His success was a stroke of luck. If his volunteers had all, by some strange coincidence, been chefs or hunters, they would have offered similar definitions: A duck is a bird (noun). If the

OED contributors were by chance all soldiers, they would have provided a different definition: Duck means to dive (verb).

The biologist Ernst Mayr argued that competition does not exist and evolution is not promoted when individuals are similar. Furthermore, he asserted that diversity cannot be assured when the contributors are anonymous.[25] Because CI contributors are not screened to ensure their diversity, CI makes it possible to collect many answers, but CI cannot assure that many answers will indeed be identified and, therefore, CI does not guarantee that the optimal solution will be found.

Collaborative Intelligence

The non-anonymous version of CI whereby the contributors are screened to ensure heterogeneity is called *collaborative intelligence* (CQ). The 4th-century B.C. philosopher Aristotle wrote in *Politics,* "A feast to which many contribute is better than a dinner provided out of a single purse." His statement is often interpreted as one of the earliest references to CI, when he must have been thinking about CQ. After all, a feast would be less interesting if the guests had no knowledge of each other and each guest brought the same dish. I actually put this theory to the test. One Sunday afternoon, I called several friends and told them I was starting my grill and going to watch the football game on my patio. I invited them over. Five friends showed up, three brought hot dogs, one brought sausages, one brought potato salad, and they brought two brands of cheap beer. No one brought buns, ketchup, mustard, sauerkraut, pickles, chips, salsa, or soda.

The Good Judgment Project (GJP) founded by Philip Tetlock, Barbara Mellers and Don Moore is a hugely successful CQ platform. In their book *Super Forecasting,* Tetlock et al. describe how they harnessed the wisdom of thousands of experts representing many disciplines to forecast world events.[26] GJP teams are created by intentionally combining individuals with disparate skills and know-how. The assignment for the teams is to predict the likelihood of certain events. For example: "Before 1 October 2017, will Ban Ki-moon announce this candidacy for president of South Korea?" "Will a new Supreme Court Justice be confirmed before

30 April 2017?" "Will Canada legalize recreational marijuana nationally before 1 October 2017? "The GJP results are amazing. The heterogeneous GJP forecasting teams are consistently more accurate than teams of homogeneous intelligent officers, even though the intelligence officers have access to volumes of classified information.

Although CQ satisfies Mayr's condition for evolution in that the diversity of contributors is guaranteed, implicitly some sort of selection will take place. Every group is at risk of experiencing a *tyranny of the majority*. This happens when a majority of the members suppresses a dissenting minority. Tetlock and his colleagues identified this potential weakness in CQ and devised personality tests, training methods and other tools to select and train participants in order to decrease the likelihood that dissimilar, minority opinions are ignored. As long as diversity is imposed and selection bias is managed, the CQ approach can produce all plausible responses and also the most accurate answer to a specific question,

Groupthink

Collective intelligence and collaborative intelligence are deliberate forms of social interaction that serve to optimize the results for the group albeit with different expectations. They are the means to an end.

Groupthink, a term coined by psychologist Irving Janis,[27] is not a deliberate form of interaction. Groupthink forms accidentally when people with similar views team up. It is occurs when no mechanism exists to ensure the diversity of members and to manage bias. When group members are similar and familiar with each other, something Michaela Del Vicario calls *disintermediation* occurs, which refers to the absence of critical evaluation.[28]

Members of such groups are not necessarily all stupid or fully ignorant. They simply desire harmony and this results in conformity, complacency, and the suppression of dissenting viewpoints. All groups have some sort of leader, and psychologist Michael Hogg showed that members of such groups do not follow the brightest person in the group, but rather the most average individual.[29] Rejection encourages the brightest members of the cohort to keep their dissenting opinions to themselves and take special action like amplifying false beliefs or using racial slurs to demonstrate that they are just as normal as the other members. Be honest, how many times have you agreed with or even encouraged something stupid that a friend planned, just to be polite and not come off as a know-it-all? Rare polite gestures do not mean we are part of groupthink, but when this becomes a habit and when we find that we frequently support bad decisions and encourage wrong behavior to preserve harmony, then we need to reassess our membership in such a group.

According to Jarvis, "When a group of like-minded individuals isolates itself from outside influences, the result is an inflated certainty that the right decision was made." This is called the *illusion of invulnerability*, which means "the in-group drastically overrates its own intelligence and decision-making ability, because it sees no other benchmark to gauge itself." There are indeed benchmarks, but the in-group discredits or completely ignores information from the out-group. This produces an artificial strength that can trigger a dysfunctional dynamic. The in-group is not geographically isolated from the world, just mentally disconnected from it. It knows that out-groups do exist and it has access to dissenting information, yet its social identity is so strong that it assertively dismisses and even acts against outsiders in the form of verbal assaults and possibly violence.

One reason in-groups hold such strong negative views of out-groups is explained by *attribution theory*, which sets forth two perspectives for interpreting behavior: an internal and an external view. According to Heider, we are all hobby psychologists and we tend to assign the actions of others to internal factors like character or personality, but when we examine our own behavior, we usually link it to some external factor like environment or situation.[30] If someone cuts us off on the roadway, we tend to think that person is rude or stupid, but when we cut someone off, it's because the sun was in our eyes or we were distracted by something. In essence, we tend to think that people who think and act differently have flawed characters, whereas our behavior is an acceptable response to factors outside our control.

Janis observed that these groups make more polarized decisions than their individual members, i.e. the group amplifies the beliefs of its members. This can lead to disastrous decisions or dangerous behavior. Stanley Milgram showed that people find it easier to offend others when they are remote or not physically present.[31] Through his famous Stanford Prison Experiment, Philip Zimbardo showed that certain environmental situations and social roles, i.e. group membership and role, can strip people of their individuality and trigger acts of sadism, which the individual would never think of committing alone.[32]

The modern forms of assault against a member of the out-group that are rooted in groupthink are *mobbing* or *cyber-bullying*. Mobbing and cyber-bullying involve spreading rumors about a person with the intention of convincing others to dislike and denigrate that person. A study by John Chaplin titled *Adolescents and Cyber Bullying: The Precaution Adoption Process Model* showed that 30 percent of the respondents reported being cyber bullied in the past 12 months.[33] The National Crime Victimization Survey estimates that 2.2 million students experience cyber-bullying every year.[34] Twenty teen suicides have been attributed to cyber-bullying including the tragic suicide of Brandy Vela, a teenage girl from Texas City, who shot herself in the chest after her attempts to stop cyber-bullies failed. The bullies created a fake profile for her on a dating website that included pictures of her, an offer for free sex, and her phone number.

Groups that experience groupthink are not always small, isolated fractions. Large organizations and entire business sectors can experience groupthink. The new President of the United States and many of his Alt-right and Republican colleagues dismiss all scientific evidence proving global warming as a liberal hoax. Even though the vice-premier of China announced at a 2016 meeting of UNEP that "environmental protection and low-carbon development will be top priority considerations"[35] for his country, Donald Trump continued to claim that "the concept of global warming was created by and for the Chinese in order to make U.S. manufacturing non-competitive."[36] This is classic groupthink. Knowledge is dismissed as a conspiracy and some member of the out-group is vilified.

Business sectors can suffer groupthink when managers with specific methods move from one company to the next. These so-called *one trick ponies* bring with them a static view of the market, a fixed portfolio of strategies, and sometimes even the same people. In *The Golden Passport*, the author, Duff McDonald, shows how Harvard has contributed to pretty much every crisis that has occurred in American business and the economy in the last century. By sending a disproportionate number of its graduates to consulting firms, Wall Street, and start-up companies, Harvard provided the ideological foundation for the corporate scandals of the 2000s, the egregious increase in the pay gap between chief executives and ordinary employees, the real estate mortgage bubble and ensuing financial crisis, and even the election of Donald Trump.[37] In virtually every instance, McDonald contends, Harvard provided intellectual arguments to justify its strategies.

Kodak is a famous corporate failure attributed to groupthink. Kodak invented the digital camera, but executives feared that the new technology would render the traditional film business and their fiefdoms obsolete, so they collectively resisted the digital photography evolution. They ignored analyst's reports and suppressed internal dissenters. Change always represents some level of crisis and every crisis is an opportunity, but a majority of Kodak's executives wanted to preserve the status quo. One reporter who visited the Kodak headquarters shortly before the company's imminent bankruptcy described the environment as "complacent."

Exercise in Collective, Collaboration and Cooperation

To more easily understand the differences between these different forms of social interaction, consider the following scenario. A bicycle company conducts focus groups to find out what colors it should paint a new line of beach cruisers. In the first approach, four people are asked about their favorite colors. Their responses are as follows:

Mark	Red
Judy	Yellow
Sally	Blue
Steve	Yellow

This approach produces three colors: blue, yellow, and red.

In the second approach, four people receive name tags and a white bucket containing their favorite color paint. The four people enter a room carrying their buckets of paint. They are instructed to form two groups. There are three possible groups. After forming groups, the teams are instructed to mix their paint to produce as many colors as possible. If Mark and Sally form a group, then Judy and Steve have to work together. By mixing their colors, these two groups can produce four unique colors: red, blue, purple, and yellow. If Mark and Judy form a group, then Sally and Steve have to work together. These two groups produce five colors: red, yellow, blue, orange, and green. This is the same result as when Mark and Steve form a group, leaving Judy and Sally to work together.

In the third approach, the four people receive name tags, and t-shirts that match their favorite color. They are instructed to build a group of three. Judy and Steve will automatically pick each other, because they have something in common, because they both wear a yellow t-shirt, and they will collude to convince Mark or Sally to join their team thereby excluding a color. After building a group, the team is told to mix paints to produce as many colors as possible. The two possible groups can produce only three colors each. Mark, Judy and Steve can produce red, yellow, orange. Judy, Sally and Steve can produce yellow, blue, green.

In the final approach, the bicycle company interviews the participants and deliberately picks Mark, Judy, and Sally to work together due to their diversity. They are introduced to each other and told to create as many colors as possible. They produce six possible colors: red, yellow, blue, orange, green, and purple. This result is possible for free-forming groups, if the members (a) know the assignment and (b) know the other participants' paint colors before building groups, and (c) have an incentive to break any existing relationship or color alliance. These are three big ifs. In short, the outcome is fully dependent upon the level of diversity of the members and the best possible outcome can only be guaranteed by enforcing diversity.

Digital Dysfunction

Based on research from the Pew Research Center, social media and the internet are huge, heterogeneous groups. The adoption rate for people under the age of 30 is much higher than for people over 50 years old, but the internet usage rates by education level, income groups, gender and ethnicity are pretty evenly distributed.[38] The internet was created as a platform for sharing intelligence between universities and government agencies. Today, based on its heterogeneous properties, the internet and social media should be spewing incredible volumes of intelligence, but they are not, because the internet is a form of collective Intelligence in that users are free to form groups and tend to connect with other like-minded users.

The human race has similar characteristics. As a species, we are also incredibly diverse and we should produce amazing volumes of new knowledge and advancing even faster than we are owing to our ability to interact with others and exchange information easily. But our online habits mirror our offline behavior. When we segment based on nationality, religion, race, culture, age, socio-economic status, region, down to cohort, we become increasingly homogeneous and less diverse. Humans are by nature collectively intelligent and, to some extent, cooperatively intelligent, but we are not naturally collaboratively intelligent. We fear and avoid diversity, because diversity represents competition.

As a result, progress has hit a plateau and it appears we are actually becoming lesser intelligent. A study conducted in 30 countries by James Flynn showed that each generation since the early 1900's had consistently outperformed the previous generation on standardized intelligence tests.[39] A similar albeit shorter and smaller study conducted by Thomas Teasdale and David Owen in 2004 showed that, for the first time in 100 years, the results were significantly lower than in 1998. Test results got worse in just six years, coincidentally during the early days of public internet.[40] The initial implication is alarming. It appears the internet is making us dumber, so more studies are being conducted to check these results.

It is worth noting that intelligence tests are a gauge of a person's actual or acquired knowledge and not a measurement of someone's intellectual potential, which can be realized through education and training. Humanist psychologists believe people have enormous potential that can be realized when it is identified and nurtured. Therefore, there is always a gap between actual and potential intelligence. This gap appears to be growing. Our potential has not decreased, but our acquired knowledge has, because we are becoming increasingly dependent on technology and, therefore, mastering less.

Maria Wimber from the University of Birmingham in England conducted a study that shows that the habit of using technology to look up everything "prevents the build-up of long-term memories." She examined the memory habits of 6,000 adults in the UK, France, Germany, Italy, Spain, Belgium, the Netherlands and Luxembourg and found that more than a third turned first to computers to recall basic information like telephone numbers and birthdates. Another study by Kaspersky Lab shows that people have become so accustomed to outsourcing their memories to computers and smart phones that they have *digital amnesia*, meaning they purposely do not memorize information, because they believe it can be readily retrieved from some digital device.[41]

A study by researchers at the University of Waterloo showed that technology also makes us lazy. This is because most of us are *cognitive misers,* meaning we prefer to be heuristic or intuitive versus analytical.[42] Working out the answer to a problem takes more time and energy than searching online for the solution. This creates three problems:

First, intuitive thinking more often produces a wrong answer than analytic thinking. Here's a simple problem: Jim has a 5 gallon bucket and a 3 gallon bucket. How many buckets does Jim have? The impulsive thinker answers quickly and confidently, "Eight." The correct answer is two.

Second, we get used to quick and easy answers and do not develop skills that result from exercising our brains. Try this simple test: A ball and a bat together cost $1.10. The bat costs $1.00 more than the ball. How much does the ball cost? Most people answer, "ten cents," but the correct answer is five cents. Here's the math:

x = ball and y = bat
x + y = $1.10
x + (x + $1.00) = $1.10
2x = 0.10
x = $0.05, therefore y = $1.05

Third, when we are confronted with a problem to which we cannot find an answer online in a few minutes we tend to give up. We do not learn perseverance, which is necessary for invention and achievement. Solve for x, where x = 9 − 3 ÷ 1/3 + 1. In the 1980s, 90 percent of all high school seniors could solve for x without a calculator or the internet. Today, even with internet access and scientific calculators, only 60 percent of high school seniors can solve for x. The answer is x = 1.

Our decrease in actual intelligence combined with the trend to groupthink and our growing digital dependency is resulting in an innovation blockage. Many of the important advances made during the 20th century in mathematics, natural sciences, information technology and engineering came from tax-funded research or popular movements. Indeed, at a global level, tax-funded research continues to grow and it is producing incremental improvements in medical and environmental technology, but the results of popular movements are mostly frivolous. According to the science journalist Michael Hanlon, "Today, progress is defined almost entirely by consumer-driven, often banal improvements in information technology"[43] and the American technologist and founder of PayPal, Peter Thiel said in a speech at Yale University, "You wanted flying cars, you got 140 characters."[44] These "fripperies" do little to advance human knowledge or the human condition.

The Noble Laureate in Economics, Edmund Phelps, agrees. In an interview in *Wirtschafts Woche* in January 2017, Phelps explained that the high standard of living has made people lazy and stifled innovation.[45] The new innovators like Airbnb and Uber have enormous market capitalizations and they are often celebrated as *disruptive business* models at technology and business conferences worldwide, although these companies have done little to improve the human condition and actually have cost many people their jobs and security. Oddly enough, even though innovations in medicine, environment, and energy can improve the human condition, popular technologies today receive more attention and more funding. In 2016, for example, the top 5 biotech IPOs raised $6.9 billion cumulatively, whereas SnapChat raised $3.5 billion alone.

A look at the lists of Most Innovative Companies published by Forbes and FastCompany shows that popular priorities have been corrupted. Although the Forbes list includes some truly innovative bio-tech companies, the list also includes sports apparel and energy drink companies ahead of three bio-tech companies. How can Monster Beverage be seriously considered more innovative than Vertex, the producer of Orkambi, a breakthrough treatment for cystic fibrosis? The list created by FastCompany can't be taken seriously at all. It is dominated by social media, ecommerce, and entertainment companies and ranks Taco Bell as a leading innovative company.

Forbes[46]		FastCompany[47]	
1.	Tesla	1.	Buzzfeed
2.	Salesforce.com	2.	Facebook
3.	Regeneron	3.	CVS Health
4.	Incyte	4.	Uber
5.	Alexion	5.	Netflix
6.	Under Armyour	6.	Amazon
7.	Monster Beverage	7.	Apple
8.	Unilever	8.	Alphabet
9.	Vertex	9.	Black Lives Matter
10.	BioMarin	10.	Taco Bell

Illustration 8. World's Most Innovative Companies 2016

I did not deliberately pick these lists to prove my point that popular priorities are corrupted. I simply searched online for the phrase "most innovative companies" and the search engine presented links to these lists. This is what search engines do wrong. They do not display the best results. They display the most relevant results based on popularity and this can validate wrong perceptions. In order to find a list of the really important innovative companies, i.e. the ones that can have a significant impact on the human condition, you have to deliberately use Boolean logic to filter the results.

Managed Diversity

That is exactly what is missing from popular discourse today. We need a filter or some mechanism that can assure diversity and the accuracy of information. In society and in social media, groups are free to form. Through confirmation bias and selective content exposure, the group insulates itself from outside influences, search engine algorithms exacerbate this situation by displaying links to the most popular content, the *filter bubble* blocks dissenting information and the resulting *echo chamber* enables rumors and fallacies to foster. This is not the kind of filter we need. If someone searches online for the words cook meth, we really don't want them to immediately find dozens of step-by-step recipes and simple instructional videos for producing crystal methamphetamine, but rather some words of caution against using drugs.

The GJP organizers developed an immune system against groupthink. I call it *managed diversity*. Some experts assert that access and exposure to diversity are sufficient to produce intelligent outcomes, but access and exposure are not enough. Users of the internet are already able to read dissimilar opinions and get information from different sources. But we often don't. Only by imposing and managing diversity can we minimize groupthink, guarantee intelligent outcomes, and promote progress that matters. Furthermore, to combat the volume of fake information, managing diversity also entails implementing some measures to enable screening information such as dating all content, clearly classifying it as commentary or fact, and citing the author and any sources. Regarding the two lists above, Forbes and FastCompany are major publications, yet neither bothered to date their lists, describe their methods, or provide the authors' names.

Imposing diversity is exactly what the monk Greg Mendel, the father of modern genetics, did in the late 1800's when he conducted experiments crossing different breeds of pea plants to produce hybrids. Mendel's intent was not to produce better peas, but to understand how diversity works. His experiments established the rules of heredity and today genetically modified crops account for more than 90 percent of all produce in America.[48] By inserting traits that do not occur naturally, many crops today are resistant to certain pests, some diseases, and also harsh environmental conditions. A 2014 analysis showed that genetically manipulated crops reduced the use of chemical pesticides by 37 percent, increased crop yields by 22 percent, and improved farmer profits by 68 percent.[49] Diversity is effective.

The school desegregation program started up in the United States in the 1970's is another good example of the benefits of managed diversity. Back then, in a federal program known as *forced bussing*, black children were transported on buses and placed in integrated classrooms with white children. A 2011 study by the Berkeley public policy professor Rucker C. Johnson concluded that "black youths who spent five years in desegregated schools earned 25 percent more than those who never had that opportunity. Now in their 30's and 40's they are also healthier - the equivalent of being seven years younger."[50] Unfortunately, the benefits of forced diversity via bussing were only recently validated. Early reports were not positive and the practice was stopped. According to Megan McCardle, the biggest problem was self-interest. White parents worried that integration would lower performance standards and decrease their property values. Whites were not the only group against desegregation. Many black leaders like the Wisconsin Democratic Representative Annette Williams and Cleveland Mayor Michael White believed it was "patronizing to think that minority students need to sit next to a white student to learn."[51] Many black parents were not happy about bussing their children miles away to schools in unfamiliar neighborhoods. If they only knew today the long-term benefits patronization or managed diversity would produce.

In summary, a remnant instinct drives us to form groups, because we feel safe in numbers and can accomplish more when we cooperate with others. The data shows that our society has evolved into a technology-based dysfunctional state of comfort and complacency. It is ironic that cooperative intelligence enabled humans to build societies that are so proficient at protecting and providing for most of its members, that intelligence and competition are no longer requirements for survival. Such a paradoxical state was forecast by science fiction writers and movie producers, in one case, more than a century ago.

H.G. Wells described an analogous society back in 1895 in *The Time Machine*. In his book, an inventor tests builds a time machine and travels thousands of years into the future, where he meets a childlike people called the Eloi. His attempts to communicate with these kind and meek people are hampered by their lack of curiosity and ambition. The traveler speculates that they are the result of humanity conquering nature with technology and creating a world in which strength and intellect are no longer required for survival. The time traveler concludes that intelligence is the response to competition. With no real challenges facing the Eloi, they lost their intelligence and physical fitness.

The bleakest portrayal was made in the 2006 satirical film titled *Idiocracy,* which the Los Angeles Times described as a "spot on" and "hilarious vision of an American future." In the film, an average army corporal, Joe, is selected to undergo suspended animation. Average Joe awakens 500 years in the future and finds that mankind has become stupid. "Genetic engineering could not correct the evolutionary trend, because the greatest minds and resources where focused on conquering hair loss and prolonging erections."[52] Everyone speaks like a redneck, the President of the United States of America is an All Star Wrestler, crops are irrigated with an energy drink, and everyone thinks Joe is a "faggot," because he can articulate himself well. Producer Mike Judge was recently asked how he had so accurately predicted the dystopian future of America. His answer was, "I was 450 years off!"[53]

And recently, singer Katy Perry called attention to this dilemma in her song *Chained to the Rhythm,* which some reporters and critics described as "politically charged." Here are some of the lines from her song:

> Are we crazy?
> So comfortable, we live in a bubble.
> So comfortable, we cannot see the trouble.

> Happily numb. Your rose-colored glasses on.
> Stumbling around like a wasted zombie.
> Keep sweeping it under the mat
> Thought we could do better than that

H.G. Wells predicted what would happen in the absence of competition, Mike Judge forecast the impact of popularism on society, and Katy Perry is calling us out on our complacency. When the benefits of social behavior exceed the costs, social cooperation is favored. Conversely, when the costs exceed the benefit, then the form of social cooperation and group membership need to be questioned.

Chapter 4

Mature Personalities

We need information through-out the decision-making process. Good decisions are based on good information and consulting diverse sources improves the quality of information, the decisions we make and the outcomes of those decisions. Because needs trigger the decision-making process, how we prioritize needs plays an important role in our behavior and outcomes.

All Behavior is Motivated

Over the past 70 years, several different models have been set forth to explain behavior. Basically, the models make similar claims that all behavior is motivated by some deficit. We buy food to satisfy hunger or prevent hunger. We work hard to prevent failure or achieve certain goals. Everything we say and do is provoked by some scarcity or a fear of scarcity. The glass is half empty or almost empty. Even when someone acts on behalf of others, their actions are provoked by some perceived deficiency, meaning they perceive something is not fair or equitable for others. The glass is half empty, when it should be full.

The simple insight that all behavior is motivated by some deficit helps us to understand and deal with others more effectively. Someone who complains a lot or is especially demanding is usually compensating for a loss of control in other areas of their life. The person who boasts is usually compensating for low self-esteem. The person who is rude and aggressive is asserting themselves to satisfy some insecurity. Contrarily, someone who rarely complains feels generally in control, the person who never boasts is confident, and someone who is always kind, even when confronted by rude people, feels secure.

All behavior is motivated by a deficit, but it is sometimes unclear which need someone is trying to satisfy. Simple acts like eating a salad instead of a hamburger can have deeper meanings. There can be many different motivations for eating a salad. The person may not have time to eat or could be very hungry and a salad is the fastest item that can be served, the person may want to get healthy or lose weight. The person could be on a special medical diet, could be a vegetarian, or maybe the salad-eater just didn't know the restaurant has really good hamburgers. Likewise, not everyone who drives a luxury sports car or wears an expensive Rolex watch is trying to impress others. The decision to buy something expensive or luxurious can be motivated by a sense of security that comes from investing in top quality products, a respect for beauty, or a desire to project status or membership. One luxury handbag company argued that buying its fine, handmade products was better for the environment, because they were timeless, they lasted longer and would be handed down versus being thrown away. The advertisement featured a large pile of broken and worn handbags from the competitors to communicate the environmental impact of buying cheap products.

Murray	Moslow	Alderfer	Herzberg	McClelland
Autonomy	Self-Actualization	Growth	Ambition	Ambition
Accomplish	Esteem			Power
Emotional	Social	Relationship	Reward	Social
Control	Security	Existence		
Pain Avoidance	Physiological			

Illustration 9. Various Approaches to Understanding Behavior

Another assertion common for all behavioral models is that only one need can be addressed at a time. You may perceive many deficits in your life. Maybe you aren't healthy, you don't sleep well, you work too hard, you do not earn enough money, your relationship is imperfect, and global warming is concerning you. There are actions you can take that can empower you to address multiple deficiencies. For example, getting a very good education can help you to get a better job, earn more money, buy a better mattress, eat healthier food and buy an electric car, but you can only address one specific need at a time. You have to start somewhere and satisfy one need before you can turn your focus to fulfilling another.

Aside from the obvious difference that Alderfer, Herzberg, and McClelland combine needs into fewer groups, the main difference lies in their intent. Moslow's intent was to explain mature behavior, whereas the other models explain normal behavior. Moslow's model provides strict guidance for incremental personal development because the needs "are interrelated rather than sharply separated."[54] Accordingly, lower physiological needs must be satisfied as a prerequisite for fulfilling higher needs like esteem or self-actualization. Because the needs are interrelated, a deficiency at the lower level cannot be compensated for by fulfilling a higher level need. The fulfillment of higher level needs is dependent on lower need fulfillment. Simply put, buying a new Rolex when you are hungry may make you feel happy for a while, but you will eventually succumb to your hunger and have to sell your fancy watch. According to Moslow, in order to achieve our full potential, we have to act logically and incrementally. The other models do not prescribe interrelated needs, because they explain normal behavior and it is normal to act irrationally.

A Healthy Psychology

Moslow produced his valuable insights by taking a different approach. In the 1950's, when his colleagues were all busy studying mentally unhealthy people, Moslow wrote, "the study of crippled, stunted, immature, and unhealthy specimens can yield only a cripple psychology and a cripple philosophy."[55] Moslow, like all humanist psychologists, believed that every person has enormous potential and a strong desire to realize their full potential. Every person is born with some skill or talent which needs to be discovered and fostered. If you do not feel special or gifted today, then you just have not yet discovered your ability.

Moslow wanted to understand how exemplary people achieved their full potential. Instead of studying neurotic, psychotic, and mentally ill people, Moslow studied mentally healthy, altruistic, over-achievers. His subjects were academicians, authors, scientists, doctors, and politicians like Albert Schweizer and Albert Einstein. Income and wealth were not selection criteria for Moslow's study subjects, because Moslow was not trying to understand the relationship between mental health and income, or wealth and happiness. Moslow wanted to understand what motivated these model citizens and altruistic over-achievers if not compensation, prestige, or power. In other words, how did these exceptional people resist the temptations of consumerism and popular opinion to achieve their individual potential and become extraordinary people.

Moslow referred to his subjects as mature personalities in that they had mastered the fulfillment of their needs and reached a sustained and selfless stage called *self-actualization* or *self-realization*. In this stage of life, the mature personality turns their talents and energies to improving the human condition through advocacy, by developing new insights, advancing knowledge, or through community service without an expectation of compensation or personal benefit such as status or power.

That each of us has enormous potential does not mean that everyone can become whatever they set their mind to. This is a dangerous fallacy just like the silly belief that everyone is special, everybody is beautiful or every person is valuable. From the humanist perspective, we all have the potential to be special and desire to be exceptional, but the simple fact is, many of us have not recognized our talents, have not yet achieved our full potential, and are not beautiful and valuable today. To be clear, we all have enormous potential, we can all be special, but many of us are not special yet. Frankly, right now many of us are stupid, ugly, mean or ordinary.

Moslow 2.0

Moslow's work provides excellent guidelines for achieving our full potential, and there are some areas where I would like to update Moslow's approach.

First, at one point in his study Moslow observed college students, concluded they were not mature and disqualified them from further observation, because he used the terms *mature* and *self-actualization* inter-changeably. For Moslow, a mature personality had achieved self-actualization and a self-actualized person was mature. I assert that maturity and self-actualization are not inter-changeable terms and that maturity is a mindset or thought process, whereas self-realization is a state, which can only be achieved with a mature mindset. In this sense, a young person can have a mature personality and be on track to achieve self-actualization if they deliberately address their needs in a logical sequence. As a professor, I taught in America, Germany, France, and Palestine and met many young people who had mature mindsets. While some students used their student loan money to buy new cars and pay for spring break, the mature students paid tuition, budgeted for foreign summer internships and even supported community service projects.

Second, Moslow observed that his subjects coincidentally followed similar priorities and rules, which they had not written down anywhere, so he concluded that having rational priorities must have been the result of maturation. That is why older persons were, in his eyes, better equipped to achieve self-actualization. I agree that learning from experiences is a long arduous process, but there is an expeditious route. Studying history is faster, less painful and less expensive. It turns out that the priorities Moslow observed had been documented many times throughout history, and I found century old evidence describing them. For example, in Europe in the 1700's, an *honorable merchant* system[56] was established, which set forth clear guidelines for membership in guilds. One of the most beautiful and clearest examples of this merchant tradition can be viewed in the City Hall in Hamburg, Germany, where a series of enormous frescos painted by Hermann de Bruycker in the 1870's depict the stages in the life of a model citizen. The first panel features a young man leaving his parents' home to begin an apprenticeship. The second panel shows the apprentice exploring the world, seeking out and learning from different masters. The third panel shows the man returning from his adventures and graduating. In the fourth panel, the man is portrayed as a successful merchant, he marries, starts a family and builds a home. The fifth panel shows the accomplished man teaching young apprentices his trade, and the final panel depicts him sharing his knowledge with a group. Moslow's subjects probably didn't coincidentally acquire the same priorities through a hard life of trial and error, but rather through reading, after all, they were all educated people.

Third. Moslow frequently refers to mature personalities as healthy and calls immature personalities unhealthy. Moslow obviously used the word unhealthy to describe psychological development. I do not claim that immature people are psychologically ill, although an immature mindset can certainly lead to physiological and also psychological illnesses. The person who buys a Rolex watch when their children are hungry and need new shoes is not sick or mentally ill, just very immature and probably at least a little stupid.

Everyone has enormous potential and consciously or subconsciously desires to achieve their potential, but some people have simply not yet recognized their unique talents and learned priorities. Such people are not mentally ill, they are simply psychologically immature, and the root of their problem is often external. Environment, especially parenting and friends, plays a critical role in our psychological development. Just like it is wrong to categorically call someone who has never heard of Jesus or Mohammed a sinner or an infidel, it is a mistake to say an immature person is mentally sick. At the risk of sounding like a preacher or a cult leader, if you are frustrated with your state in life, it's usually because you have not been shown the way.

A Mature Mindset

Through my study of Moslow's writings and notes, I identified three key aspects that enabled Moslow's mature persons to achieve their full potential: traits, method, and rules.

1. Traits

Reflective

Here's a fun test of the reflexive or reflective mindset. Hold both hands up in front of a friend and show all your fingers spread out like in Illustration 10. Ask your friend, "How many fingers do I have?" Your friend should answer promptly, "Ten." Then reply, "You're fast. So, how many fingers would I have if I had ten hands?" The impulsive, reflexive person will answer quickly, "One hundred." Don't respond if the answer is wrong. It could take some time before they realize that the correct answer is fifty. After all, a hand has five fingers, therefore, ten hands have fifty fingers.

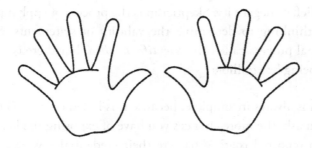

Illustration 10. How many fingers do ten hands have?

Impulsiveness is the most obvious sign of an immature personality and one of the prime examples is the terribly annoying *ad hominem* argument. It has the following structure:

>Jill: That suit is ugly. Do you have a newer suit?
>Jack: Well, you look fat in that dress.

The immature person, in this case Jack, responds immediately to anything that sounds like a critique by insulting the other person. Of course, the insult does not change the fact that Jack's suit is ugly and old and is not an answer to Jill's question, but rather an immature attempt to discredit Jill and change the subject.

Skeptical

Mature personalities are skeptical. They are able to differentiate between fact and fiction. They have a more objective and accurate perception of reality. They are not easily tricked or persuaded. They are not gullible.

Susan told me her co-workers were very confident Donald Trump would win the U.S. election, because "even the Pope voted for him," they claimed. When Susan heard this, she smirked, but said nothing. Her colleagues were confused by her grin and silence. "What's so amusing?" they asked. "I thought you had to be a U.S. citizen to vote," she answered.

It is a common misconception that skeptics are people who disbelieve everything. The true meaning of the skepticism has nothing to do with doubt, disbelief, or negativity. Skepticism is the process of applying reason and critical thinking to determine the validity of statements. Skeptics follow a formal process called the *scientific method,* but there is a simpler method for being less gullible.

First, a myth is always incomplete, because it is based on a lie. The more questions you ask, the more chances you have of exposing the lie. Dig for details. Who reported that? What are their credentials? Where did the Pope vote? When did he vote? Did he vote by mail-in ballot? Was the voting form in English or Spanish? When Susan dug deeper, her friends had to admit that the Pope Voted for Trump story had to be a rumor, because a professional news report would have had answers to at least some of these questions. No important decision should be based on incomplete information or rumor.

Second, conduct a quick fact check. During the Salem Witch Trials in 1692, spreading rumors that caused mass hysteria was easy, because there was only one official source of information and the owners of the local newspapers had a political agenda. Today, we do not have this problem. We have the internet and, even though every website, news agency, and blog has some agenda, we have access to and can read all of them. It's amazing how quick and easy we can find information online. I googled "did pope vote for Donald" and found several sources of information, including FactCheck.org, which is supported by the Annenberg Foundation. I also found information on FactCheck that refuted some Democratic narratives, which indicated to me that the website is politically neutral. The mission statement on the Annenberg website states, "We are a nonpartisan, nonprofit consumer advocate for voters that aims to reduce the level of deception and confusion in U.S. politics."[57] This website is a professional and reliable source, and it took me less than 59 seconds to shed doubt on the fake Pope story.

You can't fact check everything and so you have to ask yourself if the information really matters. Does it matter if the Pope or Madonna voted for or against Donald Trump? Madonna is an entertainer and her opinion may influence some fans, but she is not a political force like other entertainers, for example Oprah Winfrey. I paid attention to the Pope story, because the Pope has many more followers than Madonna, he is a religious leader and has significant political influence, and the story contradicted what I believed about American election rules.

We should also spend some time fact checking our beliefs to ensure they are true. I always admired Alfred Nobel, the man who established the Nobel Prizes. I always believed he donated his fortune, because he felt guilty that his invention of dynamite had made him so wealthy. When I fact checked this, just for fun, I learned that Nobel was not as altruistic as I had believed. As it turns out, Alfred Nobel's brother died in 1988, and a French newspaper erroneously published Alfred's obituary condemning him for his invention of dynamite and calling him the "Merchant of Death." Alfred Nobel was distraught over how he was portrayed in the press and concerned about how he would be remembered.[58] His decision to donate most of his estate was not motivated by some sense of social responsibility, as I had believed, but by vanity. Nonetheless, I am still an admirer of Nobel, although some of the committee's picks in the past years have been curious.

Also, it is always a good idea to fact check topics that are controversial or about which people are very passionate. The numerous mass shootings in the last decade have triggered a heated debate over the second amendment to the U.S. Constitution. This amendment reads, "A well-regulated militia, being necessary to the security of a free state, the right of the people to keep and bear arms, shall not be infringed." Many people argue that it grants individuals the right to own and carry guns and they even call themselves constitutionalists, although a strict constitutional interpretation clearly only permits individual ownership as it pertains to membership in a militia. A series of rulings by the U.S. Supreme Court in the 20th century authorized individual gun ownership for recreational purposes. After fact checking this, it's obvious that advocates for individual gun ownership are not constitutionalists. Furthermore, the NRA opponents cannot argue that the second amendment does not permit the ownership of military-style assault rifles, because these are exactly the type of arms that are required by a militia and necessary to secure a free state.

Skepticism is not simply about debunking statements using scientific methods or rational thinking. Skepticism is about redirecting attention and resources away from superstition and popular misinformation toward projects and ideas that are proven to be beneficial to humanity. Not all skeptics are real skeptics. Richard Wilson wrote in his book *Don't Get Fooled Again* that some "skeptics are disguised dogmatist who cherry pick facts to defend [an] ideological position," [59] such as the deniers of the Holocaust and climate change. An easy way to defeat the bogus skeptic is to ask if denying it is in any way beneficial to humanity. For example, does denying climate change have any benefits for humanity? Even if climatologists got it wrong and global warming is a hoax, would it nonetheless be beneficial to humanity to decrease waste and pollution? In the presence of any doubt or absence of conclusive scientific evidence, we should always err on the side of humanity.

Open-Minded

Mature personalities are accepting and tolerant of diversity and the unknown. They are open-minded, have had many unique experiences and actively seek new experiences. This curiosity is often misinterpreted as irresponsible and dangerous.

Samantha: When our girls were 7 and 10 years old, we took them out of school to move to Costa Rica for a year. When we returned to our home town, our girls could speak fluent Spanish and they made friends with some of the Spanish-speaking children. Two years later, Jack, my husband and I started planning another long adventure, this time to Asia. The other parents accused us of being irresponsible and dangerous parents. "Your girls have been bitten by monkeys and they've eaten donkey. That's not normal!" They mobbed us, but we were not deterred. We knew their girls would benefit from such experiences.

Being open-minded is easier to practice when we are alone. Robert Kraut and Robert Johnson at Cornell University conducted studies that show that we act differently when we are with others.[60] They watched thousands of frames of bowling and observed that bowlers who did well rarely smiled when they were alone or had their backs to other players, but they always smiled when they did well and were facing other players. There are two explanations for the differences in behavior. First, the bowlers smiled when they did well and were facing other players, because they were happy and wanted to show or share their happiness. Second, they smiled because it was expected and they didn't want to be perceived as arrogant. I was interested in knowing why the bowlers who did well and were alone did not smile as much, so I went to a bowling alley and asked some lonely bowlers this exact question. Their answer was simple. They were analyzing their movement in their heads trying to understand what they did right so they could repeat it. Of the dozens of bowlers I talked to, all of them agreed that they bowled better alone, because they could focus.

The internet is rich with videos, music, and content that can introduce you to different cultures and ideas. The challenge is making time for yourself to explore and insulated from any distraction or scrutiny of others.

Tom: I'm a second screener. When I watch t.v., I always have my tablet on my lap to check things online like the profiles of the actors, the dates of historical events, or the location of scenes. My wife and I were matching a movie where these guys were fist bumping each other. One of the guys said 'fist me harder,' and the other guy said dryly 'dude.' I didn't get the joke and so I entered 'fist me harder' in the search engine. I was surprised when I saw the video. I started to laugh, because I got the joke and the scene was so bizarre. My wife was shocked, so I also acted disgusted, but it was too late. It's been two months and she is still not over it. She thinks I have some weird fetish.

Finding solitude is difficult, but not impossible. First, take advantage of every chance you get to be alone to explore and experience something different. Relish the three hour lay-over at the airport, the 45 minute wait in the dentist's office, the cancelled meeting, the friend who is always an hour late, and the 12 hour flight. Use this time to read the newspapers left in the café, to page through the old magazines in the waiting room, pick up and read the back jacket of as many books as you can in the bookstore, or just surf the internet.

If you do not have these kinds of opportunities, then you can create them. Book the cheapest flight, because it usually has the most and longest lay-overs, go to the doctor's office an hour early, show up on-time even though you know your fiend will be an hour late. If you need more time, then you can create opportunities for solitude without losing the trust of your friends and family by being honesty. Honesty is the best policy so tell your friends and family, "I need some time alone to study or travel. It's important to me."

If honesty is not an option, then deception is. Yes, deception is justifiable as a means to personal development. Imagine you are a member of a group that has very strong anti-immigrant views, but you are secretly curious about foreigners and you want to learn more about them, but you know that telling your friends and family about your feelings will cause friction and you're not ready to isolate yourself. You have two options. You can fake a doctor's appointment in order to visit an immigrant center in another city. A proctologist appointment is a perfect cover, because few people know much about the colon and no one really wants to hear details about your examination. Second, you can pretend to conduct counter-surveillance. Tell your xenophobic friends, "I'm going under-cover to find out what these immigrants are all about."

Edge Experiences

Moslow described a kind of experience called a *peak experience*. These are euphoric and emotional moments that create a heightened sense of reality for the experiencer. Peak experiences are most often had in solitude by self-actualized individuals, probably because they have an open mindset and are fully comfortable being alone. There is another kind of radical experience that everyone can have independent of psychological development or mindset. I call them *edge experiences.*

An edge experience involves exposure to something new that is inconsistent with the experiencer's belief system or fully outside their comfort level and which reveals a new reality, the recognition of which can be quite emotional. In some ways, edge experiences are akin to an enlightenment or awakening in that they trigger the dissolution of selfishness and suppress the ego, although edge experiences are not necessarily spiritual in nature. Like peak experiences, edge experiences must be had in solitude so their importance can be fully experienced. Imagine you are standing on the edge of a cliff observing something that you do not comprehend or cannot believe. If you are distracted for a moment by others, you could lose sight of it or lose your footing and fall. If you think about your behavior or the reactions of others instead of focusing and fully absorbing the moment, the experience will be short-lived and its impact less significant. In order for this experience to have any meaning or permanence, it has to be fully lived out.

> Markus: Last year, my friends and I climbed Mt. Whitney. I reached the peak about five minutes before the rest of his climbing group and stood quietly and alone near a plaque marking 14,000 feet. I felt overwhelmed by the incredible 360 degree view. I could hear an eagle flapping its wings in the wind. I realized standing there that our planet is so

big and so beautiful, and we are so small. My eyes started to tear. Then the rest of the group arrived. They all started hooting, hollering, and high fiving each other. I quickly wiped the tears away and we took some selfies.

Standing alone exposed Markus to a reality changing experience, which was cut short when his friends distracted him.

The psychiatrists Thomas Holmes and Richard Rahe created a list of 43 events including the death of a spouse, divorce and imprisonment. They called these events *life changing events*, because they had dramatically impacted the lives of the people experiencing them in a negative way. The Holmes-Rahe list is described later in greater detail, but I mention it here to show that edge experiences are also life changing events, but they always change lives in a profoundly positive manner. A Holmes-Rahe event can trigger an edge experience, but an edge experience is never a Holmes-Rahe event. Here's an example of a Holmes-Rahe event that turned into an edge experience in that it was a stressful event that helped the experiencer recognize his personal potential.

> Jerome: I was an unemployed college drop-out and drug dealer when an old girlfriend called me up to give me some important news. I had nothing to do and went straight to her apartment. She greeted me at the door and wasted no time telling me I was the father of her newborn son. I was shocked. She handed me the baby and told me to hold him while she showered. I sat in her living room alone for ten minutes holding this tiny person and I instantly realized that it wasn't about me anymore. Heck, I wasn't doing a good job taking care of myself. Now I had a kid. I really don't know what went through my head, but I knew I had to change my life. I wanted to be a role model. Jimmy is two years old now, and I just started my new job. I'm a nurse in a hospital.

According to the Holmes-Rahe Stress Scale, Jerome was at high risk of a contracting a stress-induced illness. Statistically speaking, the combination of life changing events like failing in school, unemployment, relationship issues, and a new child should have triggered depression. The Holmes-Rahe scale is a reliable indicator of stress-induced illness, but no model is 100 percent perfect. Instead of triggering illness or violent behavior, this final event in a series of life changing events triggered an edge experience for Jerome, because he was left alone to absorb the implications and significance of being a father. It created a new perception of reality for Jerome, helped him to realize that he was part of a bigger picture and had important responsibilities, suppressed his selfish tendencies, empowered him to recognize his potential, and steered him to change his life and make a positive social impact.

The German poet and author, Hermann Hess, once wrote, "Only in solitude can we find ourselves." Jerome's quiet moment alone with his baby helped him to find himself. You can easily imagine how this scene could have developed in a completely different direction had Jerome and his girlfriend gotten into an argument, had the baby awoken and started crying, or had Jerome's friends appeared on the scene. The few quiet minutes alone with his baby were absolutely critical for him to fully absorb the significance of the event. He had to change his life. He had to accept responsibility and become a better person.

Many things can be edge experiences and their effect can have a drastic impact on attitudes. Many of the stories I collected deal with people overcoming fears, indifference, stereotypes and even hatred to be a positive force in their communities.

> Dennis: I admit today that I grew up in a community plagued by homophobia. When I was approved for an organ transplant, I insisted on meeting the donor who was willing to save my life. I am ashamed today that I was disgusted then to learn that the donor was gay. I made a huge mistake of telling my friends and family. They actually suggested that accepting the organ from a homo would make me gay and told me to think twice about accepting his donation. I was actually going to get

a second opinion. As I laid there in bed waiting for the doctor to come, I thought about how I would ask him without sounding like a moron. I was really going to ask a doctor if there was a possibility that I would become gay by accepting an organ from a gay person. The doctor was late and I was alone in my room. Then I realized that it didn't even matter. I started to laugh at my own ignorance and at the same time I began crying over the generosity of the donor's gift. I have never laughed and cried at the same time. Embarrassment, anger, and joy were mixed. I was an emotion mess, but I knew then that I was going to live. I wondered how many people had suffered and maybe even died due to such stupidity. I am alive today and part of a bigger community. After all, I have a gay kidney so I am part homosexual. I'm a firefighter and gay pride parades are incredible fun. I convinced my firehouse to participate and we do a lot of advocacy and fundraising for the gay community now.

You might think that Dennis' attitude adjustment was self-motivated, but that does not lessen the impact of his experience. He could have checked out of the hospital and lived out his short heterosexual life, but his experience changed his perception about sexual orientation, today he suppresses his ego and tells self-deprecating jokes, he even extended his circle of friends to include an out-group that he used to loathe, and he managed to get his old friends to accept something they used to fear.

There are thousands of stories about people having life changing experiences that motivated them to be brave or generous. Many are indeed inspiring and some of those people serve as role models for others, but singular acts of heroism and tales of courage seldom qualify as edge experiences. The edge experience always involves

1. exposure to something unfamiliar or incongruous with the experiencer's existing beliefs,
2. creates a new perception of reality,

3. changes the person's direction in life,
4. suppresses the experiencer's ego, and
5. produces a sustainable social benefit.

Autonomous

Mature personalities are curious and open to new experiences. They do not necessarily seek loneliness, but they enjoy it when they find it. Such independence can be annoying to co-dependent people and it is sometimes misinterpreted as infidelity, dislike or anti-social behavior.

> Thomas: We planned a vacation together, but I had some unexpected expenses and could not afford to go. Beth went alone. During her two weeks trip to Europe, I did not hear from her once. She was in Italy and I was jealous.

> Beth: It was an amazing vacation. I spent every day from morning to evening in galleries, cafes, shops, museums, and libraries. I didn't have cell coverage so I turned off my phone. I could not understand the shows on the t.v. I could not read the newspaper or magazines. I could not communicate with the locals. I was cut off from the world and alone. For two weeks, I did not send a single email or post a single selfie or comment. I didn't even take pictures. On some days, I did not utter a single word. It was incredibly liberating. Once I sat on a bench for four hours admiring a fountain and watching the people. I absorbed everything and thought about so many things in my life. I have clarity and feel rebooted.

Along the same lines, mature personalities make decisions without always consulting their friends and family and often have views that are incongruous with their cohort or society.

Jackie: All our friends are involved in some network marketing company or part-time gig and constantly pressuring us to also invest. Some couples are selling energy drinks, others are pushing nuts, and another couple is driving for Uber after work. Every time we get together, they try to recruit us into their business. We don't really socialize anymore. They just brag about how much money they will make and what luxury crap they will buy. I actually feel insulted, like they are underestimating us. Why should we spend our free time selling vitamins or driving taxis?

Often, the friends of autonomous people feel marginalized.

Thomas: Beth bought a car without consulting me. I'm her boyfriend.

Beth: Tom knows nothing about cars and I bought it with my money.

Instead of appeasing Thomas' emotional insecurities, Beth chose the logical, expeditious route. Her attitude is bitter for Thomas, but this kind of straightforward logic is usual for mature personalities.

Many mature personalities consider themselves outsiders or observers and they have a cautious relationship with culture. They are rarely patriotic. They adhere to cultural norms when they make moral sense or are easy, but as soon as conformance requires effort or irrational behavior, they tend to get indolent or even avoidant. Standing when the national anthem is played is a curious ritual, contributing a couple dollars to a co-workers maternity gift is illogical, and high-fiving co-workers is silly, but the mature personality usually conforms. Saluting soldiers at the supermarket or participating in inane team building exercises can be no-gos.

Simple

Mature personalities are easy and spontaneous. They have no special requests, no strict conditions, and no difficult requirements.

> Jill: My husband doesn't have an opinion. If I ask him if he wants pizza or sushi for dinner, he says, 'you decide, dear.' When I ask him what you should do on the weekend, he always says 'I'm up for everything' so I end up planning everything.

The mature personality has opinions, but he selectively asserts himself.

> Roger: I state my opinion when it is really important. Where we eat, what movie we see and what friends we meet are important for Jill, but trivial to me, so I let her decide.

The mature person appreciates order and process and they are often minimalists and neat freaks. Rules and policies make it easy to complete mundane tasks leaving more time for more exciting endeavors. Albert Einstein is said to have had only one outfit in his wardrobe when he as at Princeton, because he didn't want to waste any time thinking about what to put on every morning.

Being simple is easy. Just say yes more often. We've all heard the phrase just say no. It is used in the war against drugs ("just say no to drugs") and in the campaign against sex abuse ("no means no"). No is a verbal way of setting boundaries and limits and no campaigns makes sense when the topic is cigarettes, drugs, rape, child abuse, terror, racism, and crime. But when the invitation is to do something that is healthy, legal and moral, the answer should be yes. Saying no to healthy, legal and moral opportunities is motivated by fear and the lack of confidence. Yes is a mindset that is born out of curiosity, perseverance or positive experiences. When we say yes we are presented opportunities to test ourselves. The more often we say yes the more often we have chances to learn what works and what does not. Outcomes improve with experience frequency.

We can apply this concept to the dating scene. Finding a partner is difficult, many people are disillusioned and some have given up entirely, because they have had too many bad first dates or tumultuous relationships. But these people know today what made those dates or relationships bad and they also know what to do to make the next relationship or date a little better. We know today what traits, words, expectations, and behavior work and do not work for us in a relationship. There are billions of people living on our planet and the number of suitable partners is huge, although we can agree that it is finite. Saying yes more often will not only help you to perfect your dating skills, but also help you to eliminate incompatible partners and find the perfect partner faster.

Of course we can't say yes to everything and this conundrum was hilariously played out in the movie *Yes Man*. Jim Carey plays, Carl, a loan officer in a bank whose life is at a standstill until he enrolls in a personal development program led by the self-help guru, Terrence Bundley. Bundley's success strategy is very simple: leave the negativism aside and say yes to everything. Carl discovers the power of yes and his professional and romantic life improve overnight, but he soon learns that saying yes to everything can have some unintended consequences.

The mature personality chooses his battles. When they have demands, say no, or when they complain, it's because it is important. Remember the childhood story about the boy who cried wolf so often that when the wolf finally did appear no one took him seriously when he cried for help? If you stop complaining and stop saying no to everything, people will listen and take you seriously when you do complain and say no.

Objective

Mature personalities are empathetic, objective, and problem-oriented. When you ask a mature personality for help, be prepared for impartiality. The mature personality seeks a meaningful understanding of the situation. Dealing with the mature personality requires thick skin, because their candor can be hurtful. Do not expect blind loyalty from the mature personality.

Barbara: I am pregnant and my husband is divorcing me.

An immature personality hears this and reflexively concludes that Barbara's husband must be a real jerk. Barbara's friend Kate's initial thought was exactly that, but she did not say anything. She did not validate Barbara, because she knew there had to be more to the story.

> Kate: I knew Stephen and wanted to understand why Stephen would act like this. Here's a summary. Barb's husband was a workaholic and she felt neglected. She had an affair, got pregnant, and the other guy bolted. Her husband knows it's not his child, he's not happy, but he agreed to work things out. Now she expects her husband to cut his hours and take over some of the baby chores so she can go back to work. That's when he asked for a divorce. I'm just stating the facts and not an opinion. Those are the facts, right Barb?
>
> Barbara: Well, yes, when you state the facts, I sound like a real bitch. How does that help me?
>
> Kate: You need to reconcile with Stephen and that means do not ask him to put his career on hold so you can keep yours.

This kind of objectivity and pragmatism is common for mature, healthy personalities. When Kate and I dug deeper into Barbara's story, we learned that her husband, Stephen, had accepted the fact that she had an affair and was pregnant. He realized that he had neglected her and was incredibly open-minded.

Appreciation of the Unconventional

Mature personalities appreciate complexity and unconventionality. They love difficult challenges and find beauty in the fantastic, bizarre and unusual. Mature, healthy people have no pretense that the things they like are common. They know they prefer the peculiar and often they are deemed weird or even perverse.

Dirk: My friends are surprised every time they visit my office or apartment. "Why do you have the book *Fifty Shades of Grey* and a *Soldier of Fortune* magazine on your coffee table? Those are totally opposite genres!" I'm the kind of person who reads, watches and listens to everything. Books, fliers, magazines, videos, albums. If it's lying there, I just grab them. Last week I read a book about scrap-booking and yesterday I read a woman's fashion magazine cover-to-cover in a coffee shop. It's all very fascinating, and I'm always surprised how much I didn't know. My friends are also surprised how much I do know about miscellaneous stuff.

Their tolerance, objectivity, curiosity, open-mindedness, and appreciation for the unconventional means mature personalities rarely get disgusted.

Theresa: I returned from a business trip to Asia and the Middle East and told my friends about my experiences. "You're disgusting. How could you eat that?" They said. I explained that there are more than a billion people living there and so they can't waste anything. When they asked me if I felt discriminated as a woman working in an Arab country, I told them that I was always respected and I never felt as safe as when I was there. I could walk in the city at any time of the day or night, and no one bothered me. I am more uncomfortable in some European and American cities. They all say I "must be brainwashed." We frequently have differences of opinion. For example, last year, a school teacher was accused of molesting a pupil, and the incident received media coverage. My friends were outraged and fully supported the principal's decision to fire the teacher. But I didn't see it that way. He had not been found guilty of anything and should have been put on administrative leave, not fired. And his name and picture did not belong in the media until he was found guilty of something. He could be innocent, but his life is now ruined. They all argued, "He must be guilty of something otherwise he wouldn't have been fired." That makes no sense at all.

2. Mature Method

Mature personalities do not act based on a gut feeling, instinct, or desire. They are deliberate and rational. They are conscientious. Of course, these model citizens sometimes have fantasies and desires, they can be spontaneous, but they do not immediately speak about or act upon their urges. Even when confronted with seemingly simple decisions, mature personalities hesitate briefly to reflect on priorities. These priorities are not written down anywhere. None of Moslow's subjects had a list of priorities, yet somehow they all independently established and followed the same logical, incremental framework for deciding what to do. Moslow identified and ranked these priorities. The result is Moslow's *Hierarchy of Needs*.

The needs that motivate behavior are ranked from 1 to 5 to denote their relative priority.

Priority		Needs	Examples
1	Low to High	Physiological	Food, Water, Sleep
2		Security	Home, Health, Financial
3		Social	Friends, Family, Intimacy
4		Esteem	Respect, Status, Position
5		Self-Actualization	Knowledge, Justice, Service

Illustration 11. Moslow's Hierarchy of Needs

Your intelligence may be insulted by the following explanation, so please accept my apologies in advance. I have had many long and annoying debates with students, parents and professionals about how to rank priorities. For clarification, a lower need has a higher priority and a lower priority number, and vice versa. For example, water is one of the most basic physiological human needs. We cannot survive without water, whereas a sports car is a means for satisfying the need for esteem. We can survive without a sports car. Satisfying physiological needs are more important than satisfying the need for esteem. Even though the physiological need is lower, it has a higher priority and, therefore, a lower priority number than the need for esteem. This concept is no different than the ranking of actors, movies, products, politicians, companies, and athletes. The top performer is always number one, yet somehow the idea that a higher priority is denoted by a lower number is confusing for some people. The confusion about lower needs having higher priorities and a lower priority number and vice versa is exacerbated by the popular use of a pyramid to illustrate Moslow's Hierarchy of Needs, even though Moslow never used or mentioned a pyramid in this context.

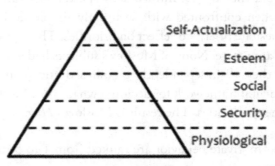

Illustration 12: Pyramid of Needs

The pyramid clearly shows that self-actualization is the highest level of psychological development. We should all strive to be altruistic, fair, selfless and charitable. The pyramid is supposed to make it clear that the higher needs for esteem and self-actualization are attainable when lower needs for nutrition and security are satisfied. Without a sturdy foundation, the pyramid would collapse. This is an important differentiation between Moslow's and some of the other models, for example Alderfer's, which states that the lower foundational needs do not need to be satisfied as a condition for fulfilling other needs. The reason for this difference is that Moslow explains mature logical behavior, whereas Alderfer's explains normal behavior. According to Moslow, we should always make sure our pantry is full and our bills are paid before we go on a vacation or buy art supplies, whereas Alderfer says it doesn't matter. To the immature person, it really doesn't matter, and that is exactly the root of the problem for most people today. Immature people do not have logical priorities.

The pyramid can be problematic, though, because it does not make it obvious that higher needs near the peak of the pyramid have a lower priority than the basic needs shown at the base and the pyramid. And sometimes, those who are acquainted with the pyramid misuse it to justify irrational decisions. Parents of a student called me one day to confront me about my teaching material. Their son recently asked if he could move back home into his old bedroom. When they asked him what he had done with the money they had given him for campus housing, he explained proudly and confidently that he bought a motorcycle instead of paying rent, because "the need for esteem is higher than the physiological need, *ergo* satisfying my need for respect is more important than fulfilling my need for shelter."

This is a perversion of priorities. Mature personalities never make this mistake. For them the ranking is obvious: a lower need at the bottom of the pyramid always has priority over a higher need. Mature people are conscientious. They always have a plan and appreciate order and they address their needs in a specific, logical order.

Priority Nr. 1. Physiological Needs

Our most basic biological need is to take in nutrition and get rest. Eating, drinking water, and sleeping are our highest priority needs. Without sufficient food, water, and sleep, we quickly grow physically weak. Our primary responsibility to ourselves and our families is to find or create a source of food, water and rest. I emphasize the word source, because our goal is to be able to satisfy these needs constantly, reliably, and without interruption. If you spend every day searching for food or a place to sleep, you cannot realize your potential, because you do not have time to focus on the next level of development.

I used to be critical of transients and low income people who eat frequently in fast food restaurants until I learned that this is actually a logical option for them. At the lowest need level, calories are the only things that count, not vitamins or minerals. Medical professionals recommend women consume 1,600 and men 2,200 calories per day to survive.[61] Humans can eat far less, but this puts our health at risk. As it turns out, there are few attractive meal options that satisfy this caloric requirement for very little money. In Michael Kirk's book *Efficiency is Everything*, he shows that there are foods like white bread, plain rice, flour, sugar and peanut butter that can satisfy the minimum requirement for less than a dollar a day per person. These foods are not meals, though. The only food on Kirk's list that can be considered a meal is Ramen noodles. Home cooked meals that meet the minimum caloric requirement start at around $3 per day per person, and Kirk's book describes "28+ mathematically proven cost efficient recipes."[62] Preparing a homemade meal requires a home with a kitchen. Fast food is convenient and tasty, and a complete meal that meets the caloric requirements for survival starts at around $5 per day per person. Instead of eating a bag of flour or a jar of peanut butter, it makes total sense to order from the McDonald's Extra Value Meal.

The long-term health effects of eating only fast food are not entirely clear. A study conducted by medical professionals at the University of Heidelberg revealed why fast food can be unhealthy.[63] For three weeks, three groups of men ate exactly 2,500 calories per day. One group of men ate Mediterranean cuisine like pizza and pasta, another group was given country-style cooking like fried chicken and mashed potatoes, and the third group consumed only fast food like hamburgers and French fries. The participants' blood and fat values and weight were checked frequently. At the end of the three week study, no significant differences in the groups' values were reported. The only difference was the participants' experiences. The men who ate only fast food were always hungry, because a 2,500 calorie fast food meal weighs on average only 940 grams, whereas the 2,500 calorie Mediterranean meals weighed 2,060 grams and the country-style meals weighed 1,335 grams each. The researchers concluded that fast food is unhealthy, because people eat twice as much by weight to feel full, and this translates into more than twice as many calories as recommended to maintain a healthy weight. Fast food is an easy, practical and logical source of calories for someone on a tight budget. Take this into consideration later when we talk about establishing self-sufficiency.

Priority Nr. 2: Security

Once you have found a source for satisfying your most basic biological needs and you do not have to wake up early every morning and search all day for water and food, because you know where to find these, you will have time to focus on the next level of needs. You can search for a permanent, safe home.

Evidence from several Housing First projects and home ownership programs around the world shows that a permanent home versus temporary accommodations has many benefits. Most of the results focus on the positive economic impact for the community, but these programs only work because individuals do better when they have stability. A home provides security and gives a person the ability to take better care of themselves. People who live in permanent homes that are warm and dry are generally healthier than transients, who visit the hospital emergency room 77 percent more frequently.[64] Also, treating health or psychological issues for someone who is transient is difficult. A permanent home provides an address and stability that people need to overcome some of the risk factors of homelessness like applying for healthcare benefits, learning a trade, and getting a job. Staying put also has social benefits like making friends and it makes it possible to save money on food, because home cooked meals cost less than eating out.

When it comes to finding permanent housing, size matters because price is a function of square footage and location. Most financial advisors agree that living expenses should not exceed 30 percent of your net monthly income. The 30 percent figure represents a threshold the U.S. government uses to decide who qualifies for public housing programs and initiatives. Households that spend more than 30 percent of their income on housing costs are said to be cost burdened, and those that spend more than 50 percent of their earnings on housing costs are classified as *severely cost-burdened households*.[65] In 2015, the Harvard Joint Center for Housing Studies reported that there were 21.3 million cost-burdened renters in 2014, meaning that almost half of all U.S. renters pay too much for rent and are at risk of losing their homes.[66] Remember, stability is important for growth and spending more than half of your income on housing is hardly sustainable and leaves little for personal development.

Some critics say that the 30 percent rule doesn't account for household size. A single person with no dependents may be able to spend more than 30 percent of their income on housing and still have enough money left over to get by, but someone supporting a large family should spend much less than 30 percent of their income on housing to have enough money for food, clothing, and education for the entire family. Speaking of size, the recommended standards to prevent over-crowding and avoid health issues differ by country, but most Western housing agencies recommend around 80 square feet (7.5 square meters) per person.[67] For reference, an average college dormitory room measures 228 square feet or 114 square feet per roommate, whereas military personnel are allocated 90 square feet per enlisted soldier.

Making ends meet is a big problem for many people and a major cause of stress, depression and divorce. A recent report from the American Psychological Association shows that among more than 3,000 adults surveyed, 72 percent reported feeling stressed about money and half reported feeling depressed.[68] According to a recent survey of 191 Certified Divorce Financial Analysts across North America, making ends meet is one of the three leading causes of divorce and 22 percent of divorces are attributed to financial problems.[69] Income is seldom the issue, spending is and spending is a function of priority.

If your standard of living exceeds your means, then you are not only burdened in the official sense, but at risk in the physiological and psychological sense. Stress is debilitating. Studies by Schneiderman and Ironson found a clear connection between stress and illness, because stress often triggers bad behavior like smoking, drinking, poor eating habits and physical inactivity.[70] Recent work by Greubel and Kecklund,[71] shows that stress also increases an individual's susceptibility to physical illnesses like the common cold and heart disease.

The message thus far is simple: become very efficient at providing the basics. Calories and a permanent home are prerequisites for your personal development and the minimum recommended requirements are quite affordable. You do not need to be affluent to achieve your full potential.

It is not enough to satisfy an acute need. The goal is not to simply get by or make ends meet. Mature personalities are keen on doing it efficiently and sustainably. They are not motivated to find the next meal, but rather to excel at preventing scarcity of food by keeping the pantry stocked. At the surface this may sound greedy or selfish, but this thinking is logical and it ultimately facilitates human development. Being an excellent provider of basic needs is important, because it enables stability, which is a cornerstone for advancing the human condition. An under-nourished homeless person can be happy, they can be charitable on occasion and experience short-term happiness, but they cannot physiologically and financially afford to be generous constantly. They cannot be altruistic for long. Eventually, the elements and a lack of nutrition will take their toll, they will grow weak, lose their independency and require assistance. The person who practices and becomes excellent at satisfying their own needs has the time, energy, and resources to explore, learn, experiment, create, and produce knowledge and insights that can help others, not just momentarily or occasionally, but permanently. Simply put, a person can serve others better when he is very good at serving himself. Both Muslim (Quran 13:11) and Christian (Colossians 3:23) texts offer similar teachings.

Being able to efficiently and constantly satisfy the basic priorities in the hierarchy of needs is a critical turning point in personal and human development. Over time, our ability to satisfy basic needs and produce surpluses has improved and empowered humans to make huge advances in our standard and quality of living. Isaac Newton wrote in 1676, "if I have seen further, it is by standing on the shoulders of giants." Newton was probably referring to his colleagues when he wrote this and not thinking about our prehistoric ancestors, but the ability to produce surpluses and then spend time exploring and inventing started many thousands of years ago. A starving prehistoric hunter did not have time to paint pictures on the walls of caves or forge metal into tools. Painting on cave walls and making tools was only possible, because our cavemen ancestors became excellent providers, they had surplus food, a safe permanent shelter and, therefore, time to create. Bread only exists today, because someone thousands of years ago had become so efficient at satisfying their basic needs that they had free time and surplus food. Instead of eating the raw ingredients, which is what a starving person would do, some prehistoric person conducted fireside experiments with wheat, eggs and milk, and invented bread. The advances made by our ancestors made it easier for the following generations to have the time and resources to think, experiment, learn, and discover.

Probably the best example of our progress as a species is the remarkable decline in birth mortality since 1900. At the beginning of the 20th century in the United States, for every 1,000 births, 100 infants died and six to nine women died of pregnancy-related complications. By 1997, the infant mortality rate declined to 7.2 per 1,000 live births, and the maternal mortality rate declined to 0.0077 deaths per 1,000 live births.[72] These remarkable improvements were made possible by constant advances in environmental conditions, nutrition, medicines, access to health care, disease monitoring, standards of living, and education. But this kind of progress is not widespread. Majid Ezzati and his team from the Imperial College in London published a report showing that most people born in rich countries after 2030 will live to be more than 90 years old.[73] Scientists once believed an average life expectancy beyond 90 was impossible, but medical advances coupled with improved social programs are helping to break the barriers. While some genetic factors might explain longevity in certain countries, social and environmental factors are more important. The researchers noted that the U.S. has the highest rates of maternal death, infant death and homicide of high income countries. The U.S. is also the only high income country without comprehensive health care.

In most modern cultures, many young people do not have to worry much about satisfying their basic needs, because parents and social programs assume this responsibility. The idea that our children have almost two decades, from birth to age 18, to explore, learn, discover and create is an incredible luxury. Obviously, this period is meant for identifying and developing our talents so that our transition from dependent child to head-of-household is easier. There should be no doubt that this transition is easier with a formal education. The U.S. Department of Education's National

Center for Education Statistics (NCES) analyzes employee earnings data biennially. The findings indicate that workers with college degrees earn significantly more than those without. In 2015, adults with bachelor's degrees earned $48,500 a year, while high school diploma holders earned only $23,900.[74] The National Association for Colleges and Employers looks at the career placement rates and salaries for college graduates. The recent report[75] shows that only five percent of college graduates were unemployed. The lowest unemployment rate was for Agriculture at 1.8 percent, and the highest rate of unemployment was for Geologists, although it was only 8.8 percent. The starting salaries ranged from $28,400 for Family Sciences to $71,000 for Chemical Engineer. The report also shows 29 majors that have an under-employment rate greater than 50 percent, although the average starting salaries for these people were still at least 25 percent higher than for workers without a college degree. In other words, almost half of the college graduates did not have their dream jobs, but that doesn't matter, because, no matter what you study in college, your chances of finding a job are very good and you will earn more money than not attending college. A formal education makes it much easier to be independent and efficient.

The first two need levels are foundational in that personal and human development depends on them. When one can efficiently satisfy basic needs then surplus time, resources, and money are available to focus on other needs. Having a surplus is necessary because developing meaningful relationships requires time and energy. It takes frequent communication, interactions, and meetings to get to know other people and establish a strong connection. Relationships require effort and time. The inefficient person spends much of their energy and time trying to make ends meet and has too little time for relationships. It is, therefore, no surprise that finances are the leading cause of stress in relationships.

Kate, Mary and Sally grew up in the same neighborhood and attended the same high school and college together. They work together and their monthly incomes are similar. Kate and Mary are efficient. They spend 50 percent of their monthly income on rent, car loans, utilities and other living expenses. They pay their bills on time, have growing saving accounts, and $250 per month pocket money. After work, Kate and Mary each spend about ten hours a week shopping for groceries, cooking, and housekeeping. On the other hand, Sally is inefficient. She spends more than 80% of her income to pay rent, her car lease, credit card debt, utilities, subscriptions, and other living expenses. As soon as Sally gets paid, she catches up on her bills and puts $200 in her wallet for groceries and pocket money. Sally procrastinates shopping for groceries, because then she would have less money in her wallet for the rest of the month. Instead, she buys food on-demand and often eats out.

Kate and Mary have time, energy and resources to meet frequently. Sally can't afford to meet her friends frequently without putting her financial security at risk. The efficient person manages risk by preventing it, but the inefficient person is constantly confronted with risk. Sally could easily run out of money before pay day. Their friendship is strained.

> Kate and Mary: Sallly never has time. She never has money. We have to cover her drink tab all the time. When we meet she only complains. Sally recently made us feel guilty when we talked about planning a wellness weekend. "Why are you planning something without me? You know I can't afford that." And once when the bill came, she pulled out a coupon for 20 percent off instead of forking out $10 cash. There were three of us so it should have been a 33 percent coupon!

Efficiency and stability at the basic need levels provide options that can be exercised without adversely affecting financial security and health. Kate and Mary have energy, money, and time to take art classes, attend night school or volunteer at the community center. They can join clubs and meet people. They can afford to cut their hours in order to attend college or apply for better jobs. Sally needs to down-size, but she has no time to look for a cheaper apartment. She needs a better job, but she has no money and time to take classes or search for a new job.

The person who follows rational priorities and is efficient produces surplus food and resources and has time and energy to meet friends, socialize, entertain, be intimate, and eventually start and provide for a family. According to the *Cost of Raising A Child* report from the U.S. Department of Agriculture, it costs nearly $300,000 to raise a child, including housing, food, clothes, furniture, supplies, healthcare, little league, dance lessons, toys, electronics, memberships, cars, class trips, college, etc.[76] A growing family needs a larger home so housing represents 30 percent of this expense. The *Journal of Marriage and Family* reported that the amount of time parents spend with children has been climbing since the 1970s. Fathers' time with children nearly tripled from 2.6 hours per week in 1965 to 7.2 in 2010, and mothers' time with children rose from 10.5 hours a week in 1965 to 13.7 in 2010.[77] The amount of time parents spend with their children is less important than the quality of time. Melissa Milkie, a sociologist at the University of Toronto and one of the report's authors, explained, the amount of time parents spend with their children has virtually no relationship to children's academic achievement, behavior and emotional well-being. A study in the *BMJ Open* showed that the quality of time parents spend with children is more important than the quantity of time. "Fathers who took pleasure in caring for their young children were 28% less likely to have children with behavioral problems at both nine and 11 years old."[78] Enjoying the time with children can be difficult when parents are distracted by other issues like health, finances, and home. The conclusion is that a childless couple needs to efficiently and consistently earn $1,200 per month surplus to be able to provide for the basic needs and enjoy a few good quality hours every week with a child.

The point is, when we are healthy and efficient, we have the time, money and energy required to work on relationships and family.

Priority 3. Social

According to Moslow, mature persons have fewer albeit deeper relationships, because they are curious, cautious, and objective. When it comes to relationships, the mature personality seeks collaborators and partners.

Mature friendships are functional. Friends need to be engaging and challenging. They need to expose the mature person to new ideas and beliefs. Friends are for learning from and with. The mature person seeks diverse and meaningful relationships. They make a clear distinction between casual acquaintances and true friends. Their circle of friends is small, because they are selective, they believe friendship is earned, and there are few people who appreciate their traits and can keep up with them intellectually. A reporter told Jeff Bezos, the founder of Amazon.com, that she heard he had very few friends and she was curious if this was true and why. Mr. Bezos explained that a friend for him was someone who could break him out of a Mexican jail without asking how he got there.

Mature persons have unique humor. They appreciate word puns, sarcasm, and dry and sophisticated jokes. Mature people do not make jokes at the expense of other individuals, races, or cultures. Self-deprecation is common.

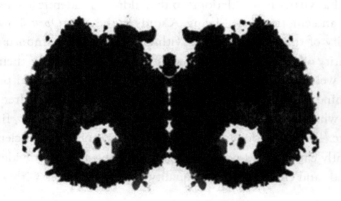

Illustration 13: Rorschach Blot

A man visits a psychoanalyst. The analyst takes a stack of cards containing Rorschach ink blots, shows the first card to the man, and asks him to say whatever comes to mind. The man looks at the first card and says, "Sex." Then he looks at the second ink blot and says, "Sex." The analyst goes through the whole stack of Rorschach cards and the man says every card reminds him of sex. The analyst looks serious and says, "I don't want to worry you, but you are clearly obsessed with sex." The man looks at the psychoanalyst surprised and exclaims, "I can't believe you just said that. You are the one with the pile of pornographic pictures!"

The mature person's intimate relationships are predominantly systematic, meaning that the mature person seeks someone who is a partner first and then a romantic lover. Partners can accomplish more together. This should not be misinterpreted to mean the mature personality uses people as instruments for learning and improving their efficiency. Due to the aforementioned abilities, this person is an excellent friend, partner, and lover. They are empathetic, passionate, dedicated, and honest. They have no fears and can give themselves fully to the right friends and partner. They are curious and adventurous, open to new unusual experiences, and do not get embarrassed. But the romantic connection is second to an intellectual connection.

Priority Nr. 4. Esteem

Esteem represents the desire to achieve and be accepted and respected by others. These activities give the person a sense of contribution or value. Maslow distinguished two versions of esteem. A lower version and a higher version. The lower level of esteem is the need for respect from others. This may include a need for status, recognition, fame, prestige, and attention. The higher version manifests itself as the need for self-respect, for example, the person may have a need for competence, mastery, confidence, independence, and freedom.

The mature person is introverted and, as such, they focus on the higher esteem level. They care little about what others think about them and are keener on feeling comfortable with their own achievements and status. They are modest and tend to be secretive, modest and even somewhat embarrassed about their achievements or possessions. One subject had published numerous scientific papers and two books without telling their friends and family. They were all dumbfounded when they saw the subject on television sitting as an expert on a discussion panel. "Why didn't you tell us you were some guru?" they exclaimed.

The mature person wants to be respected for the things they earned, the fruits of their labor, their creations, hard work and intellect, and less for their appearance or purchases. Nevertheless, it is a mistake to think the mature person is anti-materialistic. Indeed, they appreciate possessions, but their possessions are mostly unique and sentimental. There is almost always a story behind the things they own. They were self-created, discovered, gifted, or awarded. Mature personalities don't acquire or make things to impress others. They own things for their own enjoyment and don't like talking and never brag about their collections and possessions. For example, I noticed that a colleague was wearing a rare and very expensive vintage watch and I complimented him on it. He was impressed that I recognized it, because it was a "time piece that only an expert horologist would recognize," he said. Then he confided in me that he actually had several rare watches in various states of restoration and begged me not to tell any of our colleagues or friends. He didn't want others to think he was frivolous or a show-off. Many mature people who have reached the esteem level are reluctant to invite people to their homes.

> Maxwell: When a new friend visits my apartment for the first time, they usually act all suspicious and weird. "Who's apartment is this? Is that an original? Are you a drug dealer?" I have to laugh every time. I feel like I'm apologizing when I explain that I love flea markets and auctions and I know what to look for. I'm afraid to show anyone what's parked in my garage.

An inferiority complex is often expressed at the esteem level by immature persons. A person, who has not worked hard to satisfy their basic needs or does not sense self-pride often compensates for these deficiencies by boasting about their status or flaunting their possessions. The immature person tends to post pictures of their new stuff on social media. One sign of an inferiority complex is the use of superfluous details.

Jane on Facebook: Picking up my new 2016 Audi Q5, metallic panther paint, 21-inch BBS rims with P70s, and of course, a Bose 13-speaker sound system.

Anne on Twitter: Just got promoted to Assistant to the South West Region Executive Vice-President for After-Sales Service for Heavy Duty Off-Road Machinery.

The immature person often exaggerates their position and status.

Amanda: So, what are you doing now?
Patty: I'm the CEO of a company.
Amanda: Congratulations! What does your company do?
Patty: We're a leader in enterprise facility management services.
Amanda: Sounds important. How many employees do you have?
Patty: Um, well, we're just getting started.
Amanda: (I was thinking, it sounds like he was a janitor and works alone.)

Wanda: Hi Mark, what are you up to these days?
Mark: I'm an entrepreneur.
Wanda: What do you do?
Mark: I drive for Uber.

This is in stark contrast to the mature person who often downplays their position. If they are the Senior Executive Vice President for Global Supply Chain Management they simply tell friends "I'm in management," and when they are the Senior Project Manager for Enterprise Resource Planning and Integration, they say "I work in IT."

The mature person is happy when others succeed and is generous with complements and praise, whereas the immature person is intimidated by the achievements of others. Another clear sign of an inferiority complex is the *qualifying question*.

> Alan: I saw your new car. Did you buy it new or is it used?

> Michael: You're wearing a new Rolex. Is it real?

> Keith: This is a beautiful condo. How can you afford this?

The terribly insecure, immature person goes a step further in responding to the success of others by using antipathetic statements that express their resentment.

> Denis: What kind of car do you drive?
> Harry: I have a Jaguar.
> Denis: Oh. Well, I don't need that to be happy.

> Sam: Hey Matt, I haven't seen you in years. What are you up to now?
> Matt: I'm teaching at the university.
> Sam: Are you a professor?
> Matt: Yes, I teach biology.
> Sam: Don't you need to have a PhD to be a professor?
> Matt: Yes. I earned my Doctor in Biology at Berkeley.
> Sam: Well, you know what they say, "those who can't do, teach."

> Zachary: "I just got a really nice bonus and can finally afford to take my family on a really nice vacation."
> Bob: "Well, you're going to have to pay taxes on your bonus, so don't get too excited about that fancy vacation."

Priority Nr. 5. Self-Actualization

"What a man can be, he must be." This quotation from Moslow forms the basis for self-actualization. Maslow defines this need as the desire to accomplish everything that one can, to become the most that one can be.

Achieving self-actualization is difficult, because it requires mastering all previous needs. Once someone has learned to efficiently satisfy basic needs, established stability, built a network of trustworthy friends, and earned intellectual and professional recognition, they can focus their energy, time and resources on promoting advancement in their field. Mastery of the previous needs is an imperative for self-actualization, because often the person has to fight the system, do things out of the box, create and test entirely new approaches. Some resistance and failure are inevitable so the person needs to have stability to sustain their efforts. The tenure system at universities was designed to facilitate self-actualization. A tenured professor is an appointment that lasts until retirement age. The justification of such a position is the principle of *academic freedom*, which holds that it is beneficial for state, society and academia in the long term if scholars are free to examine, hold, and advance controversial views.

Collaborative Intentionality

There are two levels of self-actualization: internal and external. A teacher who observes that their immigrant pupils need targeted mentoring may endeavor to develop new teaching materials or methods in order to (a) become a better teacher, and then (b) help other teachers to become more effective. These activities serve to help immigrant children in their classroom to succeed and then helping immigrant children everywhere. Likewise, a mechanic may tinker in his workshop to build a better machine that can make them more productive, more competitive, produce better quality, or lower their energy consumption. It may take them many years and thousands of dollars to perfect their invention, but every failure incrementally improves their knowledge making them more productive. Eventually, when their machine is perfected, they will share their knowledge with others by filing a patent, which becomes public record, licensing their design, publishing their plans for others to use, or producing and selling a new product that makes others more efficient.

The Wright brothers did not finish high school. Yet, as teenagers, they built their own printing press and started a successful daily newspaper. They sold the printing company to open a bicycle repair shop to capitalize on the bicycle craze of the late 1800's and, in 1896, they began manufacturing their own bicycles to fund their growing interest in flight. In 1903, the Wright brothers made the first controlled and sustained flight of a powered, heavier-than-air aircraft. They continued to improve their design and, in 1904–1905, the brothers developed their flying machine into the first practical fixed-wing aircraft. The Wright brothers dedicated themselves for nearly ten years to developing their flying machine, which in terms of scientific discoveries is short. Their commitment and investment were only possible because they could efficiently and consistently satisfy their lower needs. Their impact on mankind is enormous. It is difficult to quantify the enormous positive impact that air travel and transportation has had on our world. According to the Air Transport Action Group, the industry supports 63 million jobs and transports 3.6 billion passengers per year.[79]

The chances today of high school drop-outs inventing something that can have as significant an impact on society as an airplane are slim. Today, almost everything that has promise of advancing mankind is being developed or produced by multi-disciplinary teams. At the European Organization for Nuclear Research (CERN), physicists and engineers are investigating the fundamental structure of the universe using the world's largest and most complex scientific instruments. This kind of advancement takes a team of diverse experts. Surprisingly, less than 3 percent of the staff members at CERN are physicists and engineers. CERNs 2,500 employees represent 17 different job categories and possess some combination of more than 400 different skill sets.[80] Even seemingly mundane professions like dairy farming are a magnitude more complex today than they were 50 years ago. The modern dairy farm team has mechanics, electricians, veterinarians, nutritionists, as well as environmental, breeding and waste management experts. The modern dairy is creating new positions for various IT specialists and engineers to build and maintain robots and automated, remote controlled systems for feeding, grooming and milking cows.

The point being, a person can reach the first level of self-actualization by becoming the best musician, the best doctor, the best teacher, or the best hair stylist that they can be. However, due to the increasing complexity of most things today, it is difficult for most people to have a meaningful and sustainable impact on society by working alone. Fortunately, you don't have to be rich or a genius to have a sustainable impact on others. There is no limit to the type of skill that can be leveraged for social good. You just have to have time, energy, resources, and the right friends.

In April 2009, two Germans, Titus Dittmann and Dr. Rupert Neudeck, traveled together to Afghanistan. Six years earlier, Dr. Neudeck had helped save thousands of Vietnamese boat people in the China See and then co-founded the international Gruenhelme Peace Corps, which built many schools in Afghanistan, Africa and Palestine. Dittmann's idea was to promote unity, gender equality, self-confidence and self-worth by bringing skateboarding to children in areas of conflict and deprivation.[81] He wanted to use the Gruenhelme's existing school infrastructure to build outdoor skate-board parks. Sounds crazy, but it worked. Since founding Skate-Aid and opening the first skate park in 2009, Dittmann and his fellow skater activists have built dozens of skateboarding parks in Asia, the Middle East, Africa, South America and Europe. On an on-going basis, the parks provide jobs to locals, as well as, training, equipment, clothing, and a safe environment to children. Dittmann is no Tony Hawk on the half pipe and he was not rich, but he had a passion for skateboarding, he achieved efficiency, he identified and developed his talent as a teacher, and he befriended the right people.

3. Mature Rules

In addition to having certain traits like being reflective, skeptical, spontaneous, and open-minded, and having clear priorities like stocking the pantry before buying the sports car, mature personalities follow simple rules:

Rule 1. Always sacrifice a higher need in order to satisfy a lower need. If you drive to McDonald's in a Cadillac and order from the Extra Value Menu, because you can't afford groceries and the family is hungry, then take a critical look at your fulfilled higher needs and sacrifice something in order to establish more stability with your lower needs.

Rule 2. Never sacrifice a lower need in order to fulfill a higher need. If the pursuit of some higher need is causing stress, making you lose sleep or gain weight or skip meals or putting your health or life in danger, then you need to reassess your priorities. It is not physiologically or psychologically healthy to constantly sacrifice health and security for esteem, entertainment or pleasure.

Rule 3. Compromise a lower need in order to fulfill a higher need. Being proficient at satisfying lower needs does not mean doing so in high-style. You can trade the free range filet mignon and exotic organic vegetables for hamburger and mash potatoes in order to afford a club membership or sports car - without putting your health and security at risk.

Rule 4. Be flexible. The situation or circumstances can change making it necessary to reassess priorities. If basic physiological and security needs are met, the refrigerator and pantry are full of groceries, the family has warm clothes, rent is paid and there is money in the savings account, it is sensible to plan a party or vacation. But as soon as a sudden storm damages the home or the refrigerator breaks, then the party or vacation may have to be cancelled or postponed.

Exercise in Mature Priorities

There's a fun exercise for teaching or learning the mature method. Here's what you need:

> 1 16 oz. (500 ml) canning jar
> 1 cup (240 ml) coffee beans
> 1 cup (240 ml) salt
> 1/2 cup (120 ml) water
> 1 small apple
> 1 medium egg

Spread the items out in front of your child, friend or subject and explain:

This glass jar represents a fulfilled life and these food items represent all the things that can make you a good parent, a good friend and a good person. The apple represents your basic human needs like food, sleep and water. The eggs represent security like a home and a job. The coffee beans represent your friends and family. The salt represents achievement and rewards. The water represents the good things you do for others like volunteering and donating. You want your life, this jar, to be as full as possible. Emptiness represents sadness. Now pack as much of this food in the jar as you can without crushing, cutting or breaking them.

When you add up the volumes of the five items, it appears that not all of the food items can possibly fit in the jar, but they do - if you plan carefully how you fill your jar of life. You can pour the coffee beans and salt into the jar first, but there will not be enough room for the apple and the egg. In other words, prioritizing friends means compromising health and security. The optimal packing method is to place the apple in the jar, then the egg. Then pour the coffee beans and roll the jar slowly to help the coffee beans settle into the crevasses. Not all coffee beans will fit at first. Then pour the salt and shake the jar gently to help the salt fill the empty spaces. Not all of the salt will fit. Finally, add water. This will dissolve the salt and create more room for the remaining coffee beans and salt. Amazingly, everything fits.

Illustration 14: Jar of Life

There are many lessons to be drawn from this exercise:

1. The jar is completely full only when you use all ingredients, i.e. living a fulfilled life means satisfying all needs.
2. Even though the volumes for coffee and salt add up to 480 ml, the 500 ml jar will only be half full if you add only the coffee beans and salt, i.e. if you focus on friends and esteem, you can be happy, but you cannot be completely fulfilled.
3. If you add the coffee beans and salt first, you will have to sacrifice either the apple or the egg, i.e. if you focus on friends and esteem, you have to sacrifice health or safety.
4. Once you have placed the apple and the egg in the jar, you can alternately add more coffee beans, salt and water to fill the jar completely, i.e. health and safety are constants.
5. Adding the water makes room for more coffee beans and salt, i.e. being a good charitable person creates new friends and more rewards.

Take caution because the internet is full of stupid "jar of life" lessons, like the one that instructs you to use a beer mug to represent life. Place two ping pong balls in the mug to represent friends, then pour the peanuts into the mug to represent fun, and finally pour the beer into the mug. The stupid lesson is: there is always room in life to have beer, fun and peanuts with your friends. It is exactly this kind of populist wisdom that promotes irrational priorities. I'm not saying that having a beer with friends is wrong, but the lesson is incomplete. Sometimes there is no room in life for a beer with friends. Sometimes friends and fun have to be compromised or even sacrificed to satisfy one's needs for health, job, safety or family.

Happiness and Fulfillment

Happiness and fulfillment are often linked to each other, although there is a difference. Someone can be completely happy living a deliberate self-reliant life like the one Thoreau described in his book *Life in the Woods*, or following the typical path of college, job, marriage, home, children, vacation and retirement. But happiness in these two cases does not equate to fulfillment. Having a dry bed, warm food, and a safe home can be satisfying. Having a successful career, a beautiful home, great friends and a healthy family can make one very happy, but happiness is usually an unfilled jar. Fulfillment means fulfilling all needs and applying your talent to helping others.

The internet is full of advice on how to live a happier and fulfilling life. Search online for the phrase "tips fulfilling life" and you will find many lists. Illustration 15 shows the top three results displayed by Google. These lists are not very good. They promote a few mature abilities and traits like openness, diversity, and reflection, but many of the tips are fallacies, i.e. they are nice ideals, but, as you will read later, they are not conducive to self-sufficiency and personal development. For example, one of the common issues we encountered in our study related to the tip chase your dreams and never quit. As you will read later, there is an important difference between having a dream, having talent, being passionate, and earning a living. Many of our subjects chased a dream for many years only to learn that they had actually no talent or could not survive on a dream. Some ended up broke, unskilled, defeated, and very

Forbes[82] "16 Ways to Live a Happier More Fulfilling Life"	Dumb Little Man[83] "12 Techniques to Help You Live a Happy and Fulfilled Life"	Tiny Buddha[84] "10 Choices That Lead to a Happy, Fulfilling Life"
1. Prioritize your time 2. Build relationships over possessions 3. Take what you can from life, always give back 4. Be accountable for your words and actions 5. Be disciplined 6. Expunge hate from your heart 7. Forgive yourself and others quickly 8. Put your family first 9. Find purpose in your life's work 10. Chase your dreams and never quit 11. Pursue passions bigger than yourself 12. Don't hold on too tight 13. Lead by example 14. Protect those who can't protect themselves 15. Strive to improve a little bit every day	1. Keep life simple 2. Practice being satisfied 3. Beware of indecision 4. Practice cheerfulness 5. Learn to like people 6. Live and let live 7. Adversity teaches 8. Don't take yourself so seriously 9. Have a sense of humor 10. Practice objectivity 11. Tolerate your own mistakes 12. Forgive yourself	1. Don't sweat the small stuff; don't sweat the big stuff 2. Push you out of your comfort zone 3. Live fully in each moment 4. Give gratitude any chance you can 5. Life is what's happening while you're busy on your cell phone 6. Listen to your gut 7. Look for similarities 8. Let go of the fear of not being accepted and let your true self come out 9. Make time to reflect on relationships 10. No matter how far you travel in search of happiness, it can only be found in one place.

Illustration 15: How to Live a Happier and Fulfilling Life

unhappy. The tip "Don't sweat the small stuff; Don't sweat the big stuff" is also problematic. There are some things in life that are extremely important, like health and security. If you have big health issues or live in an unsafe community, all energy and resources have to be focused on improving your condition.

The Big Five Personality Traits

When Moslow made his observations and described the traits that his over-achievers possessed in his 1954 seminal book, *Motivation and Personality*, he did not use the Big Five Model to profile the mature person, even though this model already existed at that time. This model was originally developed by Louis Thurstone, Gordon Allport und Henry Sebastian Odbert in the 1930's to describe personality, it was advanced by Ernest Tupes and Raymond Christal in 1961, and reached wide-spread acceptance in the 1980s. According to the Big Five Model, the dimension of personality are openness, conscientious, extroverted, agreeableness, and neuroticism. These traits are typically referred to using the acronym OCEAN. Each of the Big Five traits contains two separate aspects.

	Factor	Low	High
O	Openness	conservative, routine	curious, imaginative
C	Conscientiousness	easy going, careless	efficient, organized
E	Extroversion	solitary, reserved	out-going, energetic
A	Agreeableness	suspicious, detached	friendly, compassionate
N	Neuroticism	secure, confident	sensitive, nervous

Illustration 16. The Big Five Personality Traits

(O) Openness reflects an appreciation for art, emotion, adventure, unusual ideas, imagination, curiosity, and a variety of experiences. It describes the person's degree of intellectual curiosity, creativity and a preference for novelty and diversity. Openness also describes the extent to which a person is independent. People who have high O scores tend to be more creative and more aware of their feelings than people with low O scores. They are also more likely to hold unconventional beliefs. They are often perceived to be unpredictable or easily distracted. Conversely, those with low openness prefer routine, are dogmatic and usually closed-minded. Moslow's mature personalities are high in openness.

(C) Conscientiousness describes a person's tendency to be organized and dependable, show self-discipline, act dutifully, strive for achievement above expectations, and prefer planned rather than spontaneous behavior. Conscientiousness also refers to the way in which people control and direct their impulses. High conscientiousness is often perceived as stubbornness and obsessive. Mature personalities are very conscientious. This may seem contradictory, because Moslow observed that mature personalities are spontaneous, but remember, they are spontaneous, but not impulsive. They can allow themselves to be natural more often, because they are so efficient and logical. Low conscientiousness is associated with flexibility and spontaneity, but can also appear as sloppiness and unreliable. Mature personalities are very conscientious.

(E) Extraversion describes a person's energy level, positive emotions, assertiveness, social skills, the tendency to seek the company of others and the breadth of activities. High extraversion is often perceived as attention-seeking and domineering. Extraverts enjoy interacting with people, and are often perceived as energetic. They possess high group visibility, like to talk, and are assertive.

Low extraversion people are reserved and reflective people, who can be perceived as aloof or self-absorbed. Introverts have lower social engagement and energy levels than extraverts. They tend to seem quiet, calm, deliberate, and less involved in social activities. Their lack of social involvement should not be interpreted as shyness or depression. Instead they are more independent of their social group than extraverts. Introverts need less stimulation than extraverts and seek more time alone. This does not mean that they are unfriendly or anti-social, but rather they are reserved in social situations. Mature personalities are more introverted.

(A) Agreeableness refers to the ability to be compassionate and cooperative rather than suspicious and antagonistic towards others. It is also a measure of one's trusting and helpful nature and whether a person is even-tempered. They are generally considerate, kind, generous, trusting, trustworthy, helpful, and willing. High agreeable individuals value getting along with others, they seek social harmony and are willing to compromise their interests.

Disagreeable individuals place self-interest above getting along with others. They are generally unconcerned with others' well-being and are less likely to effort themselves for others. Sometimes their skepticism about others' motives causes them to be suspicious, unfriendly, and uncooperative. Because agreeableness is a social trait, research has shown that one's agreeableness positively correlates with the quality of relationships. Low agreeableness personalities are often competitive or challenging people, who can be seen as argumentative.

Mature personalities are generally agreeable people, although they do not compromise their values for harmony.

(N) Neuroticism describes the person's tendency to experience negative emotions easily such as anger, anxiety, depression, and vulnerability. Neuroticism also refers to the degree of emotional stability and impulse control. Those who score high in neuroticism are emotionally reactive and vulnerable to stress. They are more likely to interpret ordinary situations as threats and minor frustrations as hopeless. Their negative emotional reactions tend to persist for unusually long periods of time, which means they are often in a bad mood. Problems with emotional regulation can diminish the ability of a person scoring high on neuroticism to think clearly, make decisions, and cope effectively with stress.

At the other end of the scale, individuals who score low in neuroticism are less easily upset and are less emotionally reactive. They tend to be calm, emotionally stable, and free from persistent negative feelings. Low neuroticism manifests as a stable and calm personality. Mature personalities are not neurotic. They are very confident and optimistic.

Because openness, consientiousness, extroversion and agreeableness are desireable traits, whereas neuroticism is not, I often replace neuroticism with positivity when describing certain personalities. A person who is low in neuroticism is high in positivity.

In summary, mature personalities are open-minded and curious (high O), disciplined and organized (high C), introverted and reserved (low E), agreeable although not high in conformity (medium A), as well as, confident and secure in their identities (high P ore low N). This combination of traits insulates the mature personality from stress, enables them to effectively manage life changing events, and gives them time, resources, and energy to focus on higher needs.

Personality as a Predictive Indicator

The predictive power of personality traits is evident across many domains of life like private, work, and relationships. Openness and conscientiousness are strong predictors of vocational success. Several studies including those published by teams lead by Komarraju[85] and Berings[86] show that openness has a positive relationship with cognitive ability, which is an important factor in academic and professional achievement. Research by Mount and Barrick shows that job performance and income are positively correlated to openness and conscientiousness, because these traits promote proactivity. I emphasize again the efficiency aspect, because income alone is not an insulator against stress.[87] An educated, wealthy, especially an inexperienced or suddenly rich person, who is not conscientious, is at risk of experiencing stress and poorly managing it. Extroversion and agreeableness are not strong drivers of individual career success as these often lead to complacency in the workplace, but they are strong predictors of team and organizational success. Openness and conscientiousness are strong predictors of personal success. Studies show that high levels of openness and conscientiousness can add as many as five years to a person's life. Simply put, preparation prevents poor performance. Curious and organized people are smart and stabile. These traits improve job stability and financial security, decrease the risk of experiencing avoidable life changing events like termination, and improve the ability to cope with unavoidable stressors like death of a family member. Finally, recent research by Holland and Roisman demonstrates that relationship quality is strongly related to openness, conscientiousness, extroversion and agreeableness.[88] Neuroticism is a predictor of failure in all domains of life, and recent research indicates that high neuroticism predates the development of all common mental disorders.[89]

Chapter 5

Depression is a Process

Nothing suddenly breaks. Mechanics and engineers are aware of this. Geologists know this. Physicians and psychologists know this. Dissatisfaction, failure, sadness, anger, stress, and illness develop according to a clear process. It starts with something seemingly insignificant and can grow into something serious. There are always early indicators that something is wrong.

Major Depressive Disorder (MDD), also known as depression, is a mental disorder characterized by at least two weeks of low mood accompanied by low self-esteem, loss of interest in normally enjoyable activities, low energy, and pain without a clear cause.[90]

MDD can negatively affect a person's family, work and school life, sleeping or eating habits, and general health. Some people have periods of depression separated by years in which they are normal, while others may always display symptoms.

Depression is a big problem. According to the Global Burden of Disease Study published in 2013, about 3.6 percent of the global population (253 million people) was diagnosed with MDD. The percentage of people who are affected at one point in their life varies from 7 percent in Japan to 21 percent in France. Lifetime rates for depression are higher in the developed world (15 percent) compared *to the* developing world (11 percent).[91] Steven Richards and Michael O'Hara found that 2 to 7 percent

97

of adults with major depression die by suicide, and up to 60 percent of people who die by suicide had depression or another mood disorder.[92]

There are several theories explaining the cause of depression including biological, genetic, psychological, and environmental influencers. Today, the biopsychosocial (bio-psycho-social) model, also known as the diathesis–stress model, is widely accepted as the most logical explanation. It postulates that depression results when a pre-existing vulnerability is activated by stressful life events. The vulnerability for MDD can be a biological, genetic and/or schematic. Accordingly, genetics and biology do not trigger depression, but rather they increase the risk that stress turns into depression.

Vulnerabilities for Stress and Depression

1. Biological Vulnerabilities

According to various biological approaches like the *permissive hypothesis* and the *monoamine hypothesis* of depression, a deficiency of certain neurotransmitters is responsible for the features of depression like low mood, low energy, or pain without an obvious source.[93] This is why most antidepressant medications alter the levels of one or more of the monoamines like serotonin, norepinephrine and dopamine. Medications can normalize neurotransmitter levels and reduce the features of depression, but they do not resolve the causes of the dysregulation. Something triggers this dysfunction and it is usually an external factor. A lifestyle adjustment is, therefore, the first advice from Harvard Medical for treating depression. According to Doctors Joanna Saisan, Melinda Smith, and Jeanne Segal, lifestyle changes are just as effective as medication and sometimes all that is needed.[94] The recommended changes include:

1. Exercise regularly to boost the production of neurotransmitters.
2. Eat small, well-balanced meals made up of complex carbohydrates.
3. Sleep at least eight hours a night.
4. Reduce isolation by taking classes and volunteering.

5. Eliminate the aspects of your life that cause stress, such as work overload or bad relationships.

Only when these simple do-it-yourself measures do not work does Harvard Medical recommend seeking therapy or medical treatment and cautions "the depression won't lift until the underlying causes are identified and addressed."[95]

Another biological explanation deals with hormones. Females are affected by MDD twice as often as males and so the hormone estrogen has been implicated in depressive disorders, although the correlation is unclear, because episodes of depression in females are associated with increases in hormonal levels after puberty and also with decreases in estrogen levels during the premenstrual, postpartum and menopausal periods.[96]

2. Genetic Vulnerabilities

According to the American Psychiatric Association, about 40 percent of the risk of MDD is related to genetics.[97] Like biological vulnerabilities, neurotransmitters and hormones, the presence of certain genes can increase the vulnerability for depression, but genes do not cause MDD. Genes require activation and the most common time of onset is in persons in their 20s and 30s. Kendler et al. showed that stressful events in adulthood are strongly associated with the onset of major depressive episodes. In other words, the genetic predisposition for MDD exists already at birth, but depression only manifests decades later.[98] Robert Plomin proved that environment can even trump genetics. In one study of persons with the MAOA gene, the gene responsible for aggressive behavior, Plomin found that a positive environment suppressed inherited aggression, whereas a negative environment exacerbated it.[99]

3. Schematic Vulnerabilities

The schematic factors refer to environmental influencers like social-economic status and family structure.

A recent report titled *National Health Interview Survey* published by the U.S. Centers for Disease Control and Prevention (CDC) shows that a life of poverty is devastating to psychological and physical health: 8.7 percent of the people living below the federal poverty line experienced serious psychological distress, while only 1.2 percent of people at or above 400 percent of the poverty line suffered depression.[100]

Why are poor families more than seven times more susceptible to stress than affluent families? For starters, many in poverty rely on unhealthy processed foods to satisfy their hunger. We know from previously cited studies that these foods are efficient when measuring calories per dollar, but they are more expensive than home cooking and often associated with over-eating and obesity, which can cause other more serious health complications. Another reason is that low-income, poorly insulted apartments do not mute the sounds of crime, domestic violence, and other night time activities. Sleep is a basic need and noise can cause sleep deprivation, making it difficult to focus at work or in school. Noise also has physiological effects that impede learning. In 2013, scientists found that constant noise can damage a child's auditory processing[101] and another study showed dramatic declines in IQ for people living in poverty.[102] Remember, IQ is not a measurement of intellectual potential, but a reflection of acquired knowledge. It is difficult for a young person to acquire knowledge when they are tired and can't hear the teacher. Furthermore, poor families usually live in economically disadvantaged neighborhoods where educational resources are often deficient making it more difficult, even for smart children, to acquire the material necessary to break the cycle of poverty. The higher a person's parents are on the income ladder, the more likely they are to work as an adult. Stanford economist Raj Chetty showed that children from poor families are much less likely to work as adults than children from middle-class families.[103] According to Chetty's findings, about 60 percent of children from the poorest families were working at age 30, compared to 80 percent of children from median-income families. The relationship between the income of parents and the income of children is also linear, because, not surprisingly, Chetty found a strong correlation between parents' earnings and children's chances of attending college. Americans who grow up poorer are less likely to go to college.

Research proves that socio-economic status and child abuse go hand in hand. This is not an absolute relationship, but a strong direct correlation. Using state-level data on child abuse, family structure, and economics, Paxson and Waldfogel observed that every one percent decrease in income below the poverty level resulted in a four percent increase in cases of abuse. Furthermore, Paxson and Waldfogel found that for every a one percent increase in the number of children living with a single non-working mother resulted in a 6.6 percent increase in physical abuse and a 12.6 percent increase in cases of neglect.[104]

According to Dr. Kathlene Kendall-Tackett, "people who experienced childhood abuse or severe neglect often see the world as a dangerous place."[105] Because they were powerless as children, they are fearful and overestimate danger and adversity as adults. They often underestimate their ability to deal with both real and perceived threats. Some display symptoms of post-traumatic stress disorder (PTSD) like persistent arousal, nervousness, sleep disorders, poor concentration, and attention deficit. People who were physically abused as children often become co-dependent adults, who are eager to adopt the views of others in order to avoid punishment or receive affection. This can cause them to be gullible and easily manipulated by others and lead to the acceptance of false beliefs and prejudices. Childhood abuse can manifest as coping mechanisms like substance abuse, compulsive high-risk sexual activities, eating disorders, and self-injurious behaviors. Past abuse can decrease the person's ability to trust others and cause avoidant behavior.

More alarming, is the finding that it is difficult to break the cycle of poverty. Scientists looked at more than 20,000 sites in the human genome of 3,000 people and found that people who grew up in poverty had vastly different gene expressions than people who matured with money.[106] Poverty, therefore, has a lasting impact on a person's DNA. This is consistent with the findings from Plomin that a negative environment can activate genetic vulnerabilities and a positive environment can override some biological and schematic predispositions.

In my own research, I identified dozens of children whose talents were first discovered after they were removed from a negative environment and placed in a more positive environment. These children were placed in foster homes or protective custody to rescue them from seriously neglectful or dangerous parents, some were children voluntarily given up for adoption by their parents who were admittedly unfit or unwilling to raise them, and several were children from developing countries who had been adopted by couples in America or Europe. The latter case is especially interesting, because those childrens` biological parents were not abusive. They were very loving. They just lived in extreme poverty and/or in oppressive countries. In all cases, their amazing talents were discovered after they were transplanted into a more positive environment. The uncovered talents included music, arts, language, science and mathematics. The adoptive parents of one girl reported that she taught herself a new language every year. After four years with her new family, she was literate in her mother language as well as in French, English, Dutch and Italian. Her ambition at age twelve was to work for the United Nations Organization. Another child, who could barely read and write when he was adopted, was doing 10th grade math just two years later when he was in fifth grade. His goal was to become a math teacher, because "It's actually a lot more fun than the teachers make it," he said. Clearly, in these cases, forced diversity coupled with stability created an environment in which these talents could be promoted.

Life Changing Events

In 1967, psychiatrists Thomas Holmes and Richard Rahe conducted a study involving more than 5,000 medical patients to determine the relationship between stress and illness. The patients were asked to indicate on a list of events those which they experienced in the year preceding their illness. Holmes and Rahe found that 88.2 percent of the patients experienced some combination of stressful events in the months before becoming ill.[107] Three years later, Rahe carried out another study to test the stress scale as a predictor of illness. 2,500 U.S. sailors were asked to select the life events they experienced in the prior six months. Over the following six months, detailed records were kept on the sailors' health. The sailors' scores correlated with drop-out rates due to medical problems. [108] The Holmes-Rahe Stress Scale has been assessed against different populations internationally and validated as a reliable model for predicting stress-induced illnesses.

The stress score represents the risk of the reported events triggering stress and illness. It is a statistical probability following a standard distribution curve. In this case, 88 percent of the subjects who had a high risk score suffered illness, 58 percent of the subjects with a moderate risk score suffered stress-induced illness, and only 28 percent of the subjects with a low risk score suffered illness. A high stress score does not mean stress-induced illness is unavoidable, and a low score does not denote illness is improbable. The Holmes-Rahe Stress Scale is, like all models, a statistical tool: 12 percent of the subjects with a high stress score did not get ill and 28 percent of those with a low score did. There are always exceptions.

Life Changing Events (Stressors)	Stress Units	Sample
Death of a spouse	100	
Divorce (of friend or family member)	73	
Marital (or family) separation	65	65
Imprisonment (of friend or family)	63	
Death of family member	63	
Personal injury or illness	53	
Marriage (of friend or family)	50	
Dismissal from work (of friend or family)	47	
Marital reconciliation	45	
Retirement	45	
Change in health of family member (or friend)	44	
Pregnancy	40	
Sexual difficulties	39	
Gain a new family member	39	
Business readjustment	39	
Change in financial state	38	
Death of a close friend	37	
Change to different line of work	36	
Major mortgage	32	
Foreclosure of mortgage or loan	30	
Change in responsibilities at work	29	
Child leaving home	29	29
Trouble with in-laws	29	29
Outstanding personal achievement	28	
Spouse starts or stops work	26	26
Beginning or ending school	26	
Change in relationship status	25	25
Revision of personal habits	24	
Trouble with boss	23	
Change in working hours or conditions	20	
Change in residence	20	20

(continued on next page)

Life Changing Events (Stressors)	Stress Units	Sample
Change in schools	20	
Change in church activities	19	
Change in social activities	18	
Minor mortgage or loan	17	
Change in sleeping habits	16	
Change in number of family reunions	15	
Change in eating habits	15	
Vacation	13	
Major holiday	12	
Violation of law (or legal issues)	11	
Failure	10	
Peer pressure, e.g. bullying or mobbing	10	
Accident	10	
Natural Disaster	50	
Victim of war incl. displacement	100	
Victim of violent crime, e.g. rape	100	
Victim of minor crime, e.g. burglary, identity theft	30	
Stress Score		**194**

Illustration 17. Holmes-Rahe Life Changing Events

Not all of the experiences reported by the subjects in my study matched directly to a Holmes-Rahe event, so I extended the scope of some definitions and appended some new events to the list. Holmes and Rahe asked subjects to indicate the events they experienced in the past 12 months and then add up the stress units.

Likelihood of Illness	Stress Score	Sample
High Risk	>300	
Moderate Risk	150-299	**194**
Low Risk	<150	

Illustration 18: Stress Score

This is exactly what we observed in our analysis. Even though all of my subjects reported some combination of life changing events and had moderate to very high risk scores, none had been clinically diagnosed with depression. They did not use words like stress or depression in their narratives to describe their feelings. Instead they described their emotions with words like sad, irritated, irate, annoyed, frustrated, pissed, mad, disappointed, confused, angry, and burned-out. They sensed that something was wrong and sought therapy or counseling to understand and address their feelings thus preventing depression from manifesting. This is an important learning, because it tells us that there are some simple early indicators of depression and many people already recognize them. We can't walk around with a Holmes-Rahe stress app to constantly record our experiences and measure our stress scores, although this is a clever idea, but we can monitor our emotions. When we feel certain emotions, we can take preventive action.

Just as Holmes and Rahe did, we asked 100 subjects to indicate the events they experiences and tell us how they felt. We then assigned their emotions to their stress scores. For example, the word pissed was used by 12 subjects who had accumulated lower stress scores, by 82 subjects who had moderate stress scores, and by 6 subjects who had high stress scores. Therefore, we associated the feeling of being pissed or pissed-off with a moderate stress score. The word sad was used by 90 subjects who had high stress scores and only 4 who had low scores so sadness is an emotion associated with a complex series of stressors.

Stress Score	Emotions
>300	angry, burned-out, sad
150-299	irate, mad, frustrated, annoyed, pissed
<150	irritated, disappointed, confused

Illustration 19: Emotional Escalation

This little experiment needs to be conducted on a broader scale, but it provides an initial baseline for guessing someone's stress score. It tells us that a singular stressful event or a low level combination of stressors produce simple confusion and disappointment, but not anger and sadness. When these initial events trigger other events and stress continues to grow over time, a trend or pattern emerges that makes subjects feel hopeless or powerless, and confusion turns into frustration. Eventually, this hopelessness turns into defeat, when the person realizes that the situation will continue. So, the next time you hear someone say, "I'm pissed," you can interpret that to mean that they experienced a single low level event. When that person later says, "I'm so sad," then it probably indicates they experienced a series of stressors over time and are growing desperate.

> Mervin: After I got discharged from the hospital and started receiving huge bills, I was confused, because I thought my insurance would cover those charges. When the insurance rejected my claim and the hospital started assessing late fees, I became frustrated, because I was doing my best to sort things out. When I had to be re-hospitalized for an infection stemming from the surgery, I was angry. I knew this situation wasn't going away quickly.

> Trisha: When my daughter called me to pick her up from a party, because she was too drunk to drive home, I was disappointed. I thought we taught her to be more responsible. When she got arrested for a DUI and lost her license, I got pissed. Didn't she learn? How was she supposed to get to work and school if she didn't have a job? And when she got kicked out of school for vandalism, I felt angry and sad, because I knew things could only go downhill from there.

A study of the effects of stress over time titled *Time Series Analysis of Events, Mood, Stress, and Satisfaction* by Fuller et al. showed that the impact of stress builds over time.[109] Depression is not a waterfall effect or some sudden occurrence, but rather a domino effect in that one stressful event can lead to others. The cumulative impact of a series of stressors grows over time.

Jim: I was the first person in my family to go to college and was super proud to get accepted into State. I loved campus life, made lots of new friends, joined a top fraternity, and quickly slipped into the party scene. In my first year, I was cited three times for under-age drinking. They were campus cops and I didn't think it counted, but I found out later it does. My parents didn't start a college fund for me, so I had to apply for student loans and I also worked part-time delivering pizzas. I was very bad at managing money. I blew it on video games, pizza, and beer. Half way through my sophomore year, I had a girlfriend and ran out of money. One of my friends gave me a small bag of marijuana to sell. I was such a bad drug dealer; I got arrested the same day for 'drug possession with the intent to sell.' I was too embarrassed to call my parents so I sat in jail for 3 days and missed an important test. I was also fired from my job because I missed work. When I was released, I tried to focus on doing better in school, but then I received a notice to appear in court. I pled guilty to drug possession and agreed to take a diversion class, because I my friends said the charge would get dismissed, because I was a first-time offender. They were wrong. Apparently, I had so much marijuana that it counted as a felony. When I applied for student loans to pay tuition, I was rejected due to the charges on my police record. So I had to drop out of college. Now I owe $40.000 for student loans and have nothing to show for it. I can't get a job, because I have all those charges on my police report and I had to move back with my parents. Oh yeah, I also got gonorrhea from my girlfriend, who just broke up with me because she says I'm the loser.

Maybe you noticed that words belonging to the friend group are used frequently in Jim's narrative. Jim didn't experience a heavy dose of life changing events all at once. He experienced a series of low level stressors in his freshman year when he got accepted to college, moved into a dorm, joined a fraternity, and borrowed money for college. Jim's inability to deal effectively with these events triggered a series of more serious stressors in his sophomore year that pushed his cumulative stress score over 300 and into the high risk zone. This process is shown in Illustration 20.

Even though it usually takes a combination of stressors to trigger depression, an unusual first time experience can have grave consequences. Even seemingly positive events like vacation, starting college, getting a new job and getting married can cause stress, because change always represents some level of crisis. Studies by Kessler showed that the first episode of psychological illness is more likely to be immediately preceded by a stressful event than a recurrent situation.[110]

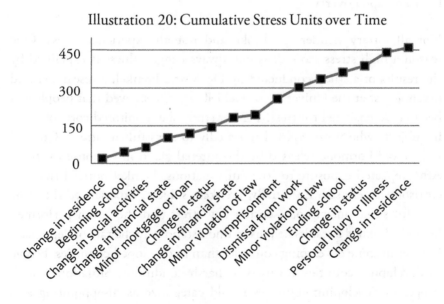

Illustration 20: Cumulative Stress Units over Time

Probably the best example of positive experiences triggering stress is an objective look at lottery winners. Winning a lottery or large inheritance is a singular life changing event that should improve the future of the recipients in that having an enormous surplus can produce stability and security for the entire family and cohort. But, like other seemingly positive life changing events, first-time windfalls can be stressors that activate other stressors and start the spiraling decline to depression. The Certified Financial Planner Board of Standards reports "nearly a third of lottery winners declare bankruptcy within three years."[111] According to the National Endowment for Financial Education, 70 percent of people who win a lottery or receive a big inheritance end up broke within a few years.[112] Steve Lewit, an expert wealth advisor, explains this phenomenon, "people who were little, ordinary people all of a sudden become extraordinary. They lose all sense of reality."[113] All change triggers some crisis and a windfall can cause an incredible crisis, because most lottery winners are inefficient at satisfying their own basic needs let alone managing a surplus. A study titled *Hitting the Jackpot or Hitting the Skids* by Blalock et al. found that lottery ticket sales rise with poverty, but movie ticket sales do not.[114] Blalock concluded that playing the lottery was not just another form of entertainment, but a bet to escape poverty.

Not all lottery winners go broke and not all experience stress. One reason a high stress score does not always trigger illness is explained by the results of a study conducted by Dr. Marie Frenkel, a researcher and psychologist at the University of Heidelberg. She showed that people can become desensitized to stress. For her study she monitored cortisol levels in subjects who were exposed repeatedly to stressful situations. Cortisol is a steroid hormone released by the adrenal gland in response to stress. After repeated exposure to stressful situations, Frenkel noticed that less cortisol was released. Eventually, Frenkel's subjects experienced the same stressful situation without sensing any stress and they even performed better.[115] Frenkel's results help us to understand why the rate of depression is lower in some developing countries than in developed countries: People in developing counties are used to harsh conditions. Situations which people in developing countries would categorize as disappointing and unacceptable are everyday realities for people living in developing countries.

Coincidentally, the desensitizing effect of stressors was also observed in lottery winners who did not go bankrupt. Researchers at Northwestern University and the University of Massachusetts interviewed lottery winners and recent victims of accidents who were paralyzed. The two groups were asked to rate the level of pleasure they got from everyday activities like chatting with friends, watching t.v., eating breakfast, or laughing at a joke. The researchers found that the recent accident victims reported more happiness from these everyday pleasures than the lottery winners.[116] Psychologists attribute this to *hedonic adaptation:* when experiences are judged based on their deviation from a baseline of past experiences, gradually even the most positive events cease to have impact as they themselves become part of the new baseline against which further events are measured. The medical explanation attributes hedonic adaptation to dopamine, a neurotransmitter that is released in the brain in response to positive experiences. When expectations are met, dopamine is released and the person senses satisfaction. Eventually, pleasureful activities become normal and the frequency of dopamine release decreases prompting the person to seek new experiences and set higher expectations for pleasure or use chemicals to stimulate dopamine. Simply put, paraplegics reported more happiness from simple activities, because their baseline included a recent catastrophic accident, whereas lottery winners did not feel joy from simple things because their baseline included receiving a check for millions of dollars.

The constant search for new experiences that produce satisfaction is a secret force driving some of the world's most innovative people. Richard Branson and Elon Musk are perfect examples. Their growing list of endeavors is bewildering. To name just a few: Branson founded the recording studio Virgin Records, went on to form Virgin Atlantic airlines, created a space tourism program Virgin Galactic, established the alternative energy company Virgin Fuel and then started the not-for-profit Virgin Earth Challenge to promote the development of environmental technologies. Musk invented the online payment platform Paypal, went on to found the electric car company TeslaMotors, opened his electric battery patents, launched a space program SpaceX, and is planning to build a hyper-speed transportation system called Hyperloop. Clearly, these two exceptional people are constantly seeking new highs and having enormous positive impacts on society. All of these contributions are made possible by a stable and secure foundation. Branson and Musk may take issue with my using them as examples of hedonism, but I am not using the urban definition of hedonism, which equates pleasure with selfishness. I use hedonism in the utilitarian sense in that maximizing pleasure and the well-being for many is the ethically goal in human life. Branson and Musk could have taken their initial fortunes and retired on a mega-yacht or tropical island, but they are self-less utilitarians. By the way, Branson did buy a tropical island and then converted it to a flamingo refuge.

In summary, depression results when a pre-existing vulnerability is activated by some combination of life changing events. Life changing events can be stressors and, whether fundamentally positive like marriage and personal achievement or inherently negative like death and illness, they can have negative and positive outcomes depending on the ability of the experiencer to manage these situations. We can't prevent dissatisfaction or disappointment completely, because we can't control others or the environment. The waitress will mess up your order, the mortgage company will post your payment to the wrong account, your boss will take credit for your fantastic idea, storm damage may force you to cancel your vacation, and someone you love will get very sick. Shit happens. People will continue to make mistakes and nature is not very happy with mankind right now. Nevertheless, we can stop getting mad, angry and frustrated by (a) reducing the chances of experiencing the avoidable life changing events like getting fired, and (b) being prepared to manage the unexpected events like the death of a family member or personal injury.

Chapter 6

Parenting

There are several phases of human development from birth to adulthood and the experiences a person has as a child impact the individual's ability to manage the next stage in their development.

Virtues

Erik Erikson, in collaboration with Joan Erikson, identified eight stages of development through which an individual passes from infancy to maturity. According to the Eriksons, all virtues are present at birth and emerge according to one's upbringing. In each stage, the person is confronted with new challenges, which they hopefully master. Like Moslow, the Eriksons asserted that the stages of development are dependent and, therefore, the mastery of a stage is not required to advance to the next stage, but unsuccessful stages produce deficits and problems later in life.

Stage	Age	Virtue	Qualities (Forces)	
			Positive	**Negative**
Infancy	0-23 mos.	Hope	Trust	Mistrust
Early Childhood	2-4 yrs.	Will	Autonomy	Shame, Doubt
Preschool	4-5 yrs.	Purpose	Initiative	Guilt
School	5-12 yrs.	Competence	Industry	Inferiority
Adolescence	13-19 yrs.	Fidelity	Identity	Role Confusion
Early Adulthood	20-39 yrs.	Love	Intimacy	Isolation
Adulthood	40-64 yrs.	Care	Generativity	Stagnation
Maturity	65-death	Wisdom	Integrity	Despair

Illustration 21: Stages of Psychosocial Development

During each stage, an individual is challenged by two conflicting forces. If an individual successfully reconciles these forces, they emerge from the stage with the corresponding virtue. For example, if parents are good providers then the infant experiences no deficits and carries the virtue of hope into the remaining stages of life. But, if parents fail to satisfy the infant's basic needs for food and security, then the infant is saddled with mistrust for the rest of its life.

1. Hope

The first stage of psychological development deals with the infant's basic needs being satisfied by the parents. This experience creates trust or mistrust. Trust is defined by Erikson as "an essential truthfulness of others as well as a fundamental sense of one's own trustworthiness."[117] A child's first trust testing relationship is always with the parents, because the infant depends on the parents, especially the mother, for sustenance and comfort. If the parents expose the child to warmth, regularity, and dependable affection, the infant's view of the world will be positive. If caregivers are consistent sources of food and affection, the infant learns that others are dependable and acquires the lasting virtue of hope.

Should the parents fail to provide a secure environment and meet the child's basic needs, mistrust will result. Mistrust can lead to feelings of frustration, suspicion, withdrawal, and a lack of confidence. If parents are neglectful or abusive, the infant advances to the next stage with the impression that the world is undependable, unpredictable, and probably dangerous.

	Positive	Negative
Experience	affection, stability, security	abuse, instability, insecurity
Perception	The world is safe. People are dependable.	The world is dangerous. People are unreliable.
Traits	trust, open-minded, positive	frustration, suspicious, withdrawal

Illustration 22: Infancy Crisis – Trust vs Mistrust

2. Will

As the child learns to control its eliminative functions and motor abilities, it begins to explore its surroundings. The parents can provide a strong base of security which enables the child to venture out and assert its will. The parents' patience and encouragement help foster autonomy in the child. At this age, children develop their first interests. A child who enjoys music may like to play with the radio or pound on pots and pans with wooden spoons. Children who enjoy the outdoors may be interested in insects, animals and plants. If parents encourage self-sufficient behavior, toddlers develop confidence that they can handle problems on their own and they acquire the virtue of will.

Highly restrictive parents, however, are more likely to instill in the child a sense of doubt and reluctance to explore. When caregivers demand too much too soon, refuse to let children perform tasks or ridicule the toddler's attempts to be self-sufficient, the child advances to the next stage with a sense of doubt about their ability to overcome challenges and handle problems.

	Positive	Negative
Experience	autonomy, patience, encouragement	ridicule, demanding, protecting
Perception	The world is exciting. People are kind.	The world is scary. People are mean.
Traits	autonomy, curiosity, independence, confidence	laziness, disinterest, unmotivated, doubt

Illustration 23: Early Childhood Crisis – Autonomy vs Doubt

3. Purpose

Initiative is the quality of planning and taking action for a reason. The child is learning basic skills like reading, writing and arithmetic as well as the principles of nature and physics. As described by Bee and Boyd, the child deals with the "complexities of planning and developing a sense of judgment."[118] Activities in this stage may include risk-taking behaviors that promote the development of courage and independence such as climbing a tree or riding a bicycle. The result is the child learns its abilities and limits.

For instances requiring initiative, the child may also develop negative behaviors when the actions produce unexpected or undesired results. Negative behaviors include a sense of guilt for not being able to achieve a goal as planned and may trigger aggressive and destructive behavior. When parents encourage and support the child's efforts, while also helping them make realistic and appropriate choices, children develop initiative and a sense of purpose. But if adults discourage the pursuit of independent activities or dismiss them as silly and unproductive, children develop guilt about their needs and desires.

	Positive	Negative
Experience	supportive	discouragement
Perception	The world is exciting. People are helpful.	Life is not fair. People are selfish.
Behavior	courage, confidence, initiative	fear, aggressive, destructive, negative

Illustration 24: Pre-school Crisis – Initiative vs Guilt

4. Competence

Children in this stage begin to learn how to be responsible and good. They understand the concepts of space and time in more logical, practical ways and gain a better understanding of cause and effect. At this stage, children form moral values, recognize cultural and individual differences and are able to manage some personal needs like grooming with minimal assistance. During this stage, children may test their independence by talking back, being disobedient or rebellious. Erikson viewed the elementary school years as critical for the development of self-confidence. Ideally, elementary school provides children many opportunities to earn the recognition of teachers, parents and peers by producing things, drawing pictures, building models, solving math problems, and writing stories. When children are encouraged to make and do things and are then praised for the results, they become industrious and diligent, they learn to persevere at tasks until completed and put work before pleasure. When children are ridiculed or punished for their efforts or if they find they are incapable of meeting their teachers' and parents' expectations, they develop feelings of inferiority about their capabilities.

At this age, children start recognizing their special talents and continue to discover interests as their education advances. They may choose to do more in the pursuit of their interests such as joining a science club, track team or marching band. If they are not allowed to discover and develop their own talents in their own time, they will develop a lack of motivation, low self-esteem, and lethargy. They may become couch potatoes if they are not allowed to develop their interests.

	Positive	Negative
Experience	encouragement, support	ridicule, punishment
Perception	The world is my oyster. People are so interesting.	Everything is stupid. Nothing makes sense.
Traits	responsibility, diligence, perseverance, productivity	disobedience, inferiority, laziness

Illustration 25: School Crisis – Industry vs Inferiority

5. Fidelity

Each stage that came before and that follows involves a crisis, but the crisis is greatest during adolescence. Adolescence is a turning point in human development, because it requires reconciliation between the person someone was raised to be, the person one is, and the person one thinks society expects one to become. The adolescent is primarily concerned with how they are perceived by others and ponders the role they will play in the adult world. They are apt to experience some confusion about vocation, religion, sexual and political orientation. Erikson calls this conflict an *identity crisis*. When society is open and tolerant, the adolescent can balance these conflicts and establish a secure identity or self-image. The result of this stage is the virtue of fidelity, which refers to the ability to keep true to oneself in spite of disparate external expectations and influences. Erikson noted that identity formation today tends to take longer, because it takes us so long to gain the skills needed for adulthood tasks in a technological world.

	Positive	**Negative**
Experience	encouraging, supportive	strict, demanding
Perception	I know my purpose in the world.	I don't know who I am.
Traits	reliable, stabile, secure, true, trustworthiness	Indecisiveness, insecure, unreliable, untrustworthy

Illustration 26: Adolescent Crisis – Identity vs Role Confusion

6. Love

Establishing identity is a pre-requisite for being able to make long-term commitments to others. The person becomes capable of forming intimate, reciprocal relationships and making the sacrifices that such relationships require. This entails managing the expectations of intimacy with isolation. If people cannot form these intimate relationships, perhaps because of their own deficits, isolation may result in feelings of *Angst*.

	Positive	Negative
Experience	affection	rejection
Perception	Life is an adventure.	People are bad.
Traits	extroversion, compromising, empathetic	avoidant, withdrawal, anti-social

Illustration 27: Adult Crisis – Intimacy vs Isolation

Parenting Styles

Mastering these virtues depends to a great extent on the individual's relationship with its parents. Parenting refers to the styles and practices of promoting the physical, emotional, social, financial, and intellectual development of a child from infancy to adulthood. Research in parenting and child development found what we would expect: children develop higher levels of competence, better social skills and proficiency when parents provide them with a proper combination of nurture, independence and control. During the 1980s, researchers began exploring how specific parenting styles influence a child's development. The most relevant material is the research conducted by Diana Baumrind on parenting typology.[119] In her research, she found four basic elements that define parenting. Parents have either very high expectations (demanding) or low expectations (undemanding) of their children, and they are either emotionally supportive (responsive) or insensitive (unresponsive). Maccoby and Martin[120] expanded upon Baumrind's findings and the result is a matrix showing the four parenting styles that result from combing these four elements.

		Expectations	
		Demanding	Undemanding
Support	Responsive	Authoritative	Indulgent
	Unresponsive	Authoritarian	Neglectful

Illustration 28: Parenting Styles

1. Authoritative Parenting

Authoritative parents are demanding and responsive. Authoritative parenting is characterized by an approach that involves goal setting and holds high expectations for development. Authoritative parents try to understand how their children are feeling and teach them how to regulate their feelings. Even with high expectations of maturity, authoritative parents are usually forgiving of failure and shortcomings. They often help their children to find the appropriate approach to solving problems. Authoritative parents encourage children to be independent, but still place realistic limits on their activities. They allow the child to explore more freely, which empowers them to make their own decisions based upon their own reasoning. Often, authoritative parents produce children who are more independent and self-reliant.

Authoritative parents will set clear standards for their children, monitor the limits that they set, and also allow children to develop autonomy. They also expect mature, independent, and age-appropriate behavior of their children. Punishments for misbehavior are measured and consistent, not arbitrary or violent. Often behaviors are not punished, but the natural consequences of the child's actions are identified and discussed. This allows the child to understand the difference between avoiding behavior that is inappropriate versus avoiding behavior to avoid punishment. Authoritative parents set limits and demand maturity. They also tend to give more positive encouragement at the right places. However, when punishing a child, the parent will explain his or her motive for their punishment. Children are more likely to respond to authoritative parenting punishment because it is reasonable and fair.

These individuals have acquired the virtues hope, will, purpose, and competence, which are cornerstones of a secure identity. They have also acquired openness, conscientiousness, extroversion, agreeableness and positivity. They have no or few deficits and seek friends with whom they can learn and develop.

2. Authoritarian Parenting

Authoritative parents are demanding, but unresponsive. Authoritarian parents focus on discipline and punishment. They make their children follow their directions with little to no explanation or feedback and have a strong focus on the child's and the family's perception and status. Corporal punishment are forms of discipline frequently used by authoritarian parents. The goal of this style, at least when well-intentioned, is to teach the child to behave, survive, and thrive as an adult in a harsh and unforgiving society. In addition, advocates of this style often believe that the shock of aggression from someone from the outside world will be less for a child accustomed to enduring both acute and chronic stress imposed by parents.

Authoritarian parenting has distinctive effects on children. Children raised by authoritarian parents may have less social competence, because the parent generally tells the child what to think and do instead of allowing the child to choose for themselves, making the child appear to excel in the short term, but limiting development in ways that are increasingly revealed as supervision and parental control decline.

Children of authoritarian parents are conditioned to behave and do not learn creative-thinking and reasoning skills. These individuals acquired the virtues hope and competence, but they did not acquire will and purpose. Their parents did not allow them to conduct self-discovery. They are conscientious and agreeable, but not open, extroverted or positive. They are very disciplined. Because they have a deficit on will and openness, they seek friends that can facilitate their independence and courage. Children of authoritarian parents become dependent, conformist, highly obedient, and quiet.

3. Indulgent Parenting

The indulgent parent is responsive, but not demanding. Indulgent parenting, also sometimes called permissive, non-directive, lenient or libertarian parenting, is characterized by having low behavioral expectations for the child. Indulgent parenting is a style of parenting in which parents are very involved with their children, but place few demands or controls on them.

Parents are nurturing, accepting and responsive to the child's needs and wishes. Indulgent parents do not require children to control themselves or behave appropriately. Permissive parents try to be friends with their children. Permissive parents permit their children to make their own decisions and give them advice as a friend would. This type of parenting is very lax, with few rules and little punishment. Permissive parents also tend to give their children whatever they want and hope that they are appreciated for their accommodating style.

Results of the indulgent parenting style are individuals with trust, autonomy and initiative, but adults who are less socially adept, and may behave in ways that cause aggression in others. They often do not learn to control their own behavior, they lack concentration and diligence, do not like to make compromises, and always expect to get their way. They tend to be more impulsive and as adolescents engage in misconduct such as drug use.

These individuals acquire the traits hope, will, and purpose, but they do not acquire competence and fidelity. It is very curious, though, that these individuals are convinced of their competence. These individuals have a deficit on competence and identity. They seek friends who accept and respect them.

Donald Trump is a contemporary example of the product of indulgent parenting. On the positive side, children of indulgent parenting have strong will, courage and confidence. They are extroverted, energetic, positive, and act autonomously. But they have weaknesses in that they lack competence, conscientiousness, and agreeableness. They are supremely confident, although not always experienced and competent. This dichotomy stems from generous liberties and the perpetual praise they received from their parents. They believe they can master all things they set their minds to, because they received praise from their parents even when they failed. They know no boundaries or limits. Despite numerous proven failures, they continue to describe their endeavors as hugely successful, because they often perceive the effort or participation as important and the outcome as irrelevant. When others do not praise their actions, the indulgent child thinks they must be using some wrong criteria, they are liars or fakes.

When someone disagrees with them, they respond using the a*d hominem* argument, meaning they attack the other person's competence, character or appearance. Children of indulgent parents are low in agreeableness and do not seek harmony. They are confrontational, provocative, and impulsive. They say and write what they think without thinking about the impact of their words on others. They are thoroughly convinced that everything they think and say is genius so they become derogatory when others don't agree with them. Children of indulgent parents often make and lose friends fast and frequently. They end up wandering from one group to the next seeking acceptance. Indulgent children are often described as spoiled rotten. This description is very appropriate, because a rotten apple cannot be made good again. It is nearly impossible to resolve the fissure between incompetence and supreme confidence, especially when the rotten apple is a billionaire.

4. Neglectful Parenting

The neglectful parent is neither demanding nor responsive. Neglectful parenting is also called uninvolved, detached, dismissive or hands-off parenting. The parents are generally not involved in their child's life, are disengaged, undemanding, low in responsiveness, and do not set goals and limits. Neglectful parenting can also mean dismissing the children's emotions and opinions. Parents are emotionally unsupportive of their children, but will still provide their basic needs like food, housing, and toiletries, or money for these, but very little encouragement or guidance.

These individuals acquired will, purpose and competence, but lack hope and are low in positivity. Many children of this parenting style had to provide for themselves and they mature beyond their years. They had to learn to be independent and are high in conscientiousness, openness, and agreeableness. They had the freedom to explore everything, and their parents didn't care what they did or who they befriended. They have an emotional deficit, namely affection and validation, which they seek to fulfill with friends.

Studies reveal some surprising insights about the relationship between parenting and success, which are summarized in Illustration 29.

1. The authoritative style imparts all traits and values and prepares children to be productive and secure.
2. The goal of strict parenting is to enable children to become self-sufficient through discipline and diligence, but these children become easily impressionable. They tend to depend on others for guidance and are eager to conform.
3. Indulgent parents believe that by giving their children lots of attention and affection, they are building their self-esteem, but these children become fixated on receiving (not earning) the admiration of others.
4. The biggest surprise, I think, is that neglectful parenting promotes maturity more so than strict or permissive parenting.

		Authoritative	Authoritarian	Indulgent	Neglectful
Virtues	Hope, Trust, Positive, Openness	●	●	●	○
	Will, Independence, Confidence	●	○	●	●
	Purpose, Courage, Initiative	●	○	●	●
	Competence, Productivity, Diligence	●	●	○	●
	Fidelity, Trustworthy, Reliability	●	●	○	●
	Love, Compromising, Empathy	●	•	•	○
Traits	Openness, Curious, Inventive	●	○	●	○
	Conscientious, Organized, Efficient	●	●	○	●
	Extroverted, Energetic, Out-Going	•	•	●	●
	Agreeable, Friendly, Compassionate	•	●	○	•
	Positivity, Confidence, Secure	●	•	●	•

Key: ○ Deficit • Weakness ● Strength

Illustration: 29: Traits and Virtues Acquired from Parenting

If instilling confidence, independence, productivity, trustworthiness and rationality in a child is the goal, then being either a good coach or simply leaving the child alone produce the best results. The latter is an approach sociologist Frank Furedi calls *infant determinism*. Furedi doesn't necessarily encourage the neglectful parenting style, but he argues that children are capable of developing well in almost any environment, writing "development really wants to happen. It takes very impoverished environments to interfere with development."[121]

My favorite evidence for this phenomenon is the story of Marshall Mathers. Mathers was born 1972 and grew up in Warren, Michigan. Mather's father was absent, and his mother was a low-income trailer park tenant. Mathers spent three years in ninth grade due to truancy and poor grades and dropped out of high school at age 17. He held several different jobs to help his mother pay bills. The Mathers family was one of only three white households on the street and Marshall was beaten frequently by his black classmates. His city was plagued by crime. Warren is a suburb of Detroit and home to General Motors, Chrysler and Ford factories. Owing to factory closures and down-sizing, Warren has been one of the fastest-shrinking cities in the U.S. since 1970. Population has declined by more than 10 percent during the 1980's and 1990's, unemployment and crime rates increased. The number of homicides peaked in 1974 at 714 and again in 1991 with 615. Despite some improvement in the last years, Detroit remains the U.S. city with one of the highest rates of homicide per capita. The schematic factors (socio-economics, family structure, and education) were stacked against Mathers and he experienced a serious combination of stressors that pushed his Holmes-Rahe score over 500. Mathematically speaking, Mathews should have become mentally ill or violent. But he didn't. He is one of the 12 percent of people who experience a series of stressors, but do not get ill. Instead, Mathers channeled his frustration into music. Today, he is better known as the hip hop artist, Eminem. With U.S. sales of 45.1 million albums and 42 million tracks as of June 2014, Mathers is the second best-selling male artist according to Nielsen, the sixth best-selling artist in the United States and the best-selling hip-hop artist of all time. Mathers` story is a perfect anecdote for a couple important points:

1. Everyone has a talent and it just needs to be discovered and developed. Giving a child the freedom for self-discovery is critical to personal development.

2. A critical level of stress does not always trigger depression. There are positive expressions of stress and some people channel stress into talent development. Mathers may not be the role model you wish for your children. His lyrics are misogynist, racist, and homophobic, but he can be nonetheless an example, because I am certain we all agree that singing about frustration and fear is better than turning to drugs, violence or terrorism.

3. Parenting is critical. Mather's family structure was imperfect, but the lack of support and affection forced him to be courageous and diligent, to build confidence, and to learn independence.

4. Income, education, community and family structure are not determinant. Attempts have been made to link parenting styles with income and there is some correlation although it is insignificant. Neglectful and authoritarian parenting are more closely linked to lower income households, whereas authoritative and indulgent parenting have a correlation to higher income households, but these correlations are not strong enough to make any meaningful generalizations.

5. Friend selection is a function of parenting. We seek to fill the deficits produced during childhood with friends. Mathers' drug and legal problems began after the release of the *Marshall Mather's LP* in 2000, which sold 1.7 million copies in its first week and became the best-selling hip hop album. Mathers won the lottery, so to say, but this positive experienced turned into a life changing event for him. The explanation is, in the absence of affection and support from his family during childhood and adolescence, Mathers sought support and love from his friends. When he eventually won their admiration, he exaggerated the behavior of his friends and fans in order to preserve his membership and improve his status in the group.

The most important learning is that that the children of authoritative and neglectful parents are better equipped for self-sufficiency, independence, and success. They are high in openness and conscientiousness, confident, independent, diligent, efficient and productive.

Children of indulgent parenting are especially disadvantaged when it comes to psychological maturity, because they do not learn competence or diligence. The most prominent examples of indulgent parenting are depicted in the 2003 documentary film titled *Born Rich,* for which the heir to the Johnson & Johnson fortune, Jamie Johnson, interviewed ten other young heirs. Johnson needed three years to make the film, because most of the socialites he contacted refused interviews due to parental objection or a fear of losing their inheritance.[122] The film reflects what one would expect from rich socialites. With the exception of Ivanka Trump, who is clearly the result of authoritarian parenting, all of the heirs interviewed were notorious for their arrogance and misdeeds. The film-maker was even sued for slander after the film's release, but the cases were dismissed, because the stars defamed themselves.

Indulgence, however, goes much further than spoiling children with cars, gadgets and brands. Emotional indulgence can be even more damaging, because it produces people who are immature, insecure, and not independent. The indulgence trend started in the U.S. in the 1990's when psychologists began observing a dramatic increase in parental involvement in child play and education. Parental behaviors included hovering close to children on playgrounds and scrutinizing school curriculum in school and even in college. Foster Cline and Jim Fay coined the term *helicopter parent*[123] to describe the practice that parents are always hovering nearby ready to intervene, defend and rescue their children. This trend has affected a generation of adults born between around 1977 and 2003 called Millennials, Generation Y, Generation Me or, more appropriately, the Peter Pan Generation. Several factors fueled the indulgent parenting trend.

First, starting in the 1980's the fear of child abduction grew in America. There was no rational trigger for this phenomenon, because the number of child abductions per year since 1920 had actually declined steadily. Russell Thomas, a data scientist and a PhD student in Computational

Social Science at George Mason University, did an exhaustive analysis of the data and showed that the *stranger danger* phenomenon began in 1980's. Even though the Bureau of Justice Statistics (BJS) reported that less than 3 percent of child abductions involved strangers,[124] Thomas found that the frequency of use of phrases like "stranger danger," "child abduction" and "child sex abuse" in American literature and news reports suddenly increased in 1983 following several highly publicized news events including the Atlanta child murders of 1979-1981, the Etan Patz missing child case of 1979, the sensational McMartin Preschool trial 1984-1987, and the popular t.v. movie *Adam,* which portrayed the kidnapping and murder of Adam Walsh, the son of John Walsh, who when on to host the popular television series *America's Most Wanted.*[125] In response to the heightened public fear, President Ronald Reagan created the National Center for Missing and Exploited Children (NCMEC) in 1983 and the NCMEC launched a campaign a year later putting photographs and descriptions of missing children on milk cartons.[126] None of these sources or programs encouraged parents to drive their kids everywhere and be omnipresent, but chauffeuring children around in mini-vans and hovering near them at playgrounds became common and expected behavior.

Second, the No Child Left Behind (NCLB) Act was adopted with the goal of improving education through standardization and frequent assessment. The unintended consequence was that school districts lowered learning goals in order to make achieving them easier, and educators focused on teaching material that was on the assessment test.[127] NCLB essentially stripped independent thinking and initiative from learning. The question, "is this going to be on the test," became a mantra of the generation that became unmotivated to do anything extra.

Third, popular ideals influenced parenting. Some celebrities are so influential that their casual opinions can affect entire markets. When Oprah Winfrey told one guest that she was not going to eat hamburger, beef prices started a two week tailspin, hit a ten year low, and cattle ranchers in Texas sued for $10 million in damages.[128] The point being, when an influential entertainer like Oprah espouses their opinion, it can become a mandate for millions of viewers. Oprah frequently welcomed parenting experts who sometimes espoused very liberal views on parenting. Dr. Shefali Tsabary, for example, promotes the *conscious parenting* approach,[129] which is clearly undemanding and non-verbal responsive, i.e. indulgent. Tsabary asserts that children cannot be fixed through scolding or punishment, parents should not respond to bad behavior, but rather they should reflect on how that bad behavior makes them feel.[130] She thinks a bad behaving child can heal itself simply through the presence of and affection from the parents. In other words, when your child does something wrong, hold your breath and hug them. It's easy to believe that millions of parents liked this approach, because it makes parenting much easier. Not all of Oprah's guests were as spiritual as Dr. Tsabary, though. Dr. Phil's seven tips for parenting,[131] for example, are very much aligned with the authoritative style.

It is interesting how the combination of misinformation about child kidnapping rates, the homogenization of education through standardization, and popular ideas can have such a significant impact on a generation. A study by SYZGY in 2016 using the Narcissistic Personality Inventory found that Millennials exhibited 16 percent higher narcissism than other generations.[132] Moreover, they were attention seekers, defensive, and had an acute sense of entitlement. The majority of research concludes that Millennials differ from their predecessors in the workplace in that their top priority is maintaining a work-life balance. They work less and play more at work than co-workers from other generations. This generation also places a strong emphasis on social consciousness, immediate feedback, and a team-oriented work environment. They don't like to work alone or independently and are heavy users of social media during work. Author Ron Alsop calls Millennials "trophy kids,"[133] because they are used to getting recognized for participation, not for performance. Employers have reported this issue and recruiters observed that this generation changes jobs more frequently than the older generations.

I know I am painting with a broad brush, but these are statistical statements corroborated by studies conducted by universities, research institutions and corporations. Sociologists and psychologists agree that every generation has unique attributes and these are statistically significant, but never 100 percent accurate. If you study the segmentation schemas like PersonicX[134] or Prizm,[135] which are produced by leading companies like Acxiom and Nielsen, you will find a fairly accurate, albeit never perfect, profile of yourself, as well as, for your family and friends. These segmentation schemas are the result of very sophisticated analyses and complex statistical modeling. Thanks to new big data and analytic capabilities, the profiles are getting more exact all the time. If you believe you are a unique, different, or an outlier, there is even a group, which some segmentation experts call the *omegas* to which people who do not match the standard profiles belong. Curiously, they may have different demographic and socio-economic attributes, but they, too, think and behave similarly. They have rational priorities and follow similar processes and rules.

Chapter 7

Identity

Parenting influences the development of virtues and traits that define our strengths and weaknesses and serve as the framework for our self-concept or initial identity, which is a set beliefs about the world and our role in it.

In *Sources of the Self: The Making of the Modern Identity*, Charles Taylor defines identity as the commitments which provide the frame or horizon which someone uses to determine what is good or valuable, what ought to be done, and what one supports or opposes.[136] Thus, in Taylor's interpretation, personal identity is a set of principles that a person uses to guide their actions. According to James D. Fearon from Standford University, identity is a set of attributes, beliefs, and principles that a person accepts and (a) the person takes pride in, (b) the person takes no special pride in, but which orient her behavior so that she would be at a loss about how to act and what to do without them, or (c) the person feels she could not change even if she wanted to. [137]

(a) I am proud to be a teacher. Teaching is my calling.
(b) I am not proud of being a teacher, but I need the benefits. Teaching is just a job.
(c) I didn't have a choice. Teaching is a tradition.

Henri Tajfel's contribution to psychology was *social identity theory*. Social identity is a person's sense of who they are based on their group membership(s).[138] Tajfel proposed that the groups to which people belong

131

are an important source of pride and self-esteem. Groups give us a sense of belonging and, in order to increase our self-image, we enhance the status of the group to which we belong by discriminating against others. Therefore, we tend to divide the world into in-group (us) and out-groups (them). Common conflicts include science versus religion, Arabs versus Jews, white collar professionals versus blue collar workers, men versus women, liberals versus conservatives, and environmentalists versus corporations.

Mullin and Hogg proposed the idea of *social proof.* Accordingly, every group expects certain behaviors, routines, rituals, and actions.[139] By performing these, we demonstrate allegiance and this reduces uncertainty and secures our membership in the group. Taken together, this means that social behavior is motivated by (a) passion, (b) security, or (c) obligation. It, therefore, implies that some expressions of pride are not true. The passionate teacher advocates for the teachers' union, because they feel the union serves an important cause. The security-minded teacher promotes the teachers' union to protect their job. And the obligated teacher only gets involved, because they think they have no choice. Cialdini and Trost asserted that social identity creates boundaries for collective intelligence and collective action or joint intentionality and consequently sets boundaries for social learning.[140] This is an especially important assertion, because it implies that conformance, whether motivated out of passion, security, or obligation, can limit personal development.

My favorite example of social proof and the us-versus-them conflict that has slowed the improvement of the human condition is the debate over stem cell research. The ability to extract cells from umbilical cord blood to artificially grow specialized cell types like muscles or nerves began in the 1960's and promises to have a very positive impact on millions of lives. Today, bone marrow transplant is the only form of stem cell therapy that is widely used without controversy. The Center for International Blood and Marrow Transplant Research reported that in 2016 20.000 Americans received life-saving bone marrow transplants.[141] Much of the criticism is rooted in religious beliefs. In the most high-profile case, U.S. President George W. Bush signed an executive order banning the use of federal funding for any cell lines other than those already in existence, stating at the time, "My position on these issues is shaped by deeply held beliefs," and "I also believe human life is a sacred gift from our creator."[142] The Bush ban was partially revoked by his successor Barack Obama and research is now underway to develop stem cell treatments for neurodegenerative diseases, diabetes, heart disease, and other conditions, but these life-saving therapies take decades to develop, test and approve. The decade long debate between religious groups, who accused scientists of playing God, and scientists, who accused religious groups of being zealots, has cost millions of people their lives.

Values and Attitudes

Decision and action are rooted in values. Values steer priorities. Everyone has values. Every group has values. And every person and group defines values and sets priorities differently. Usually, the personal and group values are aligned. We either seek out groups that share our values or we adopt the values of a group for one reason or another, which I will explore later. Values are the underlying element of identity. In order to define identity, we need to understand values.

The attributes that define a group start with broad concepts like nationality, religion, gender, and race, and become very specific and local. Most psychologists agree that it is not helpful to define groups based on broad attributes like gender, nationality, religion or race, because such definitions have no statistical significance. What does it really mean to be American or un-American? Are there values that are held by most whites or blacks, men or women, Muslims or Christians that are consistent and majority of the members of these groups? The simple answer is, no.

The three major religions have core values or tenets, which various denominations translate into sometimes very different actions. One of the most important Christian teachings is that there is value in all people, no matter their appearance or social status. Lutherans, Methodists, Mormons, Catholics and Baptists are taught to help others, but these denominations espouse conflicting attitudes about race, sexual orientation, and gender equality. For example, the Catholic Church officially opposes GLBT rights and still labels homosexuality an "objective disorder,"[143] whereas many Catholics and some Christian denominations accept gays. One value that is central to the Jewish faith involves learning, but Orthodox, Reform, and Conservative Jews promote incongruent views about technology, science, and medicine. For example, according to Alexander Nussbaum, the author of *Attitudes of Educated Orthodox Jews Toward Science*, "Orthodox Jews deny evolution and other central tenets of modern science."[144] Modesty is one of the most important Islamic values. Men and women are expected to dress modestly, covering themselves from the waist to the knees in loose fitting and opaque clothing, but Sunnis, Shi'as and Kharijites have different views on fashion and materialism. According to John Burgess, former U.S. diplomat in the Middle East, women in Saudi Arabia are expected to wear a robe and veil when outdoors and when in the presence of a non-related male, but there is no uniform rule about covering the face and some cities are less conservative than others. "In Jeddah, for example, you'll see many uncovered faces. In others, including a region south of Riyadh, women's faces are covered at puberty and not uncovered until death. These women do not show their faces even to their spouses or children."[145]

As soon as we start to discuss our values with others, we discover that there are many and they are *aspecific*, meaning there is no single definition of what it means to value things like family or freedom. Although we are often tempted, it is not a good idea to judge values. Our values may not be aligned, but it is very difficult to say that one value is better than another. There are many different perspectives for each value. These differing perspectives are called attitudes.

If we ask someone, "Do you value family?" and that person answers "Yes, very much," what does that really mean? There are different ways of prioritizing family. One person may express their family value by working 80 hours a week to provide a safe home, healthy food, excellent healthcare and a good education for their children, i.e. family value is equated with ensuring stability and security. Another person may show their commitment to family by sacrificing their career to stay home and spend time with their wife and children. In other words, by focusing on the emotional needs of the family. Both value family, but they have different ways of expressing it. Neither is wrong or better. Likewise, there are different forms of freedom. There is a freedom from and a freedom to. When asked someone if freedom is important, one could argue, "Yes, freedom from inequality and poverty is important," which is an argument used in favor of socialism. One could also argue, "Yes, the freedom to do what I want is important," which is a position in favor of capitalism. Those who use the freedom-from argument are more willing to sacrifice some personal freedoms for greater protections. Likewise, those who use the freedom-to argument are likely to compromise personal protection for more personal liberties. For many years, America used the freedom-to argument to position itself as land of the free, but Americans are more willing today to sacrifice some personal liberties in order to gain more protections, i.e. to be free from violence and terrorism. When one form of freedom is prioritized, the other form is automatically suppressed. The current U.S. administration is strongly pushing a freedom-from terrorism and illegal immigration agenda at the price of reducing or eliminating some personal freedoms to travel, for example.

It is, therefore, impossible to talk about values without also discussing attitudes. Although we should refrain from criticizing values and attitudes, we need to recognize the fact that some attitudes are detrimental to personal and human development. Some attitudes can create vulnerabilities for stress and depression and make it difficult for a person to achieve self-actualization. It is highly desirable that fewer people suffer stress and depression and that more people achieve self-actualization. It would be wonderful if more people realized their full potential and were in a position to make long-term beneficial impacts on society. We would be better off and further ahead as a race. But self-actualization is not a categorical imperative. You are not a bad or immoral person for not fully developing your talents and becoming altruistic, although you are psychologically immature for not trying and you are more likely to become sad, angry, stressed and ill.

We know that mature personalities possess certain virtues and traits that are conducive to achieving self-actualization. High openness and conscientiousness correlate to academic and vocational achievement, which insulate against some types of stress. Low openness and low conscientiousness combined with high neuroticism are negatively correlated to academics and vocational success, which can increase the likelihood of experiencing some types of stress. But how do we know what virtues or traits a person possesses? We need to examine values, specifically attitudes.

Personality Traits	Values
Openness	acceptance, curiosity, creativity, knowledge, learning, adventure, artistry, awareness, brilliance, change, adaptability, diversity, exploration, expressiveness, freedom, growth, imagination, inspiration, inventiveness, resilience
Conscientiousness	accomplishment, accountability, accuracy, advancement, ambition, attentiveness, calmness, candor, capability, carefulness, competence, composure, concentration, consistency, dependability, diligence, perseverance, direction, education, effectiveness, efficiency, endurance, excellence, expertise, focus, initiative, intellect, knowledge, learning, logic, mastery, neatness, order, proactivity, productivity, reflection, responsibility
Extroversion	affection, cheerfulness, cooperation, approval, camaraderie, closeness, cooperation, gregariousness, intuition, involvement, optimistic, teamwork, tolerance, warmth
Agreeableness	altruism, availability, belonging, benevolence, caring, community, compassion, conformity, courage, devotion, duty, empathy, energy, enthusiasm, fairness, forgiveness, generosity, helpfulness, honesty, honor, hospitality, impartiality, justice, kindness, obedience, philanthropy, piety, sacrifice, selflessness, sharing, volunteering, unity
Positivity (opposite of neuroticism)	authority, calmness, careful, composure, conservative, control, conviction, faith, economy, firmness, frugal, hope, persuasiveness, perseverance, power, predictability, punctuality, resolve, routine, silence, stability, stubborn, thrift, trust

Illustration 30: OCEAN Values

Attitudes	
Low	**High**
• GO WITH THE FLOW • IGNORANCE IS BLISS • WHAT YOU DON'T KNOW CAN'T HURT YOU • YOU CAN'T TEACH AN OLD DOG NEW TRICKS	• BEAUTY IS IN THE EYES OF THE BEHOLDER • BEAUTY IS ONLY SKIN DEEP • EVERYONE YOU WILL EVER MEET KNOWS SOMETHING YOU DON'T • YOU NEVER STOP LEARNING • FOLLOW YOUR DREAM • EXPERIENCE IS THE BEST TEACHER

Illustration 31: Attitude Statements That Reflect Openness

Deducing Traits from Attitudes

If personality traits are a predictive indicator, how can we know which traits a person possesses? The answer is simple: attitudes mirror traits.

In the first step, I list values for each of the OCEAN traits. I cannot adequately describe the more than 500 values and the plethora of attitudes in this book, so I focus on the values that map easily to personality traits. The results are shown in Illustration 30.

In the second step, I extracted the most popular attitudes from my study notes and matched each statement to a specific value. The result is a very long spreadsheet, which I excluded from this book, because my intent is not to catalog the many ways to express values, but to show the attitudes that match to certain personality traits.

In the third step, I consolidated the attitudes by trait. Illustrations 31-33 are a collection of mottos reflecting a broad range of attitudes sorted by trait.

Because attitudes have different dimensions, e.g. freedom-to vs freedom-from, the mapping of attitudes to traits is based on context. For example, someone high in conscientiousness would say "preparation prevents poor performance," and someone high in agreeableness would probably say "forgive and forget." I show these statements in all upper case letters to remind you that these are some of the same mottos and memes shared millions of times every day on social media usually superimposed in capital letters over the image of a famous person, beautiful scenery, or a wild animal.

Attitudes	
Low	**High**
• TAKE LIFE ONE STEP AT A TIME • JUST DO IT • FOLLOW YOUR GUT • WINNING ISN'T EVERYTHING - THE EXPERIENCE IS MORE IMPORTANT • GO WITH THE FLOW • SOME THINGS ARE JUST MEANT TO BE • LIVE AND LET LIVE • EXCELLENCE IS NOT BEING THE BEST, IT'S TRYING YOUR BEST	• THINK BEFORE YOU ACT • PREPARATION PREVENTS POOR PERFORMANCE • YOU'RE ONLY AS GOOD AS YOUR WORD • IF YOU'RE GOING TO DO IT, THEN DO IT RIGHT • QUALITY IS BETTER THAN QUANTITY • WITH MONEY YOU CAN CHOOSE YOUR MISERY • KNOWLEDGE IS POWER
• YOU CAN'T BUY HAPPINESS • SHIT HAPPENS	• HONESTY IS THE BEST POLICY • BELIEFS DON'T MAKE YOU A BETTER PERSON, ACTIONS DO • JUST BECAUSE YOU HAVE THE RIGHT TO DO IT, DOESN'T MEAN IT IS THE RIGHT THING TO DO • DON'T WAIT FOR YOUR SHIP TO COME IN – SWIM OUT TO IT • WAIT IS A FOUR LETTER WORD

Illustration 32: Attitude Statements That Reflect Conscientiousness

My study showed that, with a high level of statistical significance, people with attitudes listed in the high column of openness and conscientiousness, are much better at satisfying their basic needs than those with attitudes listed in the low column. Due to their positive attitudes about learning, planning and achievement, the probability is very low that these individuals will experience avoidable life changing events like dismissal from work (47 stress units), a change in financial state (38 stress units), or foreclosure (30 stress units). People with attitudes listed in the low column, on the other hand, are more likely to experience this type of life changing events. Even if low column people earn a lot more money than the high column people, their attitudes imply that they are laidback, unprepared and inefficient. These factors increase the risk that these members will encounter more stress in life.

Furthermore, my study showed that people with attitudes listed in the high openness and conscientiousness column are better prepared to deal with unavoidable life changing events like the death of a spouse, death of a family member and personal injury or illness. Anyone who experiences a combination of unavoidable life changing events is at risk of suffering stress and illness, but people with attitudes corresponding to high openness and conscientiousness can manage such situations much better than people with attitudes listed in the low column. People with attitudes that map to high openness and conscientiousness probably had insurance policies and emergency savings accounts. They were prepared and efficient and could afford to pay unexpected expenses like legal fees, medical, funeral, and travel costs – and still satisfy basic needs like feeding their families and paying their bills. They could afford to take time off work to recover from injury or burnout, help friends, or care for a family member. People with attitudes listed in the low columns for openness and conscientiousness tended not to have insurance policies, they had low job security, no savings account, and no back-up plan, so when something negative happened, it grew serious quickly.

Traits	Attitudes	
	Low	High
Extroversion	• HOME IS WHERE I HANG MY HAT • STILL WATERS RUN DEEP • BELIEVE IN YOURSELF • DO WHAT MAKES YOU HAPPY • DON'T CARE WHAT OTHER PEOPLE THINK • WE HAVE TWO EARS AND ONE MOUTH	• TOGETHER EVERYONE ACHIEVES MORE • ONE HAND WASHES THE OTHER • ALL I NEED ARE MY FRIENDS • FAIRNESS DOESN'T MEAN EVERYONE GETS THE SAME, IT MEANS EVERYONE GETS WHAT HE NEEDS • A STRANGER IS A FRIEND YOU HAVEN'T MET YET
Agreeableness	• WE WILL NEVER FORGET • STICK TO YOUR GUNS • DO WHAT'S RIGHT • FOR YOU • GOOD THINGS COME • TO THOSE WHO WAIT • A TIGER DOESN'T LOSE SLEEP OVER THE OPINION OF SHEEP	• FORGIVE AND FORGET • YOU GET WHAT YOU GIVE • IF YOU DON'T HAVE SOMETHING NICE TO SAY, THEN DON'T SAY ANYTHING • THERE ISN'T ANYONE YOU COULDN'T LOVE AFTER HEARING HIS STORY • JUST FIT IN • BE NORMAL
Neuroticism	• EVERYTHING IS IN YOUR HANDS • WE SEAL OUR FATE WITH THE CHOICES WE MAKE	• LIFE IS NOT FAIR • TAKE WHAT YOU CAN GET • DON'T TRUST ANYONE • SPEAK SOFTLY AND CARRY A BIG STICK

Illustration 33: The attitudes in the high column reflect a tendency for conformity and dependency.

The attitudes corresponding to high levels of extroversion, agreeableness, and neuroticism correlate to conformity and dependency. Here is one example.

> Ben: My new boss was terribly under-qualified and delegated everything on me. My parents always told me to stick up for myself, so I pushed back. When he wrote me up for not getting my work done on time, I told him to stick it where the sun don't shine. He told me I needed an attitude adjustment. When I told my friends this, they agreed that I had to show backbone. I did, and he fired me. My friends congratulated me for not taking crap from that weasel. It took me several months to find another job. My friends were all very supportive – emotionally. They kept saying things like "good things come to those who wait" and "maybe this is a blessing in disguise." Well it wasn't. It took me more than a year to find another job, my credit got ruined, I gained weight and feel like crap. I'm now under-employed and making a lot less than I was a year ago.

Although most of the reports we collected and analyzed read like this one in that attitudes espoused by family and then by friends influenced a decision and action that caused some temporary negative outcome, i.e. a Holmes-Rahe event, and some subjects experienced permanent, negative outcomes. Some were beaten so badly they are now disabled, some were imprisoned, a couple contracted disease, some took drugs and became addicted, while others rejected medicine and became sick or permanently disabled. And in many cases, the action caused a domino effect in that a single Holmes-Rahe event led to another and another, etc.

Sedikides and Skowronski wrote "Self concept emerges from social processes."[146] The social process begins at birth, and parenting plays an influential role. Parents instill virtues, traits and values, they help us to develop our abilities and identity and they prepare us for social interactions. The friends we make are a function of parenting in that many of us rely on friends to fill the deficits that our parents inadvertently produced. Friends can trump parenting. Identity can be transitory. As we grow from childhood to adolescence and then adulthood, we meet new people, learn different values, change allegiances, and also develop identity.

Chapter 8

Friends

We form our initial identity during childhood, and friends finish the work. Friends can improve upon, negate, or exacerbate the outcome of parenting. The influence that friends have on our attitudes, decisions and action is a function of the strengths and weakness we acquire during childhood and the role that friends play in our lives. Adult identity is, therefore, transitory and voluntary.

Starting at adolescence and throughout adulthood, friends play important roles in our lives, albeit for different reasons. All behavior is motivated and friend selection is based on one of the following needs:

(a) Curiosity, meaning the person can efficiently satisfy her basic needs and seeks personal growth through new experiences and learning.

> Ben: Everyone I meet knows something I don't.

> Rebecca: A friend is someone who brings out the best in you.

(b) Security, meaning the person has difficulties satisfying her basic needs or has deficits and seeks support from others.

> Linda: Walking with a friend in the dark is better than walking alone in the light.

Timothy: Things are never quite as scary when you've got a best friend.

(c) Acceptance, independent of the person's ability to satisfy her basic needs, she has an emotional deficit and seeks affection, attention, and validation.

Whitney: A real friend is one who walks in when the rest of the world walks out.

Walter: A true friend is one who overlooks your failures and tolerates your success.

Following Moslow and Erikson, relationships can be the next stage in psychological development. For Moslow, people who efficiently satisfy their basic physiological and security needs have a rational need for social interaction, intimacy and friendship and they have the requisite time and energy to build meaningful relationships. For Erikson, the person who has mastered the virtues of hope, will, purpose, confidence, and fidelity is equipped to succeed at building relationships. Remember, fidelity in this context refers to identity security and not to faithfulness.

For most people, though, social interaction, intimacy, relationships and friendships do not represent the next stage in psychological development. Whereas mature people, i.e. those who have acquired all virtues and follow rational priorities, seek relationships for growth, immature people have weaknesses and need relationships to satisfy or cope with some deficit or insecurity. As shown in Illustration 34, the immature personality allows the social need for intimacy and acceptance to influence their priorities and prescribe how other needs are met. Their social need overshadows all other needs and stifles their learning and self-realization. Because everyone subconsciously wants to achieve their full potential, immature personalities are frequently faced with a crisis between the group's boundaries and the latent potential of the individual.

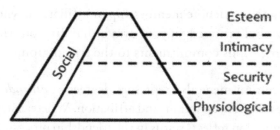

Illustration 34: Social Influence on Needs

Defining friendship is difficult, because today it can mean anything from an informal connection with hundreds of anonymous or unscreened Facebook users to an intimate relationship with a boyfriend or girlfriend. Some of the sources I consulted like the OED say a friendship is based on a bond or mutual affection, which would certainly disqualify many of the friends we have on social media. Other sources assert that friends share common interests or history, but this definition does not work for people who purposely befriend others who have very different ideas and backgrounds. One source defined a friend as someone who is not an opponent, but this definition does not work for people who have very good relationships with their competitors like some athletes, politicians and business people. The only definition that I found that works is the simple concept that friends are people with whom we are open to interact. This definition covers all types of friendships including online friends, real friends, competitors, and intimate relationships.

Attitude Assimilation

Making friends is a process, which, I observed, has five stages: awareness, interaction, integration, identification, and action. These stages can be very brief or take many years to complete, but friendships always unfold in this manner usually unconsciously and incrementally. As we progress through various stages of friendship, we engage in different activities that demonstrate more serious levels of commitment to the group. Having a conversation with someone about politics or religion is a low level of commitment that can end just as quickly as it started.

Conversations do not denote membership or affiliation, whereas getting the group's symbol tattooed on your arm or handing out fliers at a rally represent more serious commitments to the friend group.

The levels of commitment also represent degrees of *attitude assimilation:* attraction, appreciation, adoption, and affiliation. Whereas stages represent activities, assimilation reflects status in the friendship process. For example, using a group's vocabulary shows the person appreciates the group's attitudes, and speaking on behalf of a group represents membership, i.e. affiliation.

The variety of activities and status in the process are predictors of future activities. Someone who attends an event to learn about a group may appreciate the group's views, but is unlikely to begin using the group's language, identify with or take action on behalf of the group. But the person who attends events frequently, reads the group's magazines often, and uses the group's jargon is likely to begin to identify with the group through fashion. Likewise, someone who identifies strongly with a group through fashion and body art is likely to take action on behalf of the group.

The human personality has many layers and is often compared to an onion. Friendships have many layers. Think of assimilation as an onion, too. The outer skin is thin and not very valuable. You may call someone at the outer layer a friend, but this relationship is superficial and you couldn't rely on this person for much help. The deeper layers of the onion are more important. Friends who reach these deeper layers of assimilation are willing to take action on behalf of the group and its members.

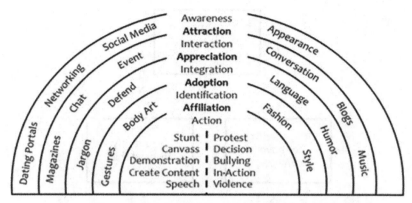

Illustration 35: Degrees of Assimilation

In addition to gauging the level of assimilation, we can also measure the intensity of assimilation. Is the person just following friends to be rebellious, as a means of discovery, or to be cool, or does the person really stand behind their behavior? To measure intensity, we can use Kelley's *Covariation Model*. This model evaluates behavior in three areas: consensus or conformity, distinctiveness, and consistency or frequency.[147]

Accordingly, when we observe someone's assimilation in a group, we can compare their behavior when they are with their friends to their behavior when they are alone or with other friends to gauge the psychological significance. Someone who engages in an activity alone or outside their group is acting genuinely, i.e. behavior is attributable to personality. This means the person has moved past just belonging to actually believing. On the other hand, behavior that is only displayed when the person is with their group is attributable to situation, i.e. peer pressure. This means the person is only trying to fit-in. Illustration 36 shows the simple process for determining if behavior is attributable to personality or situation.

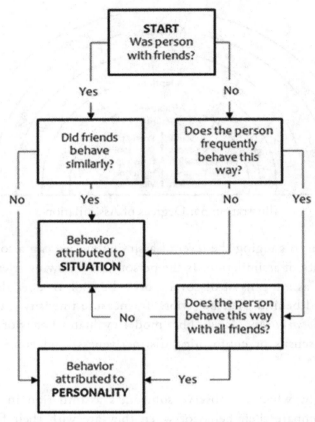

Illustration 36: Assimilation Intensity

You may think that as soon as someone wears the group's colors or takes action on behalf of the group, they are loyal members, but when apply covariation, we find that some people are just trying to fit in for some reason or another.

After the fall of the wall separating West Germany from East Germany in 1989, dozens of East German border guards were put on trial. Over the prior decades, more than 1,000 East Germans were shot and killed while trying to escape to the West. During this time, a shooting order was in effect requiring guards to aim at escapees legs. Guards were also instructed to shoot other guards who failed to follow the order. In trial, the guards admitted that they had fired at people attempting to escape, because it was required of them, and they argued they were purposely missing in order to avoid being shot themselves. They cited the fact that every year more than 2,300 people had successfully escaped, and a study by Rottman in 2008 showed that most shots fired by border guards landed in West German territory.[148] Those East German guards appeared to be fully assimilated into East German communist society. They memorized the pledges, spoke the jargon, wore the uniform, and even fired live ammunition at unarmed citizens. But, in reality, they were just pretending to fit. They had high levels of assimilation, albeit low levels of intensity.

Attributing undesirable behavior to situation versus personality does not in any way make it more acceptable. It only helps us to understand the mental health of the person committing the act. Someone who commits despicable acts alone needs psychiatric treatment, whereas someone who acts with others requires psychological therapy. In 2004, news of despicable acts of torture performed by American soldiers in Abu Ghraib prison in Iraq came out. Photographs emerged showing soldiers posing with detainees who they forced to masturbate in front of others, build a naked human pyramid, or stand naked with feces smeared on their face and torso. Even more disturbing was the fact that the soldiers were pictured holding their thumbs up and smiling. They apparently enjoyed partaking in these activities. Reflexively we think only a crazy person could take pleasure in performing such disgusting acts, but none of the soldiers involved was diagnosed with a mental illness. Had a single person committed such acts alone, they would have certainly gotten a medical discharge for psychiatric reasons and hospitalized. These acts were committed by a group and attributed to situation and peer pressure. Seventeen soldiers were dismissed and eleven were court-martialed and convicted to prison for dereliction of duty, battery and assault.

Stage 1. Awareness and Attraction

We are constantly advertising ourselves to garner attention. The objective of self-promotion is to create awareness for our attitudes and attract others. Success is measured in terms of visits, looks, friend requests, and flirts.

Online, we build profiles on Facebook, LinkedIn, eHarmony, Parship, Match.com, Timber, Snapchat, XING and other dating and networking portals to promote ourselves. These channels are always on. In some ways, online self-promotion is more effective than self-promotion in the real-world, because we share pictures online and we also provide additional information about our hobbies, religion, likes, dislikes and attitudes. Visitors to our profiles look for commonalities - maybe a shared friend, the same hometown, similar hobbies, or the same previous employer or high school. This combination of content and information helps us to determine if there is an attraction – intellectually and physically – before sending a friend request and making a date. In this sense, the awareness we create online is less superficial than the awareness we create offline, because we can learn more about a person before requesting to connect. Offline, we rely solely on our behavior or appearance to attract others.

When we walk through the city, many people capture our attention. It is hard not to notice the chanting protestors, the artist on the bus with the tattooed face, the muscle man with the shredded t-shirt in the café, the man in the movie theater wearing a cowboy hat, or the curvaceous woman in the bank wearing a tiny skirt and a tight blouse. Noticing someone means that person succeeded in calling attention to themselves. The tattoos didn't suddenly appear on the artist's face, the muscle man's t-shirt didn't accidentally rip on his way to the café, the cowboy hat didn't fall out of the sky and land on the man's head, and the women's clothing didn't shrink on her way to the bank. These are all deliberate attempts to create awareness for certain attitudes. This is called *attitude projection.*

Even though attitude projection is deliberate, it is not always obvious. Someone holding a protest sign with the words Build the Wall written on it or wearing a baseball cap with MAGA printed on it is communicating clearly what they believe. But inferring attitudes from appearance can sometimes cause problems, because fashion statements are often miscommunicated or misinterpreted.

> David Chappelle (the comedian): A guy will be out in a club or bar, kicking it with the boys. A girl walks by and she looks good. Not good in the classical way. Half her ass is hanging out her skirt, her titties are all mashed together popping out of her turtle neck. You're with your buddies. You got a couple drinks in you and you want to talk to her. So what do you say? 'Damn look at them titties!' And she says, 'Now, wait a minute, wait a minute! Just because I'm dressed this way does not make me a whore!' Which is true. Don't ever forget it, guys. But it is fucking confusing. That would be like me, David Chappelle, comedian, walking around in the street with a cop uniform. Somebody might run up on me, 'Officer! Officer! Help us, over here, help us!' Just because I'm dressed this way does not make me a police officer!' You understand what I'm saying? Alright lady, fine, fine, you are not a whore, but you are wearing a whore's uniform.

The fact that we notice some people does not mean we find them attractive. Awareness is not synonymous with attraction. While there are many people we notice, we do not want to meet and get to know everyone we see. There are also many people who we do not notice. If you are not successfully connecting with others, if your network or friend group is not growing, it does not mean you are unattractive. It only means you are either not effectively communicating your attitudes, likes and dislikes or there are few people who appreciate them.

The remote nature of social media creates a false sense of safety. Accepting a friend request is simple and unfriending is just as easy. We are, therefore, very liberal online and tend to befriend many people who we have never met and sometimes do not even know are real. They may have names and profiles, but we rarely screen these friend requests to validate the other person's identity. Academically speaking, many online friends are anonymous. This seems harmless, but in reality befriending someone online is much riskier than meeting someone in a café, because it involves an exchange. An exchange entails trading things of value. In this case, we trade information about ourselves for a connection and online friends can be costly and risky.

When we befriend someone online, we immediately share information with them. We tend to share more of our lives online than we do offline. In the real world, nobody introduces themselves to a stranger and immediately lays open their address book to show all the friends they have and they don't take out their wallet to show their family photos, their various membership cards, and their ticket stubs to the last movie they saw. But online, we are very generous. We allow new friends to read our profiles and conversations, view our pictures, see our location and movements, view our network of friends, and learn our history and habits.

This level of exposure can create a vulnerability. Social media creates a false sense of anonymity and makes people more willing to share more information. A study done by Friedland Security showed that four out of five burglars used social media to pick their targets.[149] The burglars created nice-guy profiles using content scraped from other peoples' pages and sent hundreds and sometimes thousands of friend requests. After being friended, they monitored recent posts for photos of high-value purchases like televisions and computers. Then they gathered enough personal information from posts and photos to locate the home, used Google street view to case the neighborhood, and simply waited for their victims to share vacation pictures. In other cases, friends simply stole image content from their unsuspecting Facebook friends and used it for fake fund-raising campaigns, to bully their victims, and even for extortion.

> Alicia: Someone on Facebook is stealing pics of me and has pics of my son since he was born. I have no clue who this person is. They steal my pics and send them to family members of mine overseas talking bad about me and saying they are going to kidnap my son.

This stage entails creating awareness that can lead to an attraction and eventually an introduction or connection. We should be concerned if a friend or family member is sharing too much information too quickly or attracting too much attention.

> Dick: My son bragged that he had more than 100 friends. I told him to show me who these people are. I was shocked. Some of his friends are older than me. Why is a fifty year old man connecting with a ten year old boy in an online chatroom? My son said it was a group for gamers, but I told him it's not good, because they could read his conversations with his real friends and knew where they were going and what they were doing. I told him to delete his chat profile immediately.

> Suzanne: Every time I go out with my daughter, I notice that she gets lots of looks from guys. I don't like it. It's not that I'm jealous. She's an adult, but it scares me that so many blatantly flirt with her. I told her to tone down her look, because she's attracting too many of the wrong kind of men.

Stage 2. Interacting and Appreciation

The purpose of the interaction is to learn more about the values and attitudes, background, goals, and interests of the friend. Whether or not the interaction is conducted offline or online, this activity involves a more valuable exchange. We share more information about ourselves in exchange for information about the other person and the positive emotions we feel when our attitudes and preferences are validated.

I once connected with someone online based solely on the fact that we shared the same name. We really had nothing in common and the interaction got boring fast.

> Michael 1: Are you related to Al Capone?
> Michael 2: He's somewhere in our family tree. You?
> Michael 1: Yeah, something like a second cousin to a grandfather.

Michael 2: So, you can't do any favors for me?
Michael 1: Nope. Sorry. :-)

We found 57 other people online also named Michael Capone and invited them to join our group. Weeks later we had 22 members from 7 countries. The conversation got boring fast. One day, one of the members had the fantastic idea to create a resume combining all of our qualifications and experiences and then use it to get a better job. Through the course of this silly group activity, I got to know Michael Capone, the Italian geologist. He and I both publish on academia.edu and I sometimes get invited to speak at conferences on topics like "GPS Measurements in the Neapolitan Volcanic Area," a subject about which I know nothing. I think this explains why the idea to build a consolidated resume didn't work and why the group eventually dissolved. Other than our names, we had little in common.

Media plays an important role during the interaction phase. Friends talk about their favorite t.v. shows, movies, music, books, magazines, and websites. If the new friend's views are interesting to us, we are likely to look at the content they recommended. This creates new opportunities to interact and learn from each other. We do not need to worry when we see a friend or family member reading or watching something total new. This curiosity was probably instigated by a new connection and it's actually a healthy sign that they are exploring.

We need to be cautious that friends and family do not consume too much of the wrong media. Too much exposure to some media genres can be bad. George Gerbner studied television content and how audience exposure to violent images influences their views and concept of reality. As a result, Gerbner developed *cultivation theory* to explain how long-term exposure to violent media messages alters audience perceptions of violence by cultivating a sense of normalcy.[150] Rosenberry and Vicker found that long term exposure to violence in the media goes beyond *desensitization* to *disinhibition*.[151] Viewers exposed to violent content over time become accepting of violence and also develop a stronger propensity to commit acts of aggression.

Cultivation theory can also be applied to understanding individuals' reactions to other forms of media. Reality shows are especially troublesome. Barry Morgan warned "reality television programmes prize humiliation and arrogance and are having a destructive effect on society. It seeps into our subconscious."[152] Many reality shows perpetuate negative stereotypes of rural residents, white and blue collar workers, athletes, celebrities, and urban housewives and they give fans the impression that profanity and aggressive behavior are normal and, therefore, acceptable. This is called *media priming:* The more we see reality t.v. stars misbehaving the more likely we are to mimic their behavior.[153] This trend was especially observable during the peak periods of *Jersey Shores, the Simple Life,* and *the Kardashians.* An army of Snooki, Pauli, Vinny, Paris, and Kim clones could be seen and heard on every college campus and in every shopping mall across America.

One strategy used by television producers to make shows interesting is called *superiority theory.* The premise is, people enjoy watching other people being stupid, because it makes them feel better about themselves. Reality shows purposely show people misbehaving or acting ridiculous so that viewers feel smarter, but this has backfired. A team of Austrian psychologists found that reality shows influence peoples' cognitive performance. The researchers measured the IQ of study subjects before and after viewing reality shows and found that the participants performed notably worse after watching an episode in which the central character was depicted as stupid.[154] Joanne Cantor, a psychologist and professor at the University of Wisconsin-Madison, explained that visual content is perceived at a higher level of consciousness thus predisposing the viewer for stupidity.[155] Watching people act stupid increases the likelihood that the viewer will act stupid.

Music is also an effective priming instrument. Adams and Fuller found that rap and hip hop music desensitizes individuals to sexual harassment, exploitation, abuse, and violence toward women, it "legitimizes the mistreatment and degradation of women" and creates "a social climate in which violence is viewed as acceptable."[156] The researchers also found that the more time adolescents spent watching hip hop videos, the more likely they were to accept homophobic and misogynist attitudes in their peer group and engage in exploitive activities themselves. Russo and Pirlott concluded that exposure to misogynistic messages in hip-hop music has also been shown to "increase hostile and aggressive thoughts" which may correlate to "more permanent hostility."[157]

The critics of media priming argue that a causal link cannot be demonstrated between media consumption and behavior. This is true. There is no direct link between media and violence, because media consumption is an early stage in the assimilation process that can have many paths culminating in action.

Disagreement can arise during the interaction phase when attitudes are not aligned. If both friends are mature, they will probably continue to interact, a respectful debate may ensure, and they may stay connected, because they find diversity intellectually stimulating. When disagreement arises and one of the friends is immature, a conflict can be expected. The immature personality is impulsive and usually responds to dissention with insults masked in honesty that is actually rooted in ignorance.

> Sam: Watch Trump's speech. America is land of the free.
> Tracy: I just got back from a semester in Copenhagen and I have the impression that America is not really the "land of the free" anymore.
> Sam: Sounds like you smoked too much weed over there.
> Tracy: Are you may be confusing Copenhagen with Amsterdam?
> Sam: Same difference. Socialism sucks and you're fake.

The immature person unfriends those who do not support their views, because the relationship does not give them the validation they seek. The mature person may unfriend someone, because the conversation is not respectful. Tracy would probably unfriend Sam. When this happens, the immature person may feel rejected and this sometimes escalates into cyber-bullying or stalking.

> Tina: I deleted this guy from my group, because he was rude to my friends. He started texting me that I'm fat and ugly and he didn't want to be friends anyway. He texted me like ten times.

The online relationship and exchange of information is a commitment that should be taken seriously, because once personal information is shared it cannot be retrieved. Surely, if we perceive no benefit from the interaction, we can unfriend someone, stop seeing them or block them from calling us or visiting our page again, but that person already has information about us that they may not want to return or simply cannot forget. Deleting someone from your life or group does not purge the valuable information they already have. Unfriending only makes it more difficult for others to get new information, although it is not impossible, because they already know your network and habits. For example, if we let someone know that we have a garage full of expensive tools, we live at 19 East Elm Street in Watertown, and we work Monday-Friday 11:00 pm to 8:00 am and have a long commute to work, that person retains this information and can use it against us - even if it were somehow possible to delete the internet tomorrow.

A study conducted by Dr. Sabina Datcu, a researcher at Bitdefender's research lab, showed that we really need to be careful about what we say online about ourselves and who we befriend or at least engage in conversation. Datcu created two phony profiles of a 25 year old woman. In one profile, she was portrayed as an IT worker, and in the other she was shown as an IT security worker. Over the course of several weeks, the phony profiles gradually gained the trust of more than 100 presumably real people who claimed to be security technicians or hackers. Datcu noted what kinds of personal information her new friends disclosed: 81 percent of the IT security people said they used their mother's maiden name as a password, and 78 percent of the hackers divulged this information. Similar percentages of both groups admitted they used the same password for multiple accounts, almost all of the participants shared information about their families, and 7 percent of the hacker group even divulged their passwords.[158] The results of this study suggest not only that people are too willing to accept unknown people into their group, but that they are also willing to reveal personal, sensitive information to unknown people.

Immature, extroverted and agreeable people are at risk of having bad experiences during the initial phases of friendship. They seek security and acceptance from friends and are, therefore, eager to connect and too willing to share. The positive feedback they get in the form of tags, comments, likes and shares is affirming, rewarding, and an incentive to share even more. The exchange of more and more content for immediate gratification can become an addiction for some. A study by Jonathon Kandell concluded that college students are particularly vulnerable to internet addiction.[159] The combination of an identity crisis stemming from authoritarian or indulgent parenting, a series of life changing events like leaving the family and moving away to college, and the inability to efficiently satisfy basic needs, creates a strong need for support and acceptance. Social media becomes a coping mechanism for college students. This is exactly what Lawrence Lam concluded in his paper *Factors Associated with Internet Addiction Among Adolescents.*[160] Cherly Gordon, Linda Juang and Moin Syed arrived at a similar conclusion in their paper *Internet Use and Well-being Among College Students: Beyond Frequency of Use.*[161]

Mature personalities, however, are less extroverted, lesser agreeable, and more skeptical. They seek learning opportunities and are also eager to connect, but they are more cautious with their personal information and they handle conflict better. Meeting other people online or offline to exchange ideas and beliefs is harmless for the mature, secure personality. They can befriend many different types of people and interact with them over long periods of time and they respect diversity. They may find these conversations educational, enlightening or entertaining, and the information exchanged rarely has any influence on their own attitudes and behavior.

> Nathan: I've studied abroad and have hundreds of friends all over the world. They sometimes have very different perspectives on things like healthcare, education, religion, economy, and environment. My friends do not always

agree on things, and it's interesting to learn how other cultures perceive current affairs in my country. I haven't changed my position on anything, but I understand why international relations is so hard. Heck, if things get intolerable here, I can immigrate to at least four foreign countries. My friends are all pretty tolerant of me.

A successful interaction culminates with an appreciation of the other person's attitudes. Someone can appreciate another person's views without adopting them.

Samuel: I fully understand my Muslim friends' attitude about modesty, but I don't support it, although I wish my daughter was more modest.

Becky: Most of my friends are vegetarians. I admire their will, but I love greasy pepperoni pizza and fat, juicy burgers.

Stage 3. Integration and Adoption

Awareness leads to attraction and can result in an introduction or connection. The connection starts the interaction that can lead to rejection or appreciation. In the next stage, the person may begin to incorporate the group's attitudes into her belief system.

There are several reasons for integrating the attitudes of others into our belief system. First, the messages are rational or logical. There is strong evidence to support them. Second, the messages are popular. Even when the messages are irrational, accepting them puts the individual in the in-group. Third, there is some benefit. Whether or not the message is rational or popular, if the individual sees some advantage in adopting it, they will.

The mature personality doesn't seek approval or security and only integrates attitudes into their belief system when the beliefs are logical. But the immature, insecure person conforms to win approval or to improve their status in the group. They adopt attitudes in exchange for affection and status.

> Sabine: I was brought up very strict and taught to stay away from alcohol. I always thought people who drank were weak. When I started a new job, my colleagues invited me all the time to happy hour. At first, I refused to go, but I learned quickly that I was missing out on some big things. Plans were being made over drinks, and I was not there so I wasn't being considered for some high profile projects. It was hard for me, but eventually I accepted the fact that getting drinks after work was part of team building. I still don't drink, but I am around it all the time now and I'm used to seeing my co-workers get drunk and even do cocaine. I'm the designated driver and everyone calls me 'mother,' even though I'm a lot younger than everyone else.

Integration involves mental conformity, meaning the attitudes of others are accepted as truth, but they do not yet influence the person to conform. One may believe that foreigners steel jobs, abortion is unethical, and global warming is a hoax without outwardly expressing these ideas or taking any action. Note above how Sabine adopted the unhealthy attitudes of her co-workers into her belief system in order to gain acceptance and advance her position, but she did not partake in these activities. She discarded her prude attitudes and now believes getting drunk and doing drugs are "normal." One could argue that her decision is actually good, because she benefits professionally and she can make sure her co-workers get home safely, but her acceptance of their attitudes is a bad decision for at least three reasons. Sabine is, in effect, condoning and enabling wrong behavior that makes her vulnerable, i.e. her acceptance of these attitudes increases the likelihood of her experiencing a life changing event.

First, she now runs the risk of being stopped by a police officer when one of her passengers is in possession of cocaine. Predictably, her passenger will panic and toss the cocaine under the seat of her car, in which case, she would be charged with drug possession. If it's a large enough bag of cocaine, she could be charged with intent to distribute. Both are felonies, which, depending on the terms of her employment, could result in her immediate termination, making it difficult for her to find another job. I didn't have to make this example up, because this actually happened to two study subjects.

Second, the likelihood that Sabine starts to drink and someday also tries cocaine increases with her exposure frequency. A study titled *Drug exposure opportunities and use patterns among college students: Results of a longitudinal prospective cohort* by Amelia Arria et al. showed that first time drug use is directly related to prevalence, or availability.[162]

Third, her association with the happy hour group could be used against her. In 2014 in Tempe, Arizona, white college students held an off-campus party celebrating Martin Luther King Day. Facebook pictures of the party showed attendees dressed in basketball jerseys, flashing gang signs and drinking from watermelon cups. Some perceived this as offensive against blacks and notified the authorities. The media ran the story and an investigation ensued. The university found that the organizers of the party were members of a specific fraternity. Even though it was an unofficial off-campus event, the fraternity was suspended. Several years later, one of the fraternity members, who didn't attend the party, told us:

> Ted: I was the Secretary of the fraternity at the time and this role was on my resume. Once when I applied for a job, the interviewer recalled the event and confronted me about it. I explained that the fraternity had nothing to do with organizing that party and I was out of town. I could prove that I wasn't there. Needless to say, I didn't get the job. Guilty by association?

Up to this point, the person has gained appreciation for and begun to integrate the group's attitude into their own belief system, but they haven't broadcast their membership in the group. The first tacit sign of adoption is when they defend the actions of new group, i.e. when they respond to critique from a member of the out-group, who usually has no idea that they are a member of the group. By defending the group, they effectively show affection and passively promote its attitudes, without explicitly outing themselves as a member of the group:

> Roberta: That happy hour crew is out of control. Those guys are jerks.
> Sabine: They're not bad guys. They're just letting off some steam.
> Roberta: I heard they do drugs.
> Sabine: Yeah, but only on weekends.

Sabine's response to Roberta combines empathy with defense. Empathy denotes an understanding or appreciation of attitudes, but does not denote adoption. Defense always denotes adoption. The mature person can explain unethical and degenerate behavior, without protecting and adopting it. If the attitude is ethically right, then the mature person may defend it. A defense attorney has to understand the attitudes and behavior of an abortion doctor, but does not have to adopt the doctor's views in order to defend their right to perform abortions. In other words, a defense lawyer is not defending attitudes and behavior, but the rights of the accused.

Another sign that someone is adopting the attitudes of the group is when they begin to speak the group's language or use its jargon. Learning a foreign language is an enormous benefit, because it makes it possible to connect with more people and gain exposure to different cultures. An enormous amount of work has been dedicated to language acquisition and the role language plays in relationships. Language deficiency is cited by many sources as the root cause of many historical and also contemporary international and business conflicts. It is also the single greatest barrier to integration, assimilation and success for immigrants. Although some countries mandate that students learn a second and even a third foreign language, language acquisition is voluntary and taking Spanish or French classes in high school is not equivocal to speaking the language. Speaking a language requires a serious commitment that is rooted in some appreciation for that culture's attitudes.

Lucas: I learned German when we I moved to Germany so I could get a better job.

Robert: I learned Chinese, because my first girlfriend, now my wife, is from Hong Kong.

Theodore: I learned Spanish in order to improve my chances of getting a transfer to South America.

Chris: I learned Arabic so I could read the Quran. I wanted to understand the root of the religious conflict between the monotheistic religions.

Even though learning the language spoken in a foreign country is not always a clear sign of adoption, using foreign words and pronunciations when at home and speaking your native language is. Integrating foreign words in your native language is sometimes necessary. Some foreign languages have words or phrases that English does not, it is sometimes easier or faster to describe concepts in foreign words, and using foreign words and pronunciations can also be a deliberate way of showing off.

Brenda: I worked in Tokyo for a couple years and want to implement the Japanese practice of *kaizen* in our company.

Harold: When I lived in France, it was sometimes difficult dealing with the *laissez-faire* attitude at work.

Tiffany: I just love Barthelona. The tapaths are so delithioso.

Independent of the reason someone begins to use foreign words and jargon, slang or lingo, that person is not explicitly outing himself as a member of that group, but he is clearly signaling that adoption of its attitudes has begun.

Every group has a unique vocabulary and even a simple exchange denotes attitude adoption. Rappers, body builders, college students, gamers, surfers, and athletes may speak English, but it is often difficult to understand their conversations not only because they have a repertoire of words unique to their hobby, but they use some words very differently.

> Markus: Let's get some grub.
> Steve: I'm down with that.
> Markus: The burgers here are the bomb.
> Brenda: Woohoo!
> Sandra: Woohoo!
> Brenda: You go, girl!
> Sandra: You go, too!

Professions promote certain values and the use of acronyms can link someone to a vocation and set of attitudes. One of the first challenges for new recruits is learning this new language.

> Soldier: Last night was FUBAR.

> Police Officer: You're lucky you didn't get cited for D&D.

> Paramedic: I would have declared you DOA.

Another form of jargon is the use of truncated words and text message abbreviations in spoken language. This is not only a way to exclude members of the out-group from the dialog, but also an expression of anti-establishment attitudes and laziness. Frequency denotes significance. Jargon frequency is positively related to the level of attitude adoption. If you no longer understand what a friend or family member is talking about, then they are obviously a member of another group.

> Michael: OMG, that was a brutal negosh. I need a vaca.
> Samantha: You need to be AWK for 2 weeks to respek your ship.
> Stewart: Excuse me?

The use of slang, acronyms, and abbreviations is understandable. In some cases it is important to communicate complex ideas quickly, in other cases they can enrich the conversation with more emotion. But one form of jargon that should cause alarm is the sudden intentional over-usage of bad grammar:

> Chris: Me and him and ain't gonna do nutten bad.
> Kelly: It scares me when you talk like that. I'm afraid your friends are making you dumber and we'll end up living in a trailer park.

This is the first level of assimilation where intensity is also important to monitor. When the person only uses slang when they are with other members of their friend group, then their behavior is situational, i.e. the person is behaving to fit in. As soon as the person uses group jargon outside their group, then attitudes of the group are becoming part of that person's personality.

> Oliver: My son swears a lot when he hangs out with his friends.
>
> Therapist: Does he swear when he is at home with you?
>
> Oliver: No.
>
> Therapist: "Then he's just trying to fit in. No worries – yet. As soon as he starts to swear when he's not with his friends, then take a sharp look at his friends' beliefs and behavior to make sure they are positive.

Another aspect of language that demonstrates adoption is humor. In his book *Quirkology*, Richard Wiseman describes an international study he conducted to find the world's best joke. He created a website and collected more than 10,000 jokes submitted by thousands of people from around the world. Wiseman found that there are several types of jokes. Here are some examples:

> Pun: Two fish are swimming in a tank. One fish says to another, "Do you know how to drive this thing?"

Dirty: A lady asks a pharmacist, "Do you have Viagra?" The Pharmacist answers, "Yes." The lady asks, "Can you get it over the counter?" The pharmacist answers, "Only if I take two."

Gross: How many frogs fit in a blender? It depends on if the blender is on.

Wiseman asked his contributors to submit, rate and vote for jokes. His final analysis showed that "the top jokes had one thing in common – they create a sense of superiority." [163] Also called *disparagement humor*, they "elicit amusement through the denigration, derogation, or belittlement" of a subject.[164] Sigmund Freud once (supposedly) said, "a cigar is sometimes just a cigar, but a joke is never just a joke." Superiority jokes are never just jokes. They promote prejudices and an us-versus-them thinking. Here's one of the less offensive examples:

Manager: Welcome. Today is your first day at Acme Co., so you're going to start by sweeping the factory floor.
Intern: But I'm a college graduate. I have an MBA.
Manager: In that case, let me start by showing you how to use a broom.

Superiority humor dates back to Plato and Aristotle, the first study on *superiority theory* was published in 1934 by Wolff et.al.[165] and the impact of superiority jokes is still a hot topic of research today. Recent research shows that superiority jokes can have serious consequences. Studies by Gregory Maio at Cardiff University in Wales and Jens Foerster at the University of Bremen in Germany showed that superiority jokes not only make the teller feel better about themselves, but they make the subjects of the joke feel bad about themselves - and actually perform worse.[166] In one simple study, students were instructed to read a gender joke and then take an exam. When males were the brunt of the joke, they did poorer on the test than females and *vice versa*, proving that stereotypes conveyed through jokes can influence reality.

Stage 4. Identification and Affiliation

The frequency of language, jargon or humor is a tacit indication of group affinity and a predictor of more serious commitments to come. The next level of assimilation is identification. This entails intentional, outwardly visible clues or signs of group membership.

Identification refers to the deliberate outward expression of group membership. During this stage, the effects of social proof become apparent. The person says, looks and does things to demonstrate their allegiance to the group. There are several ways that someone can demonstrate their membership and these represent various degrees of commitment beginning with identification and progressing to behavior. A combination of identification is a predictor of more serious commitments to come.

The simplest form is the gesture. Not all groups use obvious gestures, but some groups are notorious for theirs. A stiff armed salute and a goose step march are unmistakably associated with the anti-semitic and xenophobic attitudes espoused by Nazis. The book *Rappers Handbook* describes the many gestures used in the hip hop culture like the Slim Shady Chop, the Swag Walk, and the Crotch Grab.[167] Using such gestures demonstrates acceptance of the hip hop culture and support of misogynist, homophobic, and anti-authoritarian attitudes. Flashing hand signs is another clear indication of group membership. Gang members use complex, contortionist hand signs to identify their allegiance, and heavy metal fans use the *corna* or "sign of the horns" to express their neo-pagan attitudes. Jive handshakes and fist bumping were once characteristic gestures of specific groups, but have since become so common that they do no longer clearly communicate any specific group membership.

The most obvious sign of group membership is a uniform. Uniforms project attitudes and are intended to illicit a response in others. Many groups have uniforms to identify their members so that others know what to expect and how to behave. Most of us are respectful when we meet clergy, judges, physicians, nurses, barristers, paramedics, fire fighters, police officers, security guards, and military personnel. And we are courteous when we are greeted by doormen, waitress, flight crew, nurses, and hotel maids. Likewise, many groups have quasi-uniforms that are intended to trigger specific reactions from others. In some cases, the desired response is fear. Hooligans, skin heads, and biker gangs have dress codes and often use grotesque images, aggressive messages, and sometimes even forbidden symbols on their clothes to illicit a fearful response. This is akin to putting a poison symbol on a bottle.

When a dress code or uniform are not prescribed, there are other forms of group identification like make-up, clothes, jewelry, hairstyle, facial hair, and body art. These represent a spectrum of commitment shown in Illustration 37. It is very good for people, young and old, to explore different groups and experiment with different styles and identities.

Make-up	Hair Style	Tattoos
Jewelry	Hair Color	Piercings
Wardrobe	Facial Hair	Brandings
Accessories	Implants	Mutilation
Low ←		→ High

Illustration 37: Identification Levels

It is especially beneficial for young people to express themselves through fashion on their path to self-discovery. Fashion can be transitory. Someone can change their wardrobe and hairstyle frequently to match their adjusting attitudes and there is little risk of doing so. But high forms of identification like tattoos and piercings are less transient. They represent a quasi-permanent commitment to identity that reduces flexibility and increases risk later in life.

There is a saying, "One shouldn't judge a book by its cover," but this is difficult for psychologists, marketers, politicians, and sociologists, because the data proves there is a strong statistical relationship between identification, attitudes, and behavior. Low level identification is pretty much meaningless when it comes to predicting behavior, but the behavioral profile based on a combination of identification activities is very accurate.

Someone wearing a colored bandana on their head isn't communicating anything special. There are many groups that use bandanas like cancer patients, fetish groups, and gangs. If we see that same person reading a book about cancer survivors, entering a gay bar, or riding a Harley Davidson we have more signs, but still nothing meaningful. As soon as that person dons a leather vest with the Hells Angel logo embroidered on the back and has the numbers 8-1 tattooed on their neck, they are clearly signaling a very strong commitment to the attitudes of that specific group. It is very difficult to leave this group to join another motorcycle club, so this permanent commitment was, hopefully, considered carefully. Likewise, a person driving a mini-van isn't projecting any specific attitudes, but as soon as that person puts a "Baby Onboard!" or "My Child is Student of the Month" bumper sticker on their mini-van, they are signaling their commitment to specific soccer mom or soccer dad attitudes. Likewise, a young woman with a butterfly tattoo on her shoulder is signaling very little, but as soon as she pierces her tongue, dyes her hair blue, and puts on a Japanese school girl outfit, she is communicating specific attitudes.

I fully realize that this is a provocative statement, but the data proves that fashion is a statement. That's why it's called a "fashion statement." We make deliberate attitude statements with the fashion we wear. I conducted a workshop with several buyers for major department stores. We listed the most popular fashion styles today and picked one statement that best expresses the wearer's attitudes. The results are summarized in Illustration 38.

Style	Description	Sample Statement
Arty	colorful, eccentric, handmade	Be yourself
Bohemian	natural, ethnic, handmade	Go with the flow
Chic	trendy, tailored	Just fit in
Classic	conservative, timeless, elegant	Quality over quantity
Exotic	colorful, intricate, ethnic	Everything is possible
Glamorous	colorful, asymmetrical, flouncy	Beauty is skin deep
Goth	black, religious, mystical	Don't trust anyone
Preppy	practical, cheap	Knowledge is power
Punk	militant, worker, worn	Take what you can
Rocker	black, cheap, worn	Friends are everything
Romantic	colorful, flowers, loose	Follow your dream
Sexy	flirtatious, maximum skin	Everyone is beautiful
Sporty	fitted, functional	Just do it
Western	outdoor, traditional, worn	Honor tradition

Illustration 38: Fashion Statements

Appearance is a projection of attitudes. Buying clothes and jewelry, getting our hair done, getting a tan and tattoos, and working out are all investments or commitments to create and project a specific image, attitude and lifestyle. We need to be cognizant of the statement we make in public. If someone doesn't like how they are being perceived by others, then they should look in the mirror and ask themselves what attitudes they are projecting.

In one self-help session, we had three interesting identities. Donald was a 40-something physician, who complained that his boss didn't take him seriously. He was passed over several times for a promotion. Tabatha was a 30-something office administrator, who was frustrated that men were hitting on her all the time and other female co-workers shunned her. Jerome was upset that he was often stopped by security officers in hotels and stores. Donald, Tabatha, and Jerome made very clear style statements. We easily found pictures of their styles on the internet. The next time we met with Donald, Tabatha and Jerome, we showed them three pictures and asked them if they identified with the people shown. They agreed. We copied these pictures and glued them onto cue cards to make 12 sets of three cards, which we distributed in another group session. We asked the members of the other group to describe the person in the picture by writing one positive and one negative word on the back of each card.

We collected the cards and the next time we met with Donald, Tabatha and Jerome, we showed them the list of negative and positive words that the 12 other people used to describe them.

Subject	Positive	Negative
Donald	cool, laid-back, chill	skater, lazy, stoner, slacker
Tabatha	hot, sexy	slutty, porno, bitch
Jerome	strong, sexy, interesting	aggressive, scary, gang-banger

Illustration 39: Strangers' Impressions

Four interesting things happened. First, we asked Donald, Tabatha and Jerome to take a couple minutes to review the list of words and then tell us if they agreed with these descriptions of themselves. They all agreed, and this shocked us. Second, we went through the lists and it occurred to us that they had ignored or glossed over the negative words. Third, when we discussed the negative words they all felt strongly that these descriptions were unfair, "they don't even know us." Apparently, positive perceptions from strangers are acceptable, but negative impressions are not. Fourth, we told them how we obtained the pictures we used: "We got Donald's picture from a skater magazine, Tabatha 's picture was downloaded from a porno website, and Jerome's picture is from a report about prison gangs." They became quiet and reflective. We had a long discussion. Donald and Tabatha realized that they wanted to project the positive aspects of these identities and neglected to realize that these identities also had strong negative associations. Jerome admitted that the negative and positive words were accurate.

> Donald: I want to be seen as the young, cool doctor, but I realize that this is why I am not taken seriously.

> Tabatha. I like the sexy librarian image, but I see now that I'm making a statement that is easy to confuse with porno.

Jerome: I try to be intimidating. I find that I get my way when people are afraid of me.

Wearing a t-shirt or baseball cap expressing an attitude like "Mexicans Go Home" or "Fuck You" may be fun for the immature person, but when that person takes their identification commitment further by shaving their head and getting the letters F-U-C-K tattooed on their neck, they are no longer just having fun, but expressing their adoption of certain attitudes and this is a strong predictor of action. In other words, appreciation turns into identification and then action. Effectively, by making a permanent commitment to identification, they are signaling their strong commitment to attitudes, which usually means a permanent commitment to identity. Even if they have a change of heart, it will be difficult for them to promote their new attitude or be accepted for their new identity, because their old identity is permanently tattooed on their knuckles. We encountered this dilemma many times in our study. Young people took their identification too far too fast, left a group, tried to establish new identities later and were not accepted by the new group. This rejection created crises.

Jaime: I didn't do well in school and when I graduated I didn't have many options so I enlisted. I loved the extreme workouts, drills and comradery. The military was exactly what I needed. I learned discipline and reliability. When I got out, I used my GI bill to go to college and found out that I was really good in math. I graduated with honors in finance. I applied for jobs in the sector, got invited to dozens of interviews, but I didn't get a single job offer. One interviewer really liked me and told me off the record, 'you should really think about wearing gloves and saying you have an allergy or getting your tattoos lasered. Investors and gray-haired managers don't trust giving their money to someone with skulls on his knuckles and a bomb tattooed on his wrist.'

It would be nice if positions were awarded based on skills and experience alone, but skills and experience are only some of the factors businesses look for in employees. According to a survey by Futurestep, a talent management company, executives look for attitude, skills, experience, and motivation. Surprisingly, 73 percent said they would choose attitude over skill, because "skills can be taught, attitude can't." Even though Jaime's attitudes and identity had changed since his military days, his interviewers could not know this based on his form of identification. Can we blame them? Would you feel comfortable being treated by a doctor with the letters K-I-L-L tattooed on their knuckles?

High levels of identification commitment are fine when they don't negatively impact a person's ability to satisfy their basic needs and when they do not stifle personal development. In our study, we met many people who had made high levels of identification commitment that were professionally appropriate. In some cases, their commitment was visible and they had careers that accepted these forms of self-expression, for example, the computer programmer with numerous visible tattoos and piercings who became the CTO for a technology company or the body builder who became a construction manager. This is an ideal situation, but not everyone has the luxury of having a talent that can become a career that also permits all forms of self-expression. Most people have to separate talent, career and self-expression, like the math nerd who became a stock broker Monday through Friday and is the drummer in a punk rock band on weekends or the science geek who became a cancer researcher and pole dances on weekends.

One could argue that the latter group is not fully secure with its identity, because they hide their true identity from their co-workers, but this would be a wrong conclusion. They are, in fact, so mature and secure that they leverage their unique talents to ensure their self-sufficiency and, in some cases, achieve self-actualization - without concerning themselves with acceptance. It would be a shame for someone to neglect a special talent, because their friends and family do not approve of their talent or because their vocation doesn't permit their form of self-expression. Imagine a person who has incredible skills, but they refuse to apply themselves or they aren't allowed to, because their form of self-expression is not permitted.

Assimilation intensity is also important to monitor at this level. The young person who spikes their hair up, wears an anarchy t-shirt, torn jeans and army boots when they go out with friends on the weekend, but wears khakis and a button down shirt to work or class on Monday is expressing an appreciation for the attitudes of their punk friends and only experimenting with the punk identity. As soon as that person throws away their old clothes and starts to always wear punk clothes when they are alone or outside the group, when the mohawk becomes the regular look, then the person has a new identity.

Stage 5. Action

The most obvious sign that someone not only identifies with but is also affiliated with a group is when they take action starting with harmless acts of advocacy like pranks and stuns that can escalate to violence directed at the out-group.

Advocacy

People who conduct acts of advocacy are promoting the group's views in public. Stunts include simple acts like posting fliers and painting graffiti. These actions are often conducted covertly at night by anonymous persons. Spray painting stencils or messages like "The Bible is a Fairy Tale" or "No War" are communicating very specific attitudes espoused by a group. Sharing social media content, picketing and demonstrating are also acts of advocacy that show that the person is a member of a group and willing to promote its views in public.

People who perform stunts, attend demonstrations are simply repurposing content created by others or chanting simple memorized paroles and are less indoctrinated members. These actions are usually performed by new members, recruits or followers who cannot effectively explain or defend the views of the group.

Reporter: Why do you want a wall?

Demonstrator: NAFTA was a bad deal for America. Too many factories moved to Mexico.
Report: How will the wall solve the jobs issue?
Demonstrator: Mexicans are taking advantage of our social system and should pay taxes when they import their products to America.

Canvassing or handing out printed material like fliers, magazines and brochures is an act of advocacy that involves a higher level of indoctrination and training, because it requires the person be able to conduct impromptu discussions with members of the out-group. I am always impressed with the representatives of Jehowah's Witnesses who hand out pamphlets at my local train station and the missionaries of the Latter Day Saints who proactively approach others to spread their message. I frequently ask them questions and they are always very knowledgeable. It is obvious they undergo training to be able to explain and defend their attitudes and answer the most frequently asked questions. Speaking in public is also a form of high level of advocacy although speaking or reading from a teleprompter does not always denote a high level of indoctrination.

The highest level of advocacy involves creating content. Every group has a thought leader, a subject matter expert who defines the group's agenda and writes articles, books, fliers, brochures, white papers, and pamphlets. The ability to effectively communicate and defend ideals and actions demonstrates the highest level of indoctrination. Steve Bannon, the CEO of Breitbart News Network and White House Chief Strategist, is the one of the most effective thought leaders or propagandists in American today. Bear in mind though, there are many books, blogs, and articles written by people who are thought leaders, but not necessarily fact masters. Some people are leaders in their in-group, but disrespected outside their group, so creating a filter bubble is important to preserving their position. Whereas Bannon represents the thought-leader in the alt-right movement, President Donald Trump and his team of media surrogates are merely messengers. Their frequent gaffs, contradictions, distractions and misstatements are evidence of their inability to explain or defend the alt-right agenda.

Not all propagandists are villains. Al Gore is not only a popular speaker against global warming, but his lectures, book and film *An Inconvenient Truth* make him one of the leading experts on the subject. He did not invent global warming nor is he a climate scientist, but no one has explained and defended the climate crisis more effectively than he has. Granted, some of the facts he uses have been disputed, but his message is nonetheless valid and positive. Even if his facts and figures were proven inaccurate or exaggerated, we should always err on the side of humanity. Improving the environment can never be a bad idea, because we can't live without it.

"Put your money where your mouth is." Decisions include any choice made that involves a *valuable consideration* that is often documented in a legal contract or agreement to affect a purchase, lease, membership, subscription, contract, will, endowment, college enrollment, termination, employment, tuition, marriage and divorce. The decision to subscribe to Forbes or FHM magazine, to buy a trailer home or a condominium, or to pay $1,500 to attend community college or $50,000 to go to a university are commitments that mirror certain attitudes. The billion dollar pledges made by Bill and Melinda Gates to fight malaria, Mark Zuckerberg and Priscilla Chan to cure all diseases, and John and Laura Arnold to improve criminal justice and education in America demonstrate their strong commitments to specific issues and attitudes. The level of commitment is not a function of sum. The size of the valuable consideration is relative. Bill and Melinda Gates donate billions, but that doesn't mean they are more committed to helping the poor and sick than Mother Teresa, who had very little to give.

Decisions do not only involve spending or effort level. They can also be expressed as a sacrifice or compromise. No matter how one feels about President Trump's agenda, his decision to turn his business empire over to his children to serve as President signals a strong commitment to the ideals of his constituency, and we trust he will separate politics from his family's business interests. Likewise, a person who resigns their position in a company, because they feel their employer is unethical is also signaling their strong devotion to certain ideals.

Such decisions are admirable, but acts of commitment are not always positive and logical. In fact, many are irrational and have foreseeable negative consequences. Taking action that effectively compromises health and security in order to achieve higher needs is a common theme for many of the subjects in my study. Here's an example and I provide and analyze many more stories later.

> Jane: After seven years of marriage, I realized I was trapped. I wanted to travel more, but my husband was a workaholic. I needed my freedom and asked for a divorce. We arrived at an amicable agreement, but one thing you don't split in divorce is health insurance. I was on his company policy and after the divorce I had to get my own insurance. This turned out to be impossible because I have a pre-existing condition. I have no money to enjoy my freedom and I'm in no shape to travel now anyway.

Direct Acts

Assertive or direct action refers to those acts that put some person's health or life at risk. When someone is willing to take such action on behalf of the in-group or against the out-group, they have reached the highest level of assimilation. The headlines are full of reports of attacks committed by people who take action on behalf of the in-group and against members of the out-group. ISIS is leading the headlines today, but there are dozens of groups that are actively recruiting, indoctrinating and radicalizing members to carry out kidnappings, assassinations, murder, rape, and suicide bombings on their behalf. These include terrorist groups like Farc in Columbia, Boko Haram in Nigeria, the Haqqani Network and Al Qaueda in Afghanistan, Kataib Hezbollah in Iraq, and the Tehrik Talliban in Pakistan; international criminal organizations like the Russian Solntsevskaya Bratva, the Albanian Mafia, the Japanese Yamaguchi Gumi

Yakuza, the Italian Camorra, and the Mexican Sinaloa Cartel; as well as motorcycle gangs with international and regional chapters like the Hells Angels, Outlaws, Pagans, Sons of Silence, Warlocks, and the Bandidos. Aside from the international organizations there are numerous national and regional groups like the MS13, Barrio 18, the Bloods, the Crips, the Aryan Brotherhood and the Ku Klux Klan. In almost every case, members are required to demonstrate their allegiance through rituals, tattoos or self-disfigurement and prove themselves by performing various acts against the out-group and even against innocent civilians. At the local level, every town has its own rowdy gang and every office and every school has a clique that thrives on teasing, harassing, pranking and punishing others.

Toilet papering someone's house or ringing the doorbell and hiding are harmless pranks, but bullying is not. There is no deficit of Hollywood films portraying the seriousness of the us-versus-them conflict. Films like *Carrey, Mean Girls, Revenge of the Nerds, Accused, Neighbors, I am Number Four, Back to the Future, Karate Kid, the Craft,* and *Bully* call attention to the harmful effects of bullying, and reality t.v. shows like the *Biggest Loser, Jungle Camp, the Apprentice, the Bachelor, the Bachelorette,* and *Survivor* encourage bullying every week.

People with disabilities and LGBT people are especially targeted. The rates of physical abuse directed at disabled and LGBT people is more than double that reported by other groups. A study by Hatzenbuehler and Keyes showed that 36.2 percent of LGBT students were physically bullied and the National School Climate survey showed that 30.3 percent of LGBT students miss at least one day of school per month because they felt unsafe or uncomfortable, and 10.6 percent miss four or more days per month.[168] In one horrific video, which was watched more than 20 million times on YouTube, Austen Higley, a 16 year old blind student at Huntington Beach High School in California, is seen being beaten badly by another student. Moments later, Austen's friend, Cody Pines, intervenes. Cody knocks the bully out with a single punch. Pines said in an interview he had seen other videos of bullies "beating up kids and getting away with it" and told himself he would never let that happen if he witnessed it.[169]

Not all direct acts taken on behalf of a group are aimed at members of the out-group. Self-immolation is a form of protest or martyrdom involving setting oneself on fire. Self-immolations are often public and political events arranged to catch the attention of the news media. They are seen as a type of altruistic suicide for a collective cause and are not intended to inflict physical harm on others or cause material damage. Since 2009, at least 120 Tibetans performed self-immolation and more than 40 died. A wave of self-immolation suicides occurred during the Arab Spring protests in the Middle East and North Africa, with at least 14 reported incidents. These suicides played important roles in inciting the Arab Spring, including the 2010–2011 Tunisian Revolution, the 2011 Algerian Protests, and the 2011 Egyptian Revolution.

Inaction

Some direct actions taken on behalf of the in-group or against the out-group are admirable. Civil disobedience involves non-violent resistance against an oppressor. It has been used in many movements in India, in the Czechoslovakia's Velvet Revolution, in East Germany to oust the communist government, in South Africa in the fight against Apartheid, during the American Civil Rights Movement, and recently in the 2003 Rose Revolution in Georgia and in the 2004 Orange Revolution in Ukraine. It can take the form of a sit-in or sit-down, whereby participants occupy a space through non-aggressive means. Sit-ins can take place anywhere. Wall Street, the White House lawn, and Tiananmen Square have been the site of sit-ins, and protestors have peacefully occupied bridges, buildings, tunnels, cafes, buses, and burial grounds. In some cases, participants chained themselves to construction equipment or trees in protest. Julia Hill lived in a 180-foot tall, 600-year-old California Redwood tree for 738 days to prevent loggers from chopping it down. She prevailed.

Mahandas Ghandi is the world's most famous and effective advocate for civil disobedience. Ghandi spawned peaceful protests in South Africa against Apartheid and the Indian Independence Movement, which ended two centuries of British rule. The actress Daryl Hannah and her fellow

Hollywood celebrities George Clooney, Susan Sarandon, Lucy Lawless, Danny Glover, Woody Harrelson, and Martin Sheen have been arrested several times for peacefully protesting on behalf of farmers, ranchers, children, woman, disabled persons, healthcare, minorities, and veterans.

Peaceful protesting does not always end peacefully for the protestors. It requires a serious commitment to a cause - and courage. During the Indian Independence Movement, British authorities arrested more than 60,000 protestors, and policemen savagely beat thousands of peaceful demonstrators and killed more than 70. During the American Civil Rights Movement, 40 protestors were killed by police officers and more than 400 people were killed by white supremists in night time attacks. Responding to a peaceful non-anonymous action with anonymous violence has to be the epitome of cowardice.

Groups can also espouse attitudes that lead to inaction. A survey by Gallup showed that 22 million Americans are vegetarians and 9 million are vegans. These people made a cognizant decision not to buy or consume animal products. The Buy American campaign targeted foreign import products, particularly cars, involved no real sacrifice or commitment on behalf of patriotic Americans and had no measurable positive effect on the U.S. automobile industry. Boycotting certain stores and brands is also a form of inaction that projects certain attitudes without negatively affecting supporters. According to Ethical Consumer, a non-profit consumer rights group, there are presently 59 active consumer boycotts against companies like Apple, Nike and Amazon for reasons ranging from animal rights to worker conditions and political affiliation.[170] Recently, in response to President Trump's lewd comments about women, activists launched the GrabYourWallet[171] campaign to boycott 33 stores carrying Trump products like jewelry and steaks, and the Democratic Coalition Against Trump[172] published an iPhone app to help consumers boycott 250 businesses with links to the Trump family. So far, a few retailers have dropped Trump brands including Neimann Marcus, Nordstrom's, Shoes.com and Zulily.

The New York Times published a story about the growth of college-based abstinence societies like the True Love Revolution at Harvard or the Anscombe Society at Princeton. Although many of the members are Catholic, most took the celibacy pledge for health reasons, not for religious reasons. When asked why she doesn't wear a chastity ring, one of the members responded, "Why is it necessary to signify you're not doing something?"[173]

Of course, inactivity can also have negative consequences. In one study, Richard Wiseman showed how people learn attitudes that prime them for failure. Wiseman recruited subjects who agreed with two different statements: "If it's too good to be true, it is" and "Luck is believing you are lucky." Wiseman provided his volunteers with a magazine and instructed them to page through the magazines while they waited for the study to begin. Previously, Wiseman placed a full page flier in the magazines with large text stating "when you find this, see me and I will give you $50". The participants didn't know that paging through the magazine was actually the study. Amazingly, only ten percent of the participants who agreed with the statement "If it's too good to be true, it is" found the flier and most of the participants who agreed with the statement "Luck is believing you are lucky" earned $50.[174] Priming for failure is very pervasive. In my study, negative attitudes about college, white collar jobs, corporations, science, and yuppies were used by many subjects to explain why they refused to take certain beneficial action like applying for a job, applying for college or following the advice of a medical professional or lawyer.

Ladel Lewis, a Doctor of Sociology at Western Michigan University showed that there is a strong correlation between music preference and attitudes towards crime reporting. In his study titled *Stop Snitching: Hip Hop's Influence on Crime Reporting in the Inner City*, Lewis concluded that only 24.3 percent of hip hop fans who witnessed a violent crime reported it to the police, while 75 percent of those that favor rock and heavy metal and 56.9 percent of R&B and pop fans did the same.[175] A survey conducted by the Police Executive Research Forum found that 47 percent of respondents attributed the stop snitching movement to the sales of stop snitching t-shirts and songs containing stop snitching lyrics.[176]

This is called the *culture of silence* and it refers to the behavior of a group of people, who do not mention, discuss, or acknowledge an illicit practice. A culture of silence is motivated by the desire to maintain solidarity, preserving group status, or a fear of repercussions or isolation. The culture of silence is always rooted in dishonesty, cowardice and a strong loyalty to one group over another. Some practices are so well engrained in their sub-cultures they have earned their own names. The Blue Code of Silence is followed by law enforcement officers to cover up crimes committed by fellow officers. The *omerta* is the code of silence imposed by the Catholic Church on all members of the clergy under penalty of ex-communication and was used to cover up cases of child abuse.

In summary, here's a list of statements that represent assimilation level and intensity.

Level	Statement	Intensity
Awareness	I've heard of them.	○
Attraction	I'm interested in learning more about them.	○
	I know what they stand for.	○
Appreciation	I understand what they believe and why.	○
	I'm learning their language.	○
	I can explain their beliefs to others.	○
Adoption	I defend their beliefs to others.	●●●
	I use their gestures when I am with them.	●●
	I use their gestures all the time.	●●●
	I speak their language when I am with them.	●●
	I use their lingo all the time.	●●●
Affiliation	I dress like them only when I am with them.	●●
	I have hidden tattoos.	●●●
	I dress like them all the time.	●●●
	I have visible tattoos or brandings.	●●●
Action	I spend time or money to advance our views.	●●●
	I covertly spray graffiti promoting our views.	●●●
	I hand out fliers with friends.	●●
	I hand out fliers alone.	●●●
	I protest with friends.	●●
	I boycott the out-group all the time.	●●●
	I protest alone.	●●●
	I teach our stance to others.	●●●
	I speak at events.	●●●
	I act out against non-believers.	●●●

Key: ○ Curiosity ●● Situational ●●● Personality

Illustration 40. Assimilation Level & Intensity

Curiosity is always good, albeit meaningless as a predictor of behavior. Situational activities reflect a high level of agreeableness and a willing to conform under peer pressure, but are not good predictors of future behavior. Anytime behavior is attributable to personality, we expect the person will advance to the next level of assimilation quickly. When the person fully identifies with the group, the probability the person will take frequent direct and serious action against the out-group, with or without others, is high.

On Friday, November 13, 2016, a trio of suicide bombers blew themselves up outside the Stade de France in Paris. One of them was 20-year old Bilal Hadfi, the French son of Moroccan parents. Although Hadfi was born in France, spoke fluent French and attended college in Paris, there were clear signs that he was adopting extreme views, assimilating into a terrorist cell and would become violent against others.

- January 2015: Hadfi openly defended the terrorist attacks on the newspaper Charlie Hebdo in a classroom discussion. His instructor reported the incident to school authorities. Defense denotes adoption.
- February 2015: Hadfi openly defended the Nigerian Islamist terror group, Boko Haram. Other students complained to administrators. Defense denotes adoption. Hadfi was not among his friends when he made these statements indicating that these extreme believes were part of his personality and signaling that assimilation would progress.
- July 2016: Hadfi posted a picture on Facebook of himself posing with a group of other young men. He is standing on a street corner in Paris, wearing an Arab scarf on his head and pointing his index finger at the sky, i.e. the ISIS gesture representing oneness of Allah. Gestures and fashion are indications of affiliation. Passers-by can be seen in the background. This is situational behavior, but anytime promoting extreme views in public is serious. Action against the out-group was imminent.
- February 2016: Hadfi told his mother he was traveling to Morocco to visit the grave of his grandfather. In fact, he traveled alone to Syria. He posted a picture of an AK-47 on Facebook. Action taken alone indicates a serious commitment.
- October 2016: Hadfi posted to Facebook that he had stopped smoking, drinking alcohol, and listening to music. Abstinence indicates a serious conviction to attitudes. The picture shows him

flashing the West Side hand sign, which stands for a street gang or war.

- November 13, 2016. Hadfi became a suicide bomber. Fortunately, he was alone when he detonated his vest.

Chapter 9

Social Identity Disorder

In order to fit in and maintain harmony, we often adapt the attitudes of our friends and allow our social circle to define our identity. When we accept these attitudes, make decisions to appease our friends and deal frequently with crises stemming from these decisions, yet remain loyal to the same friends and continue to espouse the same irrational attitudes, then we have a social identity disorder.

At first, I wanted to understand what decisions and sources of information were behind the decisions that caused stress. Why did someone decide to drop out of college, get divorced, how did someone get into debt, or get sick or injured? We learned in the first study that most of the actions taken by our subjects were based almost solely on information or encouragement they received from friends and family.

Then I wanted to understand why friends and family play such an influential role in these decisions. The preceding chapters summarize my findings and help us to understand why friends and family are so important to us. We know that social behavior is a primitive instinct and it can be beneficial even though not all forms of social behavior are productive. Diversity is an imperative. We also know that the social process begins at childhood and continues through adulthood. We learn virtues, traits and attitudes from our parents and carry certain deficits with us into adolescence and adulthood. We try to resolve these deficits with friends, who promote their own perspectives and have expectations. We adopt to belong. Identity is, therefore, transitory. The attributes we acquire from family and friends influence our priorities, our decision-making process and our behavior. We also know that our virtues, traits, attitudes, and behavior predispose us to experience life changing events, these events can create stress, and stress can have different manifestations.

This pattern is clear and it is a fantastic pattern. Knowing it helps to understand why the stereotypical therapy session begins with the psychoanalyst saying, "So, tell me about your childhood." Like a puzzle we have seen thousands of times, we can look at a few of the pieces and work out the rest of the image. Look at the three puzzle pieces in Illustration 41.

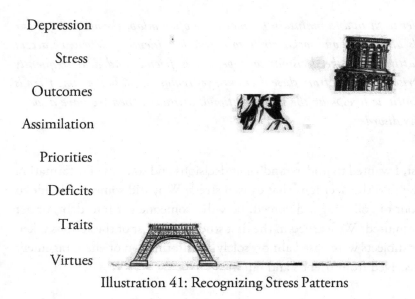

Depression

Stress

Outcomes

Assimilation

Priorities

Deficits

Traits

Virtues

Illustration 41: Recognizing Stress Patterns

Even though we only see the base of the image on the left, we roughly know what the rest of the Eifel Tower looks like and can deduce the middle and top sections. The foundation and top of the image in the middle are hidden, but we recognize the face of the Statue of Liberty and can deduce what the base and top look like. The bottom of the image on the right is masked, but we recognize the top and know roughly what the rest of the Tower of Pisa looks like. If we try to sketch the masked areas of these structures, the resulting drawing would not be precise, but it would be sufficiently accurate.

Likewise, when we identify the parenting style (the base of the Eifel Tower), we can predict the virtues and traits an individual will acquire, the deficits they will carry with them to the next stage, what role friends will play for them, and their level of assimilation (the middle section). Knowing the parenting style, however, doesn't help us to predict the attitudes they will acquire from friends, the types of stress they will experience (the top of the Eifel Tower), or how they will manage their stress, because these are group attributes.

> Arturo: My parents were too lenient with me, I hung out with the wrong crowd, and I got into lots of trouble when I was a kid. After high school, I got a bullshit college degree and it took me ten years to get my act together. It was a rough time for me. I'm going to make sure my son doesn't make the same mistakes I did. I'm going to make sure he hangs out with the right kids and picks the right career so he has an easier life than I did.

Arturo will be an authoritarian parent. His son will acquire hope and competence. He will be diligent and disciplined and high in conscientiousness. But he will lack will and purpose. As an adolescent, Arturo's child will seek friends that empower him to express himself. Because Arturo will be domineering, his son will learn to appease others, he will follow instructions and his level of assimilation will be high. Depending on the attitudes and priorities of the friends Arturo's son makes, he could become rebellious, make irrational decisions and get into trouble. If his friends are high in openness and conscientiousness, he could make better decisions.

When we pay attention to a group's or an individual's attitudes (the face of the Statue of Liberty), we can predict assimilation and the types of stress the individual will encounter (the torch) and we can deduce the traits, virtues and parenting style (the base). This is the approach

I used when I made my initial predictions. When I heard a friend complain that his new, younger manager was incompetent, saying, "I'm not letting that college weasel tell me what to do," I knew he wasn't interested in maintaining harmony, because his attitude reflected low agreeableness. When my friend dismissed my advice to take part in the training program that his manager offered, explaining, "I've been doing this for ten years, he can't teach me nothing I don't already know," his first time use of a double negative set off an alarm in my head. I knew he was spending more time with other friends who used bad grammar, so I looked closer at those friends. Most of them had similar problems at work, some were job hoppers, their careers had stalled or they were unemployed. His frequent use of double negatives over the following weeks signaled to me that he was adopting the anti-yuppie views of his other friends. I predicted he would risk his financial security for respect. Indeed, he was terminated a couple months later.

With the top part of the picture complete, we can deduce the bottom part. He was a hard-worker and conscientious, but he rebelled against authority and change, and placed a high priority on respect. He had a strong will and was very competent, but he saw the world as unfair, i.e. he did not acquire the virtue hope. I believe he viewed the younger manager with a college degree as a spoiled brat, i.e. an indulgent child, and he resented his manager. He was probably self-taught. This all points toward a neglectful parenting style.

Finally, when we see signs of stress or assimilation (the top of the Tower of Pisa), we can pretty accurately deduce the other elements (the base).

> Timothy: I just had my annual performance review and my boss reprimanded me for being late and spending too much time chatting with customers. I don't know why it's a big deal if I clock in at 9:10 am, because the bank doesn't open until 10:00 am anyway. He says I need to improve my productivity, but he doesn't realize that I'm building relationships with customers and that's more important.

Timothy places a strong priority on social connections, he is high in extroversion, but he is low in conscientiousness and agreeableness, and dislikes any sort of criticism. He acquired will, but not competence. His definition of competence differs from his manager's. Remember, it is common for the offspring of indulgent parents to over-estimate their abilities and to define performance indicators differently than others.

We know that friends and family play very big roles in our perceptions, attitudes and decision-making process. We also know why this happens. Someone suffers from what I call a *social identity disorder* when they refuse to abandon their immature attitudes and priorities in order to maintain harmony with the friends and family who are effectively making them sick, stupid and sad.

Now, let's apply this insight to understand some of the most common cases of stress, which my team documented. To uncover these relationships, I developed a simple system for recoding more than 6,000 session notes to reflect traits, priorities, stress level, level of assimilation and types of depression. We deduced traits based on the attitudes expressed by the subjects. These attitudes had to be interpreted in context, for example:

> Patricia: Life is what happens when you're not planning.
> I believe in going with the flow.
>
> Markus: I only complain when it is really important.
> Otherwise, I just go with the flow.

Patricia's use of "go with the flow" reflects low conscientiousness, whereas Markus' use reflects high agreeableness. To code priorities, we identified the need which the subject prioritized, as well as, the need which the subject sacrificed when they made a decision or took some action that triggered a life changing event. We did the same for the subject's group. To calculate the stress level, we added the stress units for the events reported by the subjects in the first part of my study. The activities reported by the subject were matched to assimilation level and intensity.

By analyzing the case data using this method, I validated some expectations and uncovered some surprises. Here's a list of the most important learnings:

1. Stress and depression are strongly linked to irrational priorities. The Holmes-Rahe stress score was medium to high in 90 percent of cases where the subject put a high priority on social or esteem and a low priority on health and security. Stress units were lowest when the subject put a high priority on health and security and a lower priority on social or esteem. Having rational priorities is an insulator against stress and stress-induced illnesses.

2. Attitudes corresponding to high agreeableness equate to a high priority on the social need and high level of assimilation. All subjects with high agreeableness and high priority on social need also had high levels of assimilation. All subjects took action that resulted in a negative outcome.

3. It's sometimes ok to go with the flow. Being identity insecure and having irrational priorities are not as detrimental as I had expected - as long as certain group conditions exist. Subjects who were unorganized and inefficient had lower levels of stress when the group was high in conscientiousness and the subject as high in agreeableness.

4. The conscientiousness trait has a very strong correlation to the security priority and an inverse relationship to stress, but high conscientiousness is not an insulator against stress when it is combined with a high priority on security. Some people took financial security so seriously that they compromised their health and experienced burnout or sleeplessness, but they were in a position to manage it better and avoid more serious forms of depression.

5. The most surprising finding was that having rational priorities creates stress when the group has irrational priorities, and vice versa. There were several different cases for this. The most common case involved people who placed high priority on security or health, when friends prioritized social or esteem. Avoidant behavior was a common manifestation in such cases.

6. The most serious relationship occurred when the subject was low in conscientiousness, high in agreeableness and put a high priority on the social need, and the group was low in openness, low in conscientiousness and high in neuroticism. Substance abuse and violent behavior were prevalent when this combination of factors existed.

7. Another dangerous combination is when the subject is low in conscientiousness and high in agreeableness, and the group puts a high priority on esteem. This combination was frequently linked to cases of illegal activity.

The application of these results has limitations. The most obvious limitation is, these results reflect input from thousands of confessed sad, angry, stressed or depressed people. I did not study people who had no problems and were happy go lucky. If you recognize a combination of factors that fit your situation and are asking yourself, "Why am I not totally stressed, an addict or a terrorist?" The answer could be:

- a. You are an exception. The results are statistically significant, but never perfect.
- b. Your combination of traits and priorities is somewhat different. Even a minor change in priorities or the degree of assimilation can produce different outcomes.
- c. There are other factors at play that I did not measure.
- d. You may have received rational advice, had an edge experience or an intervention.
- e. None of the above.
- f. All of the above

Part II

Application

In the first part, we took a look at the prevailing approaches for understanding social behavior. We unified the methods from leading psychologists like Moslow, Holmes and Rahe, and Erikson to explain the relationship between parenting, virtues, traits, priorities, assimilation, stress, and depression. The resulting unified model explains <u>why</u> our friends and family and we think and act the way we do.

In the second part, we'll take a look at a collection of stories to understand how social identity actually affected thousands of my subjects. The following stories are representative. Each story is exemplary of dozens sometimes even hundreds of other similar stories. I selected these stories because they were the most common and they help to explain the different ways social identity works against us and stifles our personal development.

The entire story is not provided, just the portions necessary to make a point. I edited the stories for readability, for example, I removed fill words and replaced some jargon with more common words. I omitted some superfluous vulgarities.

There were many ways to group these stories. By attitude, by trait, parenting style, outcome, etc... Because this book is based on the humanist belief that every person has great potential and seeks to realize it, I decided to group the stories to reflect the hierarchy of needs: physiological, security, social, esteem, and self-actualization. When we look at the ways friends and family make us sick, stupid and sad, you will probably notice that some common themes emerge. The themes most commonly linked to high stress units were:

1. GO WITH THE FLOW or TAKE LIFE ONE STEP AT A TIME
2. ALL I NEED ARE MY FRIENDS (OR FAMILY)
3. DON'T SWEAT THE LITTLE STUFF or LIFE IS WHAT HAPPENS WHEN YOU'RE NOT PLANNING
4. YOU CAN'T BUY HAPPINESS or MONEY ISN'T IMPORTANT
5. FOLLOW YOUR GUT or JUST DO IT
6. BE YOURSELF or DEFEND YOUR HONOR or STICK TO YOUR GUNS or EVERYONE IS BEAUTIFUL
7. GOOD THINGS COME TO THOSE WHO WAIT or SHIT HAPPENS
8. BE NORMAL or FIT IN
9. FOLLOW YOUR DREAM (OR PASSION) or DO WHAT MAKES YOU HAPPY
10. WINNING ISN'T EVERYTHING - THE EXPERIENCE IS MORE IMPORTANT or THE JOURNEY IS THE REWARD

These attitudes reflect low conscientiousness and low openness and high agreeableness. They also indicate a focus on higher needs like social and esteem over basic needs like health and security. They are not necessarily bad attitudes, they are just not conducive to self-sufficiency, achievement and self-actualization. Furthermore, their strong link to stress lies in the false expectations that they create.

Chapter 10

Sick

Health is the most basic human need and it should not be sacrificed for any other need. Granted, there are times when a short term unhealthy effort is necessary to achieve financial security. For example, it may be necessary to work two shifts a day every day for a couple months to afford something important or pay bills. Also, there are some people who admirably risk their health every day in careers as police officers, fire fighters, and soldiers, but they undergo extensive training and follow strict protocol in order to reduce the risk of injury. They know that compromising health is not viable in the long-term.

Many of us suffer health issues because our friends and family set expectations, or they are compassionate to a fault, establish specific requirements, share incorrect information and give bad advice. Our friends and family make us sick.

The attitudes that were most commonly expressed by subjects who suffered health issues were:

- GO WITH THE FLOW
- JUST DO IT
- FOLLOW YOUR GUT
- LIVE AND LET LIVE
- ALL I NEED ARE MY FRIENDS (OR FAMILY)
- EVERYONE IS BEAUTIFUL
- BE NORMAL

The first type of case deals with friends and family who set expectations and communicated certain attitudes that required the individual to compromise their health. Friends and family did not explicitly instruct the individual to do something unhealthy or dangerous, but the person found that they must in order to satisfy others' expectations.

> Jeremy: This huge, asshole bouncer wouldn't let me in this club. Yeah, I was drunk, but it was a bar. That's like not letting a fat person in a Wendy's. Anyway, I turned away and my friends said "Are you gonna let him dis you?" I knew if I didn't defend myself, they'd ride me all night. So I swung around to punch him, tripped on that velvet rope thing, fell and hit my eye on a post. I'm almost blind in that eye now. That kind of limits my career choices. I have no depth perception so I can't catch a ball or drive yet.

Jeremy's initial response was to turn away. However, he placed a high priority on acceptance and belonging. Jeremy's friends didn't tell him how to act, but they expressed clear attitudes about honor and created an implied expectation for him to defend himself to earn their respect. Jeremy sought approval from his friends and made a rash decision to sucker punch a huge, sober bouncer. Jeremy took action without any sort of reflection and risked his personal safety to win the approval of his friends. Poor health was an unintended consequence that caused a series of life changing events and frustration.

Any time we succumb to peer pressure and take action against others without reflection, we put our health at risk. Recent studies in Australia, England, and America show that 80 to 90 percent of altercations involved a group of male friends, happened between 9:00 pm and 3:00 a.m. in or on the street in front of a bar or nightclub, and involved alcohol. Twenty-four percent of altercations resulted in arrest. We do stupid things when we get drunk and we seldom get drunk alone. The NTSA reports that more than 90 percent of DUI arrests, car crashes and deaths involved drunk drivers who were drinking with friends.

Friends and family also influence poor health decisions by showing compassion for our weaknesses. They do this out of kindness or love. The truth sometimes hurts, but not hearing the truth can be even more unhealthy.

> Stacey: I've got a big butt. I know it. And it keeps getting bigger. My doctor's been telling me for years, I need to change my diet, get fit, even have a surgery, but my husband is so sweet. He keeps telling me, there's more of me to love.

Stacey decided not to follow a physician's advice. Her decision was influence by her husband's compassion. She enjoyed her husband's affection and put her health at risk. Her husband was compassionate and sought harmony. If she continues to refuse treatment and if he continues to remain empathetic versus telling her to take the doctor's advice, she will likely experience more serious health issues later and they will both experience stress.

> Daryl: I was on career cruise control. I worked hard and moved up the corporate ladder quickly. I had a retirement plan, insurance policies, profit share. We had a beautiful home in a great neighborhood, our mortgage was affordable, and we took nice vacations. My wife complained that I was gaining weight, but most of the guys I worked with were big. We worked like dogs and called had nick names for each other like "Bull" and "Beast." Our customers were also big. We called the biggest clients "whales." Once a skinny co-worker poked fun at one of the bigger partners, "What are you growing there, big guy?" The partner patted himself on the belly and said dryly, "Success." We laughed our asses off and this became a mantra in our office. A couple months later I had a heart attack. I missed some work, but fortunately, I'm insured up the ying yang. I was out a couple weeks, but I'm back in action. I'm on a strict diet and fitness plan now and some of the other guys are thinking about joining me.

Daryl did not make a deliberate decision to gain weight in order to win the acceptance of his colleagues. Daryl focused on his career too much and neglected his health. Growing over-weight and then suffering a heart attack were unintended consequences of putting a high priority on financial security. Daryl's colleagues also placed a high priority on financial security, but no one said, "You have to be big to be successful." Colleagues did not promote over-eating, but they tolerated obesity as a side-effect and perverse sign of success. Colleagues also promoted some us-versus-them mentality, whereby the members of the in-group were perceived as more successful than the members of the out-group. Daryl defended his group, because it validated his weakness. It was easier to justify being over-weight than to lose weight. Being big was a form of identification, and having a belly to pat was a group gesture. Fortunately, Daryl was high in conscientiousness. A heart attack created 53 stress units and Daryl was out of work for some time thus producing another 20 stress units for a total of 73 stress units, but his illness did not trigger a critical combination of other stressful events because he was prepared.

Daryl's health issues were avoidable. Fortunately, he was prepared to deal with the costs of them. In the following case, the health issue was unavoidable and the subject wasn't prepared to deal with the outcome.

> Zach: Another driver came out of nowhere and t-boned me. I was unconscious and when I awoke, I was in an ambulance and the other driver was gone. My car was totaled, I missed lots of work and I'm stuck with huge medical bills.
> Therapist: That's terrible. Did you have health insurance?
> Zach: Well, no. I'm young and don't need it. No one has health insurance.

Zach made a decision not to get health insurance, because his friends didn't have health insurance. They were all young and took their health for granted. His decision made him vulnerable and an unavoidable accident triggered more stress. Nevertheless, Zach still stands behind his decision, because it was normal.

Beth: My friends and I must have each spent more than $10,000 last year on beauty - botox, lifts, and implants. We even got our anuses bleached. I'm not sure why. None of us ever questioned what we were doing to our bodies. Some of our friends said we looked unnatural, but we dismissed them as being envious. I can't smile naturally because my face is tight, my hair is thinning, and I can't run because my bobs are too big.

Beth made a decision to get plastic surgery because her friends were also optimizing themselves. She and her friends didn't intentionally compromise their health in their pursuit of beauty. They probably thought health and beauty were synonymous, but they are not. Their priority was esteem *visavis* beauty and they inadvertently risked their health. Beth and her friends were low in openness, surgery demonstrated a high level of commitment to the group, and synthetic beauty was the group's form of identification. The women who did not have cosmetic surgery were members of the envious out-group.

These cases are different in subtle ways.

- Jeremy's behavior is attributable to personality. His friends didn't tell him to punch the bouncer. They only urged him to defend his honor. Jeremy acted alone, and his friends did not behave similarly.
- Beth's behavior is attributable to peer pressure. Her friends defined the actions that members had to take in order to belong to the in-group and they also participated.
- Daryl's and Zach's behavior is attributable to personality, but their stress can be attributed to situation. Their friends did not tell them what to do and they did not act to impress their friends. However, because their friends made similar decisions, they felt validated and did not correct their behavior.
- Jeremy and Beth suffered permanent disabilities.
- Daryl's condition was health related and temporary.
- Zach's stress is just beginning.

We see in these four examples how focusing on high needs like respect and esteem can create vulnerabilities for illness. These subjects did not purposely compromise their health. They simply neglected to consider health in their decision-making process.

We also see that the group never actually set priorities for the individuals. The group did not give members a clear choice between health and some other need. The individuals set their own priorities.

Collaborative Compassion

We see already two examples of groupthink. Daryl and Beth belonged to an in-group that formed negative opinions against the out-group. Daryl's case is interesting in that it is an example of a form of groupthink or solidarity that I call *collaborative compassion*. This refers to groups that form based on a weakness. There are other forms of collaborative compassion, which I discuss later. In the context of health, collaborative compassion exists when (a) someone prioritizes higher needs over heath, (b) the person experiences health issues, and (c) the health issue is a condition for group membership. Collaborative compassion was prevalent among gang members, drug addicts, and gay fetishists. These subjects compromised their health to fulfill other needs, suffered injuries or illness, and then used their illness or handicap as a form of group identification. You will note that, in these cases, too, the group never said explicitly, "You have to sacrifice your health to belong to our group," but the group sent a clear message that unhealthy behavior was favored.

> Will: I'm a huge soccer fan and my friends and I were always getting in trouble at matches. Mostly drunk and sometimes vandalism. We hated the other team and wanted to kick their asses and so we decided to join the local fan club of Hooligans. When we met them, they told me to get lost. They said I was too pretty and looked like a bitch. I knew what they meant. They all had missing teeth, scars, black eyes, broken noses. My friends got in and they said it was very structured. There was a dress

code, a chain of command, and rules. They worked out, partied, and went to every match together. And sometimes they got into brawls with the other fan clubs. No one wanted to lose a front tooth or break his nose in a brawl, but scars were like medals. I was missing out. So I got this stupid idea of shaving my head and then slashing my face and scalp. I went a little too far and had to get more than 20 stitches. I looked pretty scary. I went back to the hooligans and my friends told them I did the scars myself. They said anyone who is crazy enough to slash his own face is tough enough to run with them. I ran with them for just over a year and had to get out, because I had a serious concussion and lost too many teeth. My jaw clicks, I can't eat normal now, and I have constant headaches. I never had a problem picking up girls, but now I look like an extra in a Mad Max film. I'm very conscious of my looks and have problems dating. Everyone says beauty is only skin deep, but I know the girls see me as thug.

No one wishes to be ugly, but looking tough was a condition for group membership. Will acted alone to win acceptance in a group and his behavior is, therefore, attributed to personality. Will prioritized acceptance over health. Once accepted, Will and his friends took part in brawls, which created more opportunities for injury that could improve their status within the group. His decision resulted in him getting disfigured and having self-esteem and dating issues.

Our drug addicted subjects tended to form groups based on a common weakness. No one sets out to become an addict. Drug use starts as a recreation or a coping mechanism, and the choice of drugs is set forth by the group. Remember, access is a factor in drug use and abuse. When collaborative compassion exists, friends do not help other friends to get well. Instead, the friends validate the decisions and condition. The members knew the background stories of other members, they showed incredible empathy for each other and appreciated their unhealthy choices.

Collaborative compassion was especially strong among subjects who were involved in the gay fetish scene and this is problematic from a health perspective. A blend of alcohol, poppers, marijuana, cocaine, and other drugs lowers the inhibition for high risk sex acts involving multiple partners.

> Robert: I attended sex parties a couple times a month. There are always at least 50, sometimes 500 guys at these parties. Everyone is drunk, high, naked and horny. When there wasn't an event, I could always find a private party online. It was not uncommon for me to have ten or more partners on a weekend. I always tried to be safe, but when you're flying and having a good session, things get out of control sometimes. I contracted HIV and it was diagnosed early so I started treatment before it turned into full blown AIDs. For months, I was still contagious and I didn't want to infect anyone. I didn't want people to fear me so I didn't talk to anyone and kept to myself. I was withdrawn and really lonely. After about six months my virus count was below the detectable limit, which means I wasn't contagious. I don't have AIDs. Then I got out more and bumped into some other guys who also had HIV and were below the limit. We talked and I was happy to have friends who were not afraid of me. They showed me that my sex life wasn't over. Actually, it would only get better, because we didn't have to worry about getting HIV. We already had it. I started attending bare back and fisting parties and going to meat markets. These parties are totally extreme. Everything goes.

This behavior is not as novel as one would think. I documented many dozens of similar cases. Robert and other subjects in this category prioritized intimacy over health. The unifying group attribute was based on an illness. By showing compassion for HIV and using positive psychology, "Look at the bright side, we can do whatever we want now," members felt validated in their past decisions and continued their risky behavior. A study by

Schackman et. al. found that 34 percent of HIV infected persons reported not using a condom every time and 21 percent reported never using a condom.[177] My gay fetish subjects even considered HIV "empowering" and "liberating," because it enabled a higher level of sexual promiscuity. Having HIV was an element of Robert's group's identity. They wore colored blindfolds or armbands at naked sex parties and used other gestures and symbols to signal their preference for unprotected "bareback" sex, fisting, pissing, as well as to communicate their role as a top, bottom, active or passive partner. Robert's behavior was mostly situational. He only participated in high risk sex and drugs with others.

In some cases, uninfected subjects reported purposely having unprotected sex. Subjects said unprotected sex was forbidden and dangerous, and therefore, very erotic. It's called *bug-chasing* and this trend is described by Esben Elborne in *When HIV is Considered a Gift*.[178] Hardcore unprotected sex is also being fetishized in the gay porn industry. This is alarming, because we know that media can influence viewers' attitudes and behavior. A study conducted in Sweden by *The Journal of Developmental and Behavioral Pediatrics* found that 96 percent of teenage males watched porn (versus 54 percent of females) and that youngsters had approximately the same rates for porn-influenced fantasies and attempts to recreate pornographic scenes.[179]

High risk sexual behavior and drug use are typical signs of depression, but these subjects were psychologically mature in many other aspects. They were high in conscientiousness and openness. They were self-sufficient, honest, and curious. Many subjects who suffered from other diseases like cancer felt unfairly victimized and often posed questions like, "Why me?" Whereas most of the hundreds of subjects that had HIV accepted it as their new reality. Most were not stressed about their illness, because they knew that contracting HIV was the result of their own decisions and behavior. The primary source of stress for them was reconciling societal norms with their sexual preferences and experiences. They wanted to express themselves openly and freely, but they were afraid of being judged by others. They were avoidant and socialized almost exclusively with others who had similar sexual preferences.

Daniel: When I'm at work and the other hetero guys are bragging about nailing some waitress on the weekend, it all sounds so boring and normal to me. Guys can have three different types of orgasms, but most men only know one. I want to tell everyone about them. It's incredible. But I know they will be shocked, probably disgusted.

Obviously, not all of our subjects with HIV accepted it as their new reality, felt liberated, and started or continued to have unsafe sex. Contracting HIV influenced many subjects to modify their behavior, i.e. practice safe sex, carefully select partners, attend fewer sex parties, and consume less alcohol and drugs. Nevertheless, they, too, were avoidant and highly neurotic. The subjects fell into four categories: (1) those who are still dealing with the disease; (2) those who accept having HIV, but are ashamed or cautious; (3) subjects, who accepted having HIV and have come out; and (4) those who came out and are involved in safe sex or HIV/AIDs advocacy."

Alex: I still can't believe I have HIV. I'm so mad at myself and scared, I can't sleep.

Arnold: I'm afraid. I haven't told anyone, even my closest friends.

Betsy: I've confided in my closest friends, but I can't tell my family, because I know they'll judge me, probably shun me.

Roger: Getting diagnosed with HIV was very stressful for me and my relationships. I've been through it all from denial to shame, rejection and ridicule. I'm helping others to deal with it.

Robert experienced a life changing event and made a decision to curb his promiscuous behavior, he became withdrawn and his loneliness made him vulnerable, because he needed intimacy. The price of having friends was his health. Other subjects had similar experiences in that they experienced life changing events, realized they needed to set rational priorities and put health first, but the group actively opposed their new, healthy decisions. The group didn't want to lose a member and collaborative compassion was strong.

> Frank: I always worked hard and partied harder. I drank way too much, used drugs and got involved with the wrong people. I had some really close calls and I realized that I had to slow down. I'm avoiding some people and, when we do meet, I'm more careful. Everyone's always asking me, 'What's wrong? Why are you such a prude now?' Nothing's wrong. I'm just trying to be more responsible.

> Jim: I was drinking too much and it was affecting my relationship. I had to stop. I wanted to stop, but my friends didn't accept this. They say I'm "pussy whipped."

> Ralf: I wanted to quit many times, but my friends always said, "AA is for quitters."

> Marisa: My weight issues started to cause other more serious health issues and I knew I had to do something drastic. I was contemplating surgery, but I postponed the decision for several months, because every time I talked to my girlfriends about it, they said "We are beautiful the way we are."

A crisis can develop when new, rational priorities conflict with the group's existing irrational priorities. If the group is low openness and agreeableness, the person who suddenly espouses different priorities faces the prospect of rejection and loneliness. In most cases, to avoid being ostracized, the subject procrastinated a decision until their stress score reached a critical level:

> Arnold: I know I made serious mistakes in my relationship. I worked too hard and drank way too much. I justified my drinking by saying it was normal office behavior. My wife and I had frequent arguments, but I didn't think it

was serious. I was paying the bills, we had everything, and I had never gotten into any legal trouble. My friends said they had the same issues with their wives who didn't understand the stress we had. I got home late one night to find a Dear John letter taped to the toilet. That she didn't leave it on the kitchen table tells you a lot about my habits. My wife took the kids and went to her parent's house because "It was safer there," she wrote. I broke down. It was too much. I couldn't function. I started AA right away, but it was too late to save my job. I couldn't concentrate at work. I looked like shit, I was argumentative and other employees started to complain about me. I got reprimanded, written up for sexual harassment, demoted, transferred, and fired – all in just 6 months. By the time the divorce went through, I had lost everything. I couldn't even afford to buy my son a birthday present. That was embarrassing. I'm starting all over and I'm serious.

Arnold's behavior was situational. He prioritized social and financial security over health and safety of his family. His frequent arguments with his wife should have triggered a change in his life, but his friends validated his behavior and his relationship issues. He only changed when things got completely out of control.

The Normal Paradox

In most of the examples so far, the group established expectations and members set individual priorities to appease the group. This often entailed inadvertently compromising health for some other need. The group usually does not require specific action, but it tolerated unhealthy behaviors and outcomes. Now we'll look at cases where the group not only set expectations, but also recommended specific actions. The group told the person how to think and knowingly suggested unhealthy behavior.

Kimberly: I was recently divorced and suddenly a single mother of two. I had two daughters to care for. I needed money for day care, a nanny, school clothes, etc. I was an emergency room physician and we were expected to put our patients' needs before our own. I was working brutally long shifts and I was irritable, tired, and afraid I was neglecting my girls and would make a mistake at work. I had easy access to prescription drugs. Actually, they were being offered to me all the time. Colleagues would say every day, You look like shit, do you want something?" I started taking Provigil and everything was good for a couple months. I had lots of energy, I was positive, I enjoyed the time with my girls. But one thing led to another. I got addicted to amphetamines and my life is hanging by a thread.

Kimberly's needs in order of priority were social *visavis* family, financial security, and then health. She wanted to provide for her family and this required working harder. Kimberly's group placed a high priority on self-actualization, helping others, over personal health. Kimberly was high in conscientiousness and also neuroticism. She was fearful and, in order to earn more money, she made a conscious decision to compromise her health to meet her employer's expectations and earn more money. Her group defined expectations and recommended using prescription drugs for purposes other than their approved use. This is called *off-prescription use* and this practice is illegal. Physicians know this. Furthermore, as a physician, Kimberly must have known that taking prescription drugs for off-prescription use is unhealthy and addictive. Kimberly's behavior is attributed to situation.

A similar situation existed among athletes and college students who took drugs to enhance their performance. Drug use was not a condition for membership in such groups, but performance expectations were high and drug use was viewed by the group as a necessary evil. Subjects compromised their health for security or esteem, because they thought it was normal.

Adam: I was training hard and competing for years, but I never took first place. I was always first or second loser. It was really obvious that everyone else was doping, because they were improving much faster than I was. I wanted to get better faster and my trainer told me I needed to dope. This has nothing to do with money, because there's no money to be made in my sport even when you're famous. I just wanted to be best. The results were as expected, I started winning, but over the long-term I had some issues with baldness and testicular atrophy.

Sarah: If you want to land a decent entry-level position in a reputable firm, you have to somehow cram 20 years of experience into 6 years of college. Getting good grades isn't enough. You have to be in the honors program, write for the school newspaper, join the debate club, have work experience, speak a foreign language, do community service, and get involved in campus life. I didn't want to fail, and taking speed was normal. The problems is, employers expect you to keep up this level of activity when they hire you. My occasional amphetamine usage turned into a longer-term addiction. I've lost lots of weight and I'm aggravated all the time.

Adam's and Sarah's behavior is attributed to personality. Their friends took steroids or speed, influenced and validated their decisions, but they took the drugs alone. They both lived in a filter bubble, in which members think and behave similarly, and create a defective definition of normal. These are examples of groupthink that I like to call the *normal paradox*. The normal paradox exists when (a) the group believes something is normal, when facts show that it is not, and (b) even if the behavior is normal, it is not acceptable. Facts show that steroid and drug use is not normal, and not acceptable. Claudia L Reardon and Shane Creado published a study titled *Drug Abuse in Athletes* that showed that only two percent of elite athletes took a substance banned by the World Anti-Doping Agency (WADA).[180] Furthermore, a survey released by the Partnership for Drug-Free Kids titled *Under Pressure: College Students and the Abuse of RX Stimulants* showed that only 20 percent of college students abused prescription stimulants like Adderall or Ritalin.[181] Both are classified as Schedule II drugs under the Controlled Substances Act. Most universities expel students for possessing illegal drugs or using legal drugs without a valid prescription. If you don't get expelled, you could face prison. According to Section 844 of the Controlled Substances Act, the first offense for the simple possession of a Schedule II controlled substance without a prescription can be up to a year of imprisonment, a fine of $1,000, or both. A second offense can cost up to two years in prison and $2,500, and a third offense can result with multiple years of jail time and $5,000.[182]

Young adults are especially susceptible to the *normal paradox*. Colleges and military boot camps have intensive orientation programs. These are basically fast track indoctrination programs and hazing is common. Hazing is an extreme form of pledging and another example where groups establish clear expectations, set priorities and dictate specific behavior. A University of Maine study concluded that 55 percent of students who join fraternities, sororities, sports teams or other student groups experience hazing.[183] The pledges make a conscientious decision to partake in sometimes dangerous challenges in order to gain acceptance to the group. The catalog of dares is very long. It includes acts of humiliation like singing in public, eating dog food, drinking urine, public nudity, and staging embarrassing pornographic scenes. Hazing sometimes involves forced branding, tattooing, shaving one's head, sleep deprivation and can escalate to vandalism, theft, beatings, and dangerous feats. A national study of student hazing showed that, since 1970, there has been at least one hazing-related death on a college campus each year and 82 percent of hazing activities involve alcohol.

> Sam: We were duct taped naked to a chair and had to answer history questions about the college. If we got a question wrong, we had to drink a shot of vodka. The more answers I got wrong, the more I had to drink and the harder it became to get a question right. At some point I just passed out. The next morning, I woke up on the lawn in front of the Welcome Center - still bound naked to the chair. I had vomited all over myself and was covered in urine, dog feces, and used condoms. Someone wrote SAM on my forehead and LOSER with

a permanent marker all over me. Dozens of students were standing around taking pictures of me and laughing. After about 30 minutes, someone tried to cut me free, but my nuts were duct tapped to the chair. Paramedics and campus police came and diagnosed me with alcohol poisoning. My BAC (blood alcohol level) was over 3.0. I recovered from the alcohol poisoning and the duct tape rashes on my balls, but the humiliation was too much. Pictures of people putting their asses or cocks in my face, pissing on me, smearing dog shit on my face and then writing LOSER on me were all over social media. My friends all abandoned me like a leper and my only friends now are other uncool kids. I know how those kids who ran-a-mock in Columbine feel. We are constantly planning sophisticated revenge schemes.

Sam was focused on fulfilling his social need by getting accepted into a fraternity. It was no secret that fraternities have bizarre rituals. Many books and movies portray hazing, and the internet is rich with hazing stories and reports. Sam ignored this content. He succumbed to peer pressure and agreed to participate effectively risking his physical and mental health. His behavior was situational. His attempt to get accepted failed and he became a chastised member of the out-group. It sounds like Sam's depression would turn violent, but the story has a happy ending. We met Sam a couple months later and he reported on his amazing recovery:

Sam: One of my friends came up with the idea that I had been sexually assaulted and I needed to file charges. She did some research and we met with a law professor who reviewed the photos and agreed that I had been kidnapped and sexually assaulted by at least twenty other male students. We filed a law suit and wrote a cover story for the college newspaper. Date rape was already a hot topic on campus and now a male student was speaking out against sexual assault. The women's and homosexual rights groups on campus met with us and we planned a demonstration. We held signs and chanted, 'we are not your bitches.' The tables turned drastically. The fraternity was notoriously homophobic and overnight they were branded as gay predators.

Sam's new friends were high in openness and conscientiousness. They had will, purpose and competence. His new friends' basic needs were provided. They're need for social acceptance and respect were satisfied. Seeking justice *visavis* self-actualization was a rational high priority and they succeeded. Sam had a life changing event that developed into depression and, thanks to his new mature friends, he channeled his depression into something beneficial to the community. His recovery was situational. This episode in his life lasted six months and the final outcome was positive.

There is, of course, a side to this story with an unhappy ending. We know that several students were arrested and charged with sexual assault. I am pretty certain that those students who mistreated Sam while he was bound and passed-out in a chair were only trying to impress their friends. The simple fact that they posted their self-incriminating pictures on social media proves this. A study by Babson College showed that "in more than half of the hazing incidents, a member of the offending group posts pictures on a public web space." To win respect and improve their status in the group, they took turns one-upping each other in their abuse of Sam. Their behavior was situational. I didn't have contact with Sam's abusers and I can only imagine how stressful their lives became. It's difficult to get a job or rent an apartment when you're a sex offender.

Don't Try This At Home

Sometimes, we just do stupid things to gain the attention of and impress our friends.

> Monica: I was at a party with my girlfriends and we were all having fun. Everything was cool and the next thing, I

am lying on the street and someone's pointing a flashlight in my eyes. My friends showed me a video climbing up a street light and they're all chanting 'mon-key, mon-key, mon-key.' Then I'm dangling over the intersection when a semi-truck comes and knocks me down with that big wind scoop on the roof. I don't remember anything. Both my legs are broken and my hip is fractured. The doctor said I'll probably never walk normal. I have an athletic scholarship. The season starts in six weeks and I'm freaking out. That's probably all down the drain now and I don't know how I can afford college. I'm trying to get a disability rating so I can get student aid. I don't know what I'd do right now without my friends. They're all so supportive.

Monica's friends didn't set any expectations and they didn't suggest she climb the street light. Her friends are, nonetheless, complicit, because they didn't stop her. They actually encouraged her. Monica had a spontaneous stupid idea and her friends cheered her on. Her behavior is attributed to personality. As Monica lay on the street waiting for paramedics to arrive, her friends were busy taking more pictures and videos, which they immediately uploaded to Facebook. Their behavior was situational. Her friends clearly placed a high priority on the social need. I found it curious that Monica was thankful for such friends. We won't find strength in numbers when our friends don't even try to protect us from our own stupidity and then leverage the negative outcome to gain personal benefit such as improving their social media popularity. Sadly, this kind of affection was common for my subjects. Apparently, we are willing to overlook friends' flaws in exchange for their affection - even when they cause us injury and stress.

Search *neknomination* online and you'll find thousands of videos of young people speed drinking large quantities of alcohol in response to a dare from friends. In some videos, the goal is to consume excessive amounts of alcohol in a short time, while in others the goal is to do something precarious while drinking alcohol. Neknomination videos show participants dressed in chicken suits and others stripping for the camera as they consume beer and liquor.

People perform neknominations while climbing, skiing, car-surfing, etc. The craze started in Australia, but spread internationally when tourists in Australia challenged their friends at home to out-drink them. Amanda Lenhart from the Pew Center found that one-upmanship is a central theme in online behavior. Lenhart showed that 40 percent of teens said they felt pressure to post content on social media that will garner lots of likes and comments.[184]

Not all social media challenges involve alcohol. The list reads like a report from a torture chamber: have a friend douse you with boiling water, eat a Carolina Reaper, the world's hottest chili pepper, pour a bottle of vodka into your open eye, or chew and swallow an entire cactus plant. The "cinnamon challenge" involves swallowing a whole tablespoon of the spice without water and can lead to vomiting, choking and a trip to the hospital. Already more than 500 cases of overdosing on cinnamon have been recorded. The act of mimicking a wooden plank started off as a harmless fad. Due to social media, it has become a worldwide phenomenon called *planking*. The objective is to lie face down in a strange place and then upload a picture or a video of it on Facebook or Youtube for others to see. The more dangerous the location, the more likely the planker is to get featured. Photos of teenagers planking on bridges, train tracks, rooftops and moving vehicles are common on the internet. Not to be out done, several participants have increased their danger level and already many injuries and several deaths have been reported.

Amateur Advice

In all of the cases so far, the subject made a decision to neglect, sacrifice or compromise health in order to satisfy some other need. Friends set expectations, gave specific instructions, accepted or encouraged this unhealthy behavior. Now let's look at a different set of cases where the priorities of the subject and her group were fully aligned, but their attitudes or approaches differed.

> Melinda: I was diagnosed early with cancer in my right breast and the doctor recommended a mastectomy. He said the operation was minimally invasive. I even got a

second opinion. The doctors agreed the expected results would be excellent and I'd live a normal, healthy life. My husband and I talked about it and he said it was a no-brainer. He made me feel really good about it and I had no reservations. Then my girlfriends started sending me all kinds of information about alternative treatments. I asked my doctor about the alternatives and he said exactly what the articles said he would say. He discounted the homeopathic alternatives as unproven, because he wanted to operate. My girlfriends more or less mobbed me into rejecting the science. They even sometimes did the homeopathic treatments with me. I tried the alternatives for about six months, but the results were zero. In the meanwhile, the cancer spread and I ended up having both breasts removed.

Melinda's and her friends' priorities were aligned, but they held different views about science and alternative medicine. Melinda and her husband believed in medical intervention, but their rationality was trumped by Melinda's friends, who favored a natural approach. Melinda inadvertently compromised her health to belong. Her behavior was situational.

Studies reveal how widespread the problem has become. Researchers found that the most common mistake users of herbal remedies make is believing that the substances actually work. A study by the National Institutes of Health study showed that about 19 percent of Americans take herbal supplements and more than half the time they're using the substances to treat a specific health condition instead of just for general well-being.[185] That's fine, provided the supplements actually treat those conditions, but in more than two-thirds of cases, the preparations had never been clinically proven to be effective.

Aside from making you think you're doing something to alleviate your health problem and not really treating the ailment at all, herbal supplements present other possible pitfalls. "If a supplement is not effective and not harmful, most physicians probably won't have a problem with it," says Aditya Bardia, an internist at the Mayo Clinic and lead author of the study. "It's when it's not effective and also harmful that it's going to be a cause of concern."[186] Certain supplements can have adverse effects ranging from nausea and vomiting to life-threatening conditions like liver or kidney dysfunction. For example, the U.S. Food and Drug Administration (FDA) released a warning about potential liver damage from consuming *kava* root, one of the ten most popular herbal supplements sold in the U.S. banned *ephedra*, it banned a Chinese weight-loss herb after it was linked to more than 100 deaths, and found that some ayurvedic supplements were contaminated with dangerous heavy metals, including lead and mercury. Perhaps the greatest potential risk, however, lies in possible interaction with pharmaceutical drugs. Saint-John's-Wort, which has been shown to help in treating mild to moderate depression, is also known to reduce the effectiveness of some HIV medications and heart drugs such as *digoxin* and *warfarin*, both life or death medications.

> Nancy: I met some girlfriends for lunch and told them I was planning to take some time off work. I had been working too hard and needed some downtime. A day later, they started bombarding me with information about depression. They completed an online survey for me, and the results, based on their answers, showed I was depressed. They were convinced I need to start therapy and take something. Coincidentally, they were also in therapy. It was as if they were trying to convince me to be depressed with them. I told them I wasn't depressed, just burned out. They argued, 'that's exactly what my aunt's neighbor said and she ended up committing suicide." They said denial was the first sign of depression and they're constantly pointing out all the things wrong with my life. I'm starting to believe them. Is there such a thing as a depression cult?

> Timothy: I started to gain weight for no reason. I didn't change my eating habits and my level of activity was the

same, so I was concerned. Our friends said I probably had some sort of infection. Apparently, water retention was the first sign of an infection and fat is mostly water. They said it would take weeks to get a doctor's appointment so I may as well try some natural remedies first and if they worked I'd save the cost of the co-pay. This made sense. I didn't have anything to lose so my wife ordered some herbal teas for me to try. They tasted awful, I woke up at night drenched in sweat and I got terrible diarrhea. Friends said, 'that's exactly how I felt. That's your body purging the poisons. It only lasts a couple days.' That kind of made sense so I continued. Two weeks later, my wife had to bring me to the emergency room. I had kidney failure.

Stephanie: We moved to a new school district when my daughter was five. We were going to enroll her in first grade and the school's website said we needed to provide proof of vaccinations. I asked my new girlfriends to recommend a pediatrician and they told me vaccinations were dangerous. I didn't know that. They shared lots of articles showing this. 'My grandmother never got vaccinated and she's 87 years old.' They told me we didn't need vaccinations if we enrolled her in a charter school. A year later, one of the other kids at school got the chicken pox and most of the kids in her class got them, too.

These stories have several things in common. First, friends were not subject matter experts. They were not trained medical professionals. Second, friends used unscientific information they found on the internet to make a healthcare recommendation. Third, they created a filter bubble. Friends colluded to refute scientific information, and my subjects were in the minority. The majority opinion was uneducated. Forth, friends used the *curious exception* argument. There are many different examples of this type of argument, for example, "My uncle smoked and he lived to 90 years" or "There's a video online of a lady in France who cured her cancer with leeches from her own garden."

Although studies show that most medical information online is accurate, there is a potential for harm from internet-based medical diagnoses and treatments, because there is some incomplete, inaccurate and misleading information, which can only be understood by a medical professional. [187] Online support groups are especially susceptible to sensational anecdotes and unscientific advice. A community exists to support pretty much every disease and approach. For consumers who interpret information incorrectly or try inappropriate treatments, this can be hazardous to one's health. Another problem with the internet is that it is now possible for pharmaceutical companies to promote their products directly to consumers. These new ways of disseminating medical information carry important risks of conflict of interest and over-consumption of medication. Indeed, it is difficult for internet users to distinguish between content promoting drugs and non-promotional information about health problems and their treatment. Furthermore, although the knowledge of various therapeutic alternatives allows patients to be better informed and to make enlightened choices, it can also lead them to press health professionals to prescribe medication to treat health issues that actually do not exist. Finally, it is now possible to make legal online purchases of drugs, something that can pose a threat to people's health due to over-consumption, dangerous products, and adverse interactions.

Too many of my subjects tried some traditional family remedy and suffered more complications before seeking professional medical treatment. Friends recommended herbal teas, weird compressors involving mustard and urine, difficult and funny exercises, homemade inhalation therapies, and even do-it-yourself surgery and acupuncture. And some shared expired prescription drugs, illegally imported unapproved medicines, or recommended doing nothing.

> Gerald: I fell off a ladder while doing some home improvement and hurt my neck. I asked my neighbor

to drive me to the hospital. He said his wife was a yoga instructor and she could fix it. She did some stretches with me and then I heard a loud crack. I couldn't move my neck and started to freak out. I've had serious neck problems ever since. She blames me for not doing the pose right.

Doris: I twisted my ankle hiking and it hurt real bad. I could barely stand. My girlfriends said, "Just walk it off." I begged them to get the car, but they complained, "Don't be a diva." The next morning, it looked like I had elephantitis. My ankle was so swollen, I couldn't even get my pants on. I went straight to the ER and they found I had a fractured fibula. I was out of work for a week and the swelling is down, but I'm in physical therapy and it's not getting better. I still can't stand on it and I'm walking with a cane.

Now we know why and how friends and family make us sick. Friends and family set expectations, make unhealthy recommends, and tolerate unhealthy behavior. But we can't blame our friends and family when our decisions cause illness, disease, substance abuse, weight problems, disfigurement, and disabilities. None of the thousands of cases I recorded involved a person being forced to over-eat, take drugs, have high risk sex, consume alcohol, do something stupid, or do nothing at all. All of my subjects had free will. They chose to adopt attitudes and follow instructions. They wanted to belong, to fit in and be normal. They sought harmony, wanted love and affection and sought to improve their status in the group. These stories show us that the price of belonging can be poor health.

I find it especially interesting that many subjects followed the advice of friends and family, became ill, some never got fully well again, and yet so many said they were thankful for the emotional support they received from their friends when they were ill.

I started with the cases where friends and family affected personal health, because this is the most basic human need. When someone is preoccupied with poor health, it is difficult to fulfill other needs. Good health is a pre-requisite for security, a happy family, and achievement. Poor health is often a precursor for other stressors. In the next section, I focus on how friends and family influence decisions that impact our ability to be safe and financially secure.

Chapter 11

Stupid

Stress is a precursor for depression and when we look at the list of life changing events that cause stress, we see that most are related to health or financial security. There is a strong reciprocal relationship between health and security. Poor health makes it difficult to achieve financial security, and an over-emphasis on financial security can cause poor health.

It is common for a single stressful event to trigger others. An illness can cause loss of income, mortgage foreclosure, etc. and the loss of a job can trigger an illness and other stressors. These needs must be balanced. Excellent health can reduce the likelihood of contacting some illnesses or having injuries, but it cannot prevent all accidents and sickness. Being financially secure can enable someone to deal with health issues ore effectively and also prevent unexpected and unavoidable problems from spiraling out of control. Remember, when we talk about security, we do not mean wealth or affluence. We mean efficiency. Having a steady income is part of attaining and maintaining efficiency. Friends and family play influential roles in steering our priorities and our career decisions. Friends and family can make us stupid.

The attitudes most commonly expressed by subjects who had problems with security and financial stability were:

- GO WITH THE FLOW

- DON'T SWEAT THE LITTLE STUFF, DON'T SWEAT THE BIG STUFF
- BE NORMAL
- WHAT YOU DON'T KNOW CAN'T HURT YOU
- YOU CAN'T TEACH AN OLD DOG NEW TRICKS
- TAKE LIFE ONE STEP AT A TIME
- JUST DO IT
- FOLLOW YOUR GUT
- ALL I NEED IS MY FRIENDS (OR FAMILY)
- WINNING ISN'T EVERYTHING - THE EXPERIENCE IS MORE IMPORTANT
- EXCELLENCE IS NOT BEING THE BEST, IT'S TRYING YOUR BEST
- YOU CAN'T BUY HAPPINESS
- DO WHAT MAKES YOU HAPPY
- DON'T CARE WHAT OTHER PEOPLE THINK
- STICK TO YOUR GUNS
- BE YOURSELF
- GOOD THINGS COME TO THOSE WHO WAIT
- EVERYONE IS BEAUTIFUL
- FOLLOW YOUR DREAM (OR PASSION) AND DON'T GIVE UP
- LIFE IS WHAT HAPPENS WHEN YOU'RE NOT PLANNING
- THE JOURNEY IS THE REWARD
- HONOR TRADITION

The Posers

The most common problem our subjects reported was over-extending themselves. They were independent, but not efficient. They had, as one subject put it, "Champagne tastes on a beer drinkers budget." They spent too much of their incomes on luxury homes, furniture, art, boats, fashion, jewelry, electronics, and entertainment, and did not have enough left over for food, education, bills, savings accounts, college, retirement plans, and insurance policies. Their public image was impressive, but privately these subjects were in debt, stressed and unhappy, because they were trying to live up to the expectations set by friends and family.

> James: I started a new job and wanted to climb the ladder quickly. I was a new employee and didn't qualify yet for the company's health insurance plan, so I had to decide between private health insurance or leasing a new car. I chose the new car, because my colleagues all drove European sedans and our clients expected me to drive a luxury car. They laughed at my lime green Prius. It's all about projecting success to be successful. A year later, I slipped a disk mowing the lawn. I had to pay for doctor visits, physical therapy and pain killers out-of-pocket. This was expensive. I depleted my savings account fast and started using credit cards to pay my medical bills. Sitting and driving was painful, so I missed lots of work. Then the delinquent notices started to come, creditors assessed exorbitant late fees, my credit card got cancelled, the leasing firm repossessed my car. I couldn't afford physical therapy anymore, the pain was unbearable, and I started drinking. The alcohol and medicine was numbing, but I was a mess. I haven't worked in over a year, and I'm going to have to file for bankruptcy if I don't win the lottery first.

James' group placed a high priority on esteem. He placed a high priority on the social need. Leasing a luxury car is a serious decision that demonstrated a high level of commitment to the "players" in the firm. James' colleagues and clients did not tell him he should forego health insurance to afford a luxury car. They probably had no idea what James' financial situation was, but they were low in agreeableness and openness and their expectation was clear - if he wanted to be successful, he couldn't drive a Toyota. James made a deliberate decision to compromise his financial security to satisfy his group's priority for esteem and this created a vulnerability. His behavior is attributed to personality. One life changing event triggered a series of other stressors. James' stress score reached 300 points in just 12 months. James was not conscientious and he wasn't prepared to handle a combination of life changing events. Stress manifested as substance abuse.

Thousands of subjects told similar stories. Oliver and Carolyn had good jobs, a condominium in a gated community with a pool and a tennis court, and matching his and her BMWs. But they couldn't pay their bills on time and they couldn't afford to be sick.

> Carolyn: We haven't had date night in months and haven't gone on areal vacation in three years. We stay with my relatives in Ohio every year and when we get back we tell our friends we were in Hawaii or Europe for three weeks. I want to go to Hawaii - for real.
> Oliver: What are we doing wrong? Our friends have the same kind of jobs, we all drive German cars, and we all live in the same neighborhoods. They're going on vacation and eating out all the time. We're getting into debt to keep up, buying groceries on credit cards. I go to work sick, because I can't afford to miss a day.

The answer to Oliver's question is simple. Oliver and Carolyn had irrational priorities. They were conscientious and competent, probably the children of authoritarian parents. Remember, the children of authoritarian parents tend to be followers. Friends set expectations, and Oliver and Carolyn set their own priorities and lied to fit in. Their behavior is attributed to personality. In order to be accepted and respected, they prioritized esteem over their personal needs for security and intimacy. They also compromised their integrity. Should a friend learn that their annual vacations were fake, they would certainly lose face among them. In order to be able to afford to stay home when he's sick, plan a date night and take a real vacation, they need to sacrifice some luxury. They need to become more efficient.

One habit that is common for the subjects who had problems with financial security is they tend to buy things they do not use frequently instead of renting or borrowing them. Oliver and Carolyn financed a $29,000 speed boat that they used only twenty days a year. Renting a speed boat twenty days would cost less than $3,000 per year. The payment, storage and insurance for the speed boat cost them $599 per month. They also bought a $900 canoe that they used only a couple times a year instead of renting one for $49 a day.

Buck and his wife Marilyn were in a similar situation although their circumstances were somewhat different.

> Marilyn: We're retired and on a fixed budget. We eat fast food and in diners most of the time to save money. Buck needs to sell his car. It's beautiful and I love it, too, but we spend $400 to $600 a month for repairs, gas, tickets, and hotels to go to these old-timer car shows.
> Buck: She keeps telling me I need to sell my Cady, but it's my pride possession. I'm not one of those guys who's happy sitting in front of the tube. I need to be tinkering with something. Because of her, I keep busy all week and we get out of the house on weekends. Our friends are all at these shows.

Marilyn was thinking rationally. She prioritized health over esteem, but Buck clearly enjoyed the attention he got with his car. His focus was on esteem and his friends set a clear expectation for acceptance - you have to drive a classic car. I don't think selling Buck's Cadillac is the best answer. Having a hobby during retirement is very important for mental and physical well-being. Buck and Marilyn could start by reducing the costs of attending shows, for example, by packing healthy food, pitching a tent, or sharing a hotel room with friends. Another couple who had a passion for motorcycles sold their home, put $180,000 in the bank and bought a used Winnebago for $30,000. They tow their motorcycles to events. This solution wiped out their debt, lowered their monthly bills, created a comfortable savings, and kept them active.

Amateur Advice (again)

Keeping up with friends and family is always an issue when friends and family are not experts and give advice.

> Werner: I've got seven houses and the mortgages are killing me.
>
> Therapist: Why do you have seven houses?
>
> Werner: My friends got me started on real estate investing. The idea was to buy homes with very little or nothing down, let the rent pay the mortgage, and then earn the long-term rental income when they are all paid off.
>
> Therapist: Sounds like a clever plan. Is that working out?
>
> Werner: No, my renters are always trashing the place and paying rent late. I have three houses that have been empty for more than three months, I need to fix them up so I can get them occupied, but I don't have enough money, because I'm also making the mortgage payments.
>
> Therapist: How many can you afford?
>
> Werner: I can realistically afford two, but they were having so much success and the mortgage requirements were so favorable that I didn't want to miss the opportunity.
>
> Therapist: Can you sell some homes?
>
> Werner: If I do now, I'll lose money.

Werner was influenced by friends to make a risky investment decision. This is a good plan and I know several people who have succeeded with this strategy, but Werner obviously over-extended himself and put his current financial stability in jeopardy in order to keep up with his friends. Subjects told similar stories involving investing in stocks, start-up technology companies, multi-level marketing schemes, and precious metals. Aside from over-extending themselves to keep up with friends, these cases had something else in common. The subjects did not consult an expert. They relied solely on information from friends and family before making investment decisions.

Other subjects made similar mistakes. They made important financial and legal decisions without seeking the advice of an expert. Friends and family gave them amateur investment tips, tax advice, and legal counsel, and it backfired.

> Kym: I needed to refinance my home, because my mortgage rate adjusted up and my payments increased, but my credit was shit and the bank declined my application. Then, my best friend told me his lender offered him an attractive refinancing offer after he missed six months of payments. His idea was for me to skip three to four months of payments, use the money to get caught up on other bills and send them a hardship letter. He even gave me his letter as a template. It worked for him so I figured it would work for me. I got delinquent notices every month and stuck to the scheme expecting them to make me an offer. After six months, the lender started foreclosure proceedings. I almost lost my home. I had to take out huge cash advances on my credit cards to pay the six months in arrears. I got stuck with heavy late fees and penalties, and my credit score tanked so that the interest rate on my credit cards was suddenly jacked up to more than 20 percent. I can only afford to apply the interest on my mortgage and cards. I'll never be debt free.

My Friends Are My Family

Balancing esteem and financial security is already difficult for people who have an education, a job, retirement plans, and savings accounts. Imagine how hard it is for people who have no skills and no education, and no security to satisfy their needs. Crime is often the answer.

> Anthony: We lived in a crappy part of town in a nasty apartment building. It wasn't like rat infested, but the other tenants were all tweekers and gangbangers. At least

once a month, someone was shot in our neighborhood. I had my mom and sister to take care of and started selling counterfeit merch for my uncle. I was making two to three thousand a week. I gave my mom money for groceries and my sister and I wore all the hottest brands. I paid cash for an Escalade when I was only 17. I was a player and making more than the principal. College didn't make sense to me. Why would anyone waste four years to make less? So I quit school. Some months, I started to get trouble from some haters. Once they tried to hi-jack my SUV full of product, so my uncle gave me a gun. The next time I saw them, I showed them my gun and they opened fire. My sister was with me. They were not trying to kill us and just shot up engine and tires.

Anthony likes to think he was conscientious and working to care for his family, but his priority was clearly esteem. His behavior is attributed to personality. He had achieved "player" status and sacrificed education and security for respect. If his family's security was a real priority, he would have used his profits to move his family to a safer neighborhood and start a legitimate business or get some training.

We documented almost a hundred versions of this story. A young person felt obligated to take care of his family, quit school and took to dealing or trafficking drugs, stealing cars, robbing homes and stores, etc. They always gave their families enough to get by and spent most of their earnings on "bling." They all described their communities, circles and scenes as unsafe, complained about no opportunities, and boasted about acquiring "piles of money" through some illicit activity. But none of them took their pile of money and escaped. One of the questions other group members always posed was, "When you had a pile of money, why didn't you pack up your family and move somewhere safe?" Subjects in this group had four different answers to this question:

Anthony: That was my neighborhood. My friends are there.

Gary: This is my family and I am very loyal.

Bryan: If I moved to a new place, no one would know me. I'd be a no body and I'd have to start all over.

Chris: I had enough money to buy a house in one of those new, vanilla planned communities and we could have gone to nice safe suburban schools, but no one would accept people like us in that kind of neighborhood.

Jerry: I worked hard to earn that kind of respect.

Our subjects with a criminal record all put a priority on belonging and respect, over health and security. Their sense of honor and loyalty were understandably corrupted, because they received very little affection from their parents, who were either neglectful or authoritarian. Their group appreciated their circumstances and attitudes. The gang or group was collaboratively compassionate and served as the subjects' *Ersatz family*. This is a common theme in gangster cinema, for example in the *Sons of Anarachy* and the hugely successful *Fast and Furious* franchise, as well as in the recent box office hit the *Guardians of the Galaxy*, in which the word family is used hundreds of times.

Failure to Launch

The transformation from adolescence to adulthood always triggers stress. Young people move away, sign their first rental agreement, get their first job, start paying bills, get their first loans, start school. Add up the stress units for these events and it quickly reaches medium risk levels. The millennial subjects in my study, i.e. persons 17 to 37 years old, made disastrous decisions, amassed mountains of debt, were jobless, and had few and mostly bad options. I identified several reasons for this and checked data from other sources to see if my observations were correct.

First, as adolescents, they were dependent on their parents, who provided for their basic needs – a home, healthcare, school supplies, food, and clothes. They took their basic needs for granted and were used to getting everything they wanted. Remember, this generation is the result of indulgent parenting. When they moved out of their parents' homes and had independence, they continued to indulge. Few earned enough to pay their own food and housing, yet they prided themselves for "being out on my own." We found that many young people had a defective definition of independence.

> Trey: Finally, I could eat, drink, sleep, and shower when
> I wanted, how much I wanted, with whoever I wanted.

> Cody: The best part of college at first was setting my own
> rules. Going to bed when I wanted, sleeping as long as I
> wanted, making my own schedule, not making my bed.

Second, they had low incomes. All of my subjects complained that they were under-employed or unemployed and had difficulties paying rent and other bills on time.

Third, these subjects had credit card debt. Lofty desires and low income translate into credit card debt. A report by the Wall Street Journal titled *The Alarming Facts About Millennials and Debt* showed that 24 percent had over-drawn their checking accounts.[188] A meta-study by NerdWallet using data from more than 12 other sources showed that the average credit card debt for young consumers is $5,300, 22 percent had been hit with late fees, 13 percent had incurred over-the-limit fees, and 14 percent had used their credit cards to get cash advances.[189]

Forth, with basic needs paid either by parents or education loans, young people were primed to focus on the next level in the hierarchy of needs, i.e. social. The goal of attending college or trade school should be to prepare young people to become self-sufficient, but most ignored this objective and focused on other, more attractive reasons to attend college. Carolyn Martin, the President of Amherst College, provided a long list describing the many different reasons to attend college including this statement, "College is for the cultivation of enjoyment, in forms that go beyond entertainment or distraction, stimulating our capacity to create joy for ourselves and others." For my subjects, this entailed consuming alcohol, experimenting with drugs, and having sex.

> Jasper: They don't call it 'the best four years of your life' for no reason. It's totally awesome. There's a party every night somewhere and I've never met so many hot foreign chicks. I'm doing a global cunt-ry tour – get it?

Sixth, connecting with others at this level was a no-brainer, their social needs were quickly and easily fulfilled, and my subjects turned their attention to satisfying their needs for achievement and self-actualization. The prior factors created short-term crises, but choosing a major created the more stressful, long-term frustration. These subjects did not select majors or trades that were aligned with available positions, instead they picked careers that reflected their passions. As a result, in addition to their credit card debt, they amassed mountains of student loan debt to earn worthless degrees that did not help them to get good jobs. A report by Forbes Magazine showed that 44 percent of college graduates in their 20's were stuck in low-wage, dead-end jobs, and the number of young people making less than $25,000 spiked to the highest level since the 1990s.

> Ted: I majored in Communications with a specialization in omni-channel marketing, because I love social media. I'm graduating soon and looking for a job, but they pay shit. I can make more driving for Uber.

Eighth, imagine graduating college with thousands of dollars in credit card debt, holding a worthless degree, landing a low-paying job, and then having to deal with more than $30,000 in student loan debt. A report by the Wall Street Journal found that more than 40 percent of Americans who borrowed from the government's main student-loan program hadn't made payments or were in behind. The only option for millions of young people in this situation is to move home and live with mom and dad. That's exactly what many of my subjects did and this life changing event was embarrassing and also terribly frustrating for them. They enjoyed their perceived independence for four years and suddenly had to live by mom's and dad's rules again.

> Dennis: It's so humiliating when a friend asks if we can hang out at my place after work and I have to tell him that I have to ask my mom and dad.
>
> Gary: I didn't tell my girlfriend I live with my parents. She googled my address and street viewed my house and asked me how I could afford such a big house if I didn't have a job.
>
> Cady: My dad treats me like I'm 16 again. He wants to know who I'm going out with, where we're going, and tells me I need to be home by midnight. "My house, my rules," he says.

According to the Pew Center for Research, 26 percent of Millennials lived with their parents in 2016, 67 percent lived with others, and only 7 percent lived alone, i.e. had achieved real independence.

There is an excellent solution to this problem. Joseph Urgo, the President of St. Mary's College of Maryland, asserts that college is for young people to decide what and how they want to contribute to society, to the economy, to their communities, and to the well-being of their families.[190] He recommends a sort of national career draft system, whereby all high-school graduates are assessed and matched to jobs that mirror the nation's needs. This is exactly what European social democracies do. They poll businesses every couple of years to find out what skills will be required in the future, work with trade schools and universities to develop appropriate curriculum and incentives, and then assess students and match them to these jobs. Young people still have a choice to learn trades or study subjects that are not in demand, but the number of enrollments and student aid are severely restricted. The result of such an educational draft program is a low unemployment rate for young people. Germany's statistics office, Destatis, reports the rate of youth unemployment in Germany at only 7.7 percent, the lowest in Europe.[191] Compare that to the U.S., where 51 percent of high school graduates and 23 percent of college graduates are unemployed.[192]

An education draft would be an excellent solution. It would produce enormous benefits for society and the economy and also counter the bad advice from friends and family. But such reform will probably never take place in America, where the focus on individualism and self-expression are greater than the focus on societal needs and well-being. The most practical answer is to choose a career or vocation that is interesting and also has a good return-on-investment, i.e. to prioritize self-sufficiency over self-actualization.

Choosing a vocation or profession is a very serious decision - one that certainly needs to follow the formal decision-making process. A good job is a pre-requisite for self-sufficiency and income stability is a requirement for continuous personal development - along with rational priorities. Nevertheless, studies by Princeton University showed that 60 percent of career choices were made based on information from friends and family alone, while only 27 percent used career assessment tests, and only 13 percent of career seekers considered multiple sources.[193] Consulting multiple sources of information is always important when making important decisions. A meta-analysis of the data from hundreds of other studies on career mobility showed that 74 percent of those people who had considered multiple sources when making a career decision had stuck with their original choice.

Looking at the cases of stress related to financial insecurity, we uncovered an interesting pattern, namely that the subjects with income stability started with rational priorities that changed over time causing stress, whereas subjects without job security started with irrational priorities that did not change over-time. The decision to attend university or go to trade school is a rational decision. It shows that the person was conscientious and placed a high priority on self-sufficiency. When these subjects later made irrational decisions like over-spending and experienced stress like loan default, they could more effectively handle these kinds of stress, because they had an income. Even when they hated their jobs and earned low incomes, they were nonetheless conscientious; they had skills, and, therefore, more options. They could downsize, curb their luxury shopping sprees, get their debt under control, take care of their health, get re-trained, save some money, buy insurance and afford treatment or counseling. These subjects had the means to change their priorities and also start over. But the subjects without an education or training were stuck. The fact that they had no formal training shows they were low in conscientiousness and had irrational priorities to begin with. They encountered stress and had no skills, no means and, therefore, few options. Overcoming stress for them was very difficult and it often compounded into bigger problems.

Hitting a Wall

People who made good career decisions achieved self-sufficiency faster and had income stability longer. With their basic needs sustainably satisfied, they could focus on fulfilling higher needs. Meanwhile, people who made career decisions were either struggling to satisfy their basic needs or starting over. Change is stressful.

Surveys by CareerBuilder.com showed that 75 percent of its customers had changed careers at least three times in their life times and 50 percent were actively seeking a career change.[194] A career change can be forced by technology and marketplace. For example, the automation of factories, office computerization, and digitization of media made many jobs obsolete and created new, more technical jobs in those sectors. For my subjects, most career changes were motivated by personal needs. The subjects' initial career choice did not provide the flexibility, independence, or income to satisfy their longer term goals or desires.

They listened to friends and family, had become self-sufficient, but they hit a wall.

> Bernice. I love clothes and racked up huge credit card debt. I wasn't making enough money as a personal trainer so I switched to physical therapy.

> Bart: I wanted to live in a better neighborhood and have room for a family and entertaining, but I couldn't afford a bigger mortgage on my teacher's salary, so I went back to school and got a degree in human resources.

> Darius: I love to travel and really want to work abroad, but that's difficult as a tax accountant, because the laws are very local and I can't apply my expertise in this state in other countries. I'm going to engineering college.

> Tiffany: My mom didn't work and was totally dependent on my dad. She had to put up with a lot, and I didn't want to be in her shoes. Managing an art gallery was my dream job and I can afford to live alone, but I want more from life - a nicer apartment, a new car, vacations, invest in art, maybe do some volunteer work. So I have to either get married like my mom did or get a better job. I'm getting my MBA.

These four subjects didn't make any dire errors. They achieved self-sufficiency, but they did not think about what comes after basic needs, i.e. family, travel, hobbies, and volunteering. Their initial career choice was shortsighted.

R-E-S-P-E-C-T

Many of our subjects had a strong desire to be independent, even though they had no means or abilities to do so. They were either fully dependent on parents or in a relationship where the responsibilities were shared.

Nevertheless, the pressure from friends or family to be respected as an independent or equal person was so big, that they sacrificed their financial security in attempt to earn it.

> Trent: High school sucked for me. Everyone had their own car, but my parents wouldn't buy me a car and, even though I worked weekends, they wouldn't let me buy a car. They preached all the time about being frugal. I was dropped off at school every morning by my dad in his pea green station wagon. If I needed a car to go somewhere like on a date, I had to drive my mom's mini-van. When I went to college, my parents offered to pay my tuition, but because I wanted to live on campus, they said I had to make money to pay my own housing costs. Living on campus was really important for me, because I wanted to finally be able to make my own decisions. I got a part-time job in a call center and a week or so later I got an approval letter from a lender to buy a car with a $2,500 down payment. My financial aid check came and I used $2,500 for the down payment. My truck payment was only $480 and I was earning $500 a month after taxes at the call center. But, I didn't have any money for food, clothes, or books and I also needed a laptop. Then I found a job tending bar on weekends and got approved to make monthly payments for a laptop. I was working 30 hours a week between two jobs, but I ran out of money all the time, and I didn't have any time to study. I went home for Easter and when my parents saw my truck they freaked out. I thought they would be proud of me. I bought it with my own money. Then we went over my finances. I already had over $40,000 in debt and three years left to graduate. My parents said I wasn't being responsible and should think about either selling my truck or moving home. How am I supposed to learn responsibility when I don't have enough money?

Trent's parents were authoritarian and taught him to be frugal. When he left home to go to college, he rebelled. He took basic needs for granted and splurged. He prioritized esteem over his financial security, and amassed enormous debt. His income was insufficient to service his debt so he had to work two jobs. His grades suffered and this jeopardized even his future security. How would he pay his debts and become self-sufficient if he didn't graduate and find a good job?

Independence was a common theme among frustrated couples involving workaholic husbands and their desperate housewives.

> Nancy: I was married twelve years to a workaholic. His job was always super important. Yes, we had everything. A beautiful home in the best school district, new cars every three years. We took a long family vacation every summer. My girlfriends and I were all in the same boat. When the kids were in school, we worked out, went on long walks, volunteered, drank coffee and baked stuff. Then we picked the kids up from school and hung out at the park or at someone's house all day until our husbands got home. We were happy when the men got home, because then we finally had some time for ourselves. We had something planned almost every evening. Just an hour or two for ourselves. Dance lessons, yoga, art class. My husband didn't like it that I would take off when he got home. It's not that he didn't trust me, but he often complained. He said he already worked ten hours today, wanted to see me and needed some down-time. "Why do I have to fold laundry or go grocery shopping when I get home? What did you do all day?" My girlfriends had the same arguments with their husbands. Then he started coming home later all the time. I was sure he was doing it to avoid doing any house work, so I told him, "I need this so please be home on time so I don't miss my yoga class." He laughed at me. "Do you hear yourself speaking? I don't control my work load and I can't tell

my boss I have to leave early so my wife wants to go to yoga." Things started to get really nasty between us. He kept reminding me that we were a team. He works and pays the bills and my job was to cover his back at home. He made it clear that he didn't want to spend his free time doing my chores. He said he liked taking care of the kids, helping them with their homework and getting them ready for bed, but he didn't want to do laundry or clean bathrooms. My girlfriends and I were all in the same situation. Our husbands all thought they were too important to do housework. We all agreed that they needed to recognize that we were equals, we needed more independence. My girlfriends and I agreed that if we were really equal then we were entitled to decide how to spend half of our household income. I opened a bank account and the next time my husband, I mean the next time we got paid, I transferred half of it into my account. A couple days later, my husband checked our bank account balance and saw my transfer. I guess I should have talked to him about it first. He freaked out. I told him what my thinking. Our monthly income was OURS. He agreed and asked me what my point was. I told him I wanted an allowance so I could spend half of our monthly income how I wanted to. He agreed. He said I could spend half of the balance after we paid all the household and family expenses. I thought this was fair. So we made a list of all our bills and categorized them as family, his and hers. There was almost nothing in his column. He had a company car, no classes, no subscriptions. As it turned out, I was already spending more than my half. My car, my credit cards, my memberships, my classes, my subscriptions. He looked at me and said, "Looks like you have to give something up to make things fair." I felt like a big piece of shit. I knew he was right, mathematically speaking, but I was terribly sad. I felt so trapped. My girlfriends told me I was too dependent. Then I suggested selling my car, getting a smaller house, planning a less expensive family vacation. I was on this total independence trip. I thought if we could get our bills down and I got a job, I could contribute something and he'd respect me. He kept telling me, I was already contributing by helping him. Later, I told him I wanted to move out. He said he wasn't surprised. Now, I'm a single mother of two, I get a fixed allowance from him, and I work part-time. I have a tiny house, a used car, and no time or money to do anything with my girlfriends. Now I do everything - the housework, the cooking, the kids and even the yard work alone. I wanted independence, but I got isolation. I don't even know why I was so bent on independence. I had everything, no worries, and was already doing whatever I wanted.

Nancy took her basic needs for granted and focused on her social needs and satisfying the expectations set by her girlfriends to be respected as equals. She already had the respect of her husband, but her friends equated respect with independence. She may have had the potential to be independent, but she was not able to be dependent when she acted. Her girlfriends made recommendations without considering Nancy's abilities and these recommendations negatively impacted her financial security and created a series of stressful events. Her behavior was situational.

Follow Tradition

When choosing a vocation or career, one big obstacle for many subjects was over-coming tradition.

Ethan: I grew up in a small town. Everyone worked in either the mill or the furniture factory. My folks worked there for 40 years. My dad got me my first job. He told me all I needed to do was work hard and be dependable.

I started working in the mill when I was 16 years old and I worked there for 13 years. I never missed a day of work. Two years ago, the mill got taken over by a bigger company and modernized. We all got laid off. My job was replaced by a machine imported from Germany. I got a severance from the mill and used it to pay off my truck. I'm married and I have four kids. My wife is pregnant with the fifth child. I have no health insurance and no savings. My house is in foreclosure. I applied for jobs in the factory, but I don't have any certifications and I'd have to start at the bottom making minimum wage.

Ethan's parents were obviously authoritarian. His parents were conscientious and placed a high priority on obtaining financial security, but their ideas were old fashioned. Job security is no longer a function of hard work and punctuality. Machines can work longer, harder and are more reliable than humans. Job security today requires problem-solving ability, creativity, technical and team skills. Ethan had competence, but he did not acquire purpose and he lived in a community where he wasn't exposed to alternatives, so he simply followed in the footsteps of his parents and friends. This is a common conundrum in small rural towns. Diversity is missing and groupthink is strong, tradition is prized. No one questioned tradition. It worked for generations so it must be true.

Brad: My family is in all in construction, but the career assessment tests I took in high school all showed I would do well as an engineer. I wanted to go to college, but no one in my family has a college degree and they didn't see the need for one. My family was always looking for reasons for me to drop out and work for them. I told them I wasn't dropping out, but I needed a summer job. They wouldn't even give me a summer job, because they said I probably didn't want to get dirty. I graduated and I'm getting super offers now from really big construction companies. I have student loans to pay back and I will earn more and have more opportunities in a big company.

Now I have this huge problem that my family didn't want me to go to college, they didn't pay my tuition, they didn't even give me a summer job, and now they're really pissed that I'm thinking about working for the competition.

Brad's parents were conservative. They didn't have college educations and they didn't think their son needed one. They were authoritarian parents and didn't support Brad's wish to attend college. Brad acquired will and competence, and he was high in conscientiousness. A typical child of authoritarian parents, Brad rebelled - by attending college. His behavior is attributed to personality.

Dan: My parents never talked to me about what I would do after high school. It's not that they were bad parents, they just gave me lots of space and they figured I'd figure things out on my own. That's how they did it. When I graduated I did what every young person does. I moved in with some friends and started doing odd jobs. Barista, painting houses, bar tender, waiter, pizza delivery. This worked out great. I had enough money for my share of rent and if I was short, then my roommate covered me and I paid him back a week later. Then, the old car I got from my parents broke down. It needed more than $1,000 in repairs. I didn't have it, but I needed a car to get to work so I tried to buy or lease a new car. But lenders told me I had no credit and no income. I was getting paid mostly under the table, so even though I was making $1,500 a month, I couldn't prove it. I found this used car salesman who would sell me a used car and allow me to make monthly payments to him. He was pretty sleazy, but it was the only deal I got. I'll end up paying twice the purchase price and if I'm one day late with a payment, he said he'll send someone to pick up the car. I've been making payments now for 12 months perfect and I'm so nervous that I'll miss a payment that I'm working two jobs a day. Then last week, my roommate said he quit his job and I need to cover rent for a couple months until he finds a new job. I know he'll pay me back, but the problem is, I can't afford all these bills alone even thought I have two jobs. I never did the math, but I'm making only $21,000 a year now – with two jobs! I asked myself how some people afford their houses, two cars, a motorcycle and a boat? Do they have three jobs? I don't need all that. I'd just like to be able to afford my own place. I know I need to get a real nine to five job that pays $24,000 a year, but, even when my roommate gets a job, I don't have time to get any sort of training. I'm stuck between a rock and a hard place.

Dan's parents were emotionally neglectful. He did not acquire purpose and competence. He learned conscientiousness, although not from his parents. He is very responsible with his money and he knows he needs to get a better job, but he feels trapped. Dan's parents were right and we see this often in the children of neglectful parenting. He is the kind of person who will figure things out, because he has will, purpose, and competence. It will be difficult and stressful, but he will prevail.

Chasing a Dream

Harvey MacKay once said, "A goal is a dream with a plan and a deadline." We documented many stories of people chasing a dream, without a clear plan. Success requires a plan, that's why every business idea needs a business plan, and part of a business plan is a cash flow and profit-and-loss statement.

Kim: When I was a child, I created dresses and costumes for my dolls by gluing and stapling construction paper and fabric together. As I grew older, I started knitting and sewing. My friends and family loved receiving my whimsical hand-made dresses, jackets, ties, and hats as gifts. When I was a teenager, I my allowance, bought my first sewing machine, and launched my own line of hippy wear. In my senior year at high school, I had many conversations with guidance counselors, family and friends. Everyone encouraged me to follow my passion or fashion. So, after graduating from high school, I used my savings and also borrowed from friends and family to open my own shop. The encouragement from my friends and family combined with my hard work and devotion, however, are not paying off. My customer base and revenue are growing, but I can't live on this. It's been four years and I'm more than $100,000 in debt. I got thousands of likes on Facebook so I asked my friends and family if they liked my brand, why they didn't buy more in my shop. They admitted that my clothes made great 'gag gifts' for others, but they had never worn my 'funky' clothes themselves. They liked my commitment, not my clothes, and they all believed they were doing what good friends and parents do in supporting my dream. They asked me, 'were we supposed to tell you that we didn't like your style?' 'Should we have extinguished your passion?' Yes! I wish they would have throttled my passion a little or given me constructive feedback. I wish I would have gone to fashion school and tried selling my clothes online before opening a shop and incurring such debt. My friends are all graduating college now and getting jobs, and I'm starting all over.

Kim put realizing a dream before becoming self-sufficient. She believed achieving her dream would make her self-sufficient, but you need to be self-sufficient before setting out to realize a dream. She, her friends and family were all high in openness and agreeableness, but low in conscientiousness. Her parents and friends indulged her. She had no formal education as a fashion designer and no business training. She was not prepared to deal with a combination of stressful events and she accumulated 205 stress units: loan (17 stress units), business readjustment (39 units), change in financial status (38 units), change in line of work (36 units), default on loan (30 units), outstanding achievement or failure (25 units), change in work condition (20 units). Her behavior is attributed to personality.

Often in this context, the subjects or their friends and family use the *exceptional exception* argument. They justified decisions by citing examples of famous people who became hugely successful and incredibly rich, neglecting to recognize that we know about these people, because their success is so rare.

> Emilio: At the beginning of my junior year in college I had a great idea for a smart phone app. I put it online and had more than 1,000 downloads in the first month. I worked more and more on my app and by the end of my junior year I had more than 10,000 downloads. My friends all had my app and their friends were also using it. I decided to quit school to focus on my app. My friends told me Bill Gates or Mark Zuckerberg also quit college and I could be the next tech millionaire. That was two years ago and I'm making about $20,000 a year now with my app. That's not enough to survive on in the Bay Area so I started applying for jobs as a programmer. I'm getting offers, but the starting salary is low, because I didn't graduate. My friends are all starting out making more than double what I make.

It's easy for a celebrity, super star athlete or rock star to state in an interview, "I just followed my dream" or "I believe you can achieve whatever you set your mind to." This is true for exceptionally gifted people, but most of us are not exceptional yet. Moreover, success depends on more than just having passion and a dream. For many years, psychologists, managers and coaches believed in the 10,000 Hour Rule put forth by psychologist Malcolm Gladwell. Gladwell asserted that 10,000 hours of *deliberate practice* were needed to become world-class in any field,[195] but a Princeton study involving the meta-analysis of 88 other studies on deliberate practice showed that practice accounted for only a 12 percent difference in performance outcomes.[196] The conclusion is, most people can't achieve whatever they set their minds to. The kind of success super star athletes and A-list entertainers attain is rooted more in their extraordinary talent, and the success achieved by billionaires like Musk, Gates and Zuckerburg depended on a combination of extraordinary talent and uncanny timing.

Even if one could develop a world-class talent in 10,000 hours of deliberate practice, one would need to train eight hours every day for five years, and this level of effort requires financial support to cover basic needs, equipment, coaching, trainers, competition fees, and supplements. This support can come from parents or some organization that recognizes the person's talent early and sponsors the person, or the person has to work. In other words, if your talent isn't discovered early, you need to first find a way to fulfill your basic needs efficiently so you can finance and adhere to a rigorous five year training program.

One of the challenges we uncovered in our study was that subjects had a challenge differentiating between talent and passion. Most people mistakenly equated passion with talent. I, for example, have a passion for swimming, but I have no talent and probably the wrong physique. I'm five foot ten inches tall, my legs are shorter than my arms, and my feet and hands are small. I have spent thousands of hours in lakes, oceans and pools, but it would be a huge mistake for me to set my mind to becoming a competitive swimmer. If I want to do something with my passion, I have to channel it onto something other than competitive swimming. Earlier I told a story about Titus Ditmann who had a passion for skateboarding, but he recognized he wasn't a radical half-pipe talent like Tony Hawk, so he focused instead on leveraging combining his passion with his talent for teaching. Kim, the hippy designer above, had a passion for fashion, but her talent was obviously not designing clothes, but rather producing them. Her product quality wasn't the issue, it was her style. Had she discerned between passion and talent, she would have probably discovered that she could sew anything and she would have studied something like textile manufacturing.

A related challenge was differentiating between a hobby and a profession. Some of our subjects were very passionate and talented, but they couldn't make a living with their abilities. This caused low self-esteem, because they were the best, but couldn't even satisfy their most basic needs.

Alan: I've been a nature photographer all my life and have invested hundreds and thousands of dollars in equipment and travel. I've won several prizes and my work has been published in many magazines. I'm doing exactly what I've always wanted to do, but I'm always broke. I've downsized so many times, I can't downsize anymore and I refuse to live in someone's garage. Except for my equipment, everything I have is crap. My car is a junker, my furniture is from flea markets or from friends and family. I sleep in a sleeping bag. I'm 47 years old and don't have a savings account, a retirement account, or an insurance plan. I'm getting older and I don't know what to do.

Marlin: I wrestled in high school and was always division champion. I got a scholarship to wrestle in college and I've been in the top ten ranking in my discipline for the past eight years. I've won gold, silver and bronze at numerous European and global track-and-field events and I've competed in two Olympic games. My athletic career is coming to an end, because my body just can't take this punishment anymore. Nike and Red Bull aren't exactly throwing sponsorship money at wrestlers so I've been working at a home improvement warehouse the last five years. I have a degree in Sports Management and I've gotten offers to coach high school and college, but that doesn't pay much more than I'm already earning. Football coaches are earning millions, but I'd take home just over $27,000. I can't afford to support a family on that. That's almost poverty level.

Suzanne McGee wrote a short article about this problem. According to McGee, "They've devoted every waking hour and thought to perfecting their performance, and money considerations often go only to necessities plus coaching, equipment and competitions. Many top athletes live close to the poverty line."[197] Earning recognition as the best in something can corrupt priorities if being the best doesn't somehow make it easier to thrive. In Alan's and Marlin's cases, they were rational up to a point. They both became efficient at satisfying their basic needs so they could develop their talents. And they both achieved recognition, but their abilities to fulfill basic needs were not sustainable. If you've ever wondered why celebrity athletes and entertainers sometimes get depressed and then start abusing drugs or even commit suicide, this is one reason. Imagine the stress of being the best in something, the top of your game, and then it abruptly ends or you come to the realization that it has to end because you cannot survive on status alone.

> Marcel: I played professional basketball for two seasons and then got injured. Now I'm selling imports. It's really embarrassing, because some people recognize me and ask me what happened. I have a college degree, but it's worthless. What am I supposed to do with Egyptian Studies?

The NCAA's own study titled *Estimated Probability of Competing in Professional Athletics* shows that less than 2 percent of college football and basketball athletes turn professional.[198] Therefore, many schools recruit athletes who are not able to do college work and craft bogus majors to make it easy for them to focus on their sport. Performing well in college sports can be the ticket to the lucrative major leagues, which is a win-win situation for the athlete and the college. *Student athletes are routinely clustered into worthless majors that do not prepare them to succeed later in life outside sports.* The Chronicle of Higher Education reported that at least 20 schools are being investigated for academic fraud for this practice.[199] To make matters worse, most student athletes do not take academics seriously. Daniel Oppenheimer at Arizona State University surveyed 147 student athletes to find out how important academics were to them. Oppenheimer found that student athletes, in a "perverse form of peer pressure," had a mistaken belief that if they cared about academics they were uncool, so they performed poorly to fit in.[200] Not only did the student athletes not take the opportunity to earn a real degree that would improve their chances of success outside of sports, they purposely failed in the dummy majors that were tailored for them.

For many subjects, making a living with their talent was like playing the lottery, and they lost. Their passion and talents were recognized, everyone encouraged them to follow their dream, they placed a high priority on esteem and self-realization, received support and encouragement, but they were not prepared for failure or a career cut short by injury or age, which is more common than success. Just like the poor families who spend more money on the lottery than they do on education, playing the lottery is not a plan, not even a good back-up plan.

Dreams do not have to be shared. It is very romantic when they intersect or can be realized concurrently, but this is rare. It is a clear sign of love and respect when one partner supports the other partner's dream, which they do not share. I documented dozens of cases involving couples who worked together to get into a position to enable one partner to achieve self-realization, they had reached the height of personal development together, but they were talking about separating, because the self-realized partner expected the supporting partner to share his or her dream.

> Martina: My husband and I went to college together. There was this immediate attraction. I don't know what it was. I actually tried to fight my attraction to him, because he was really nerdy and I never went out with a geek like him. But he was so passionate about justice and we both loved adventure. We did everything together. Everything. We lived together, showered, cooked, ate, shopped, studied. We were awesome. We had nothing and we could always put enough money together to travel to Asia, Europe, or Africa every summer. And we did lots of volunteer work. We had top grades and ended up working in the same law firm. We had our student loans paid off no time and were saving up for a house. We kicked ass in the firm. They called us the "dynamic duo." A couple years later, my husband said he wasn't getting younger

and wanted to take some time off work and see the world and do some good before he made full partner. I told him I didn't want to quit my job, but I wouldn't stop him. He took off for almost an entire year and sent me postcards every week from some exotic place telling me to meet him a month later in some other place. It was so romantic. I thought about it a lot, but I knew it would be hard to get my job back. Besides, I was funding his adventure. Who would fund us if I took off, too?

Martina and her husband fulfilled all basic needs together - easily and quickly. They were healthy, self-sufficient, romantic, and respected. Martina's husband's wish to travel was rational, because they had fulfilled all lower needs. Her support of his pursuit of self-actualization showed her deep love for him. Nevertheless, this happy story has an unhappy ending.

Martina: When he got back, I was there at the airport to pick him up, but he didn't come home with me. He gave me a hug and a kiss and went home with his parents. I had a great relationship with his parents and I'm really hurt that they didn't tell me that he made arrangements behind my back to move in with them. Why are they supporting him in this? We talked on the phone and he said he was very disappointed that I didn't live his dream with him. I reminded him that I was the one who funded his adventure. It's been six months and we're trying to work things out. He met lots of interesting people on his trip and wants to do non-profit work now. He insists I do it with him. He's thirty three years old, he lives with his parents again and is still dreaming about changing the world. I love him, I respect his dream so much and I feel really sorry for him, but one of us has to have an income if the other one is going to work probono.

Martina is being fully rational. Her husband prioritized self-realization over his relationship, esteem and security. His behavior is attributed to personality. Her husband is acting irrationally and now he's doing nothing productive or good for anyone.

> Betty: I just started my dream job working in a nature conservancy. It took my several years to land this job and my husband held things together for us. But he works for an oil company and that can't work. He needs to quit his job.

> Amanda: I always dreamed of breeding and training dogs. My husband helped me get started and he's actually my best employee. He built my kennel, my runs, the fences, the obstacles. He fixes everything and he helped me to get a loan for my van. But he obviously doesn't love dogs. He's always yelling at them to shut up and wants me to put shock collars on them. He say's 'I'm funding your hobby and if I can't get any sleep and miss work, the funding will end.

These cases show the different ways that placing a high priority on higher needs like intimacy, esteem and self-actualization can adversely affect security and financial stability. In some cases, the conflict existed because the subjects followed irrational priorities set be their friends and family. In other cases, the influence of friends and family was not obvious.

Where does the idea come from that partners have to share dreams? It comes from media and literature, and friends and family influence what we read and watch. Romance novels and romantic films often depict couples with contradictory goals coming together after one of the partners makes an important sacrifice or they somehow integrate their dreams. The romantic story lines follow a similar structure. The woman is always portrayed as someone struggling to realize her dream of opening a chocolate store, a flower shop, a pony farm, or a bed-and-breakfast, and the man is always portrayed as an affluent developer or corporate executive who intends to use the land to build a resort, a shopping mall, or a factory. These stories have the same romantic twist. The couples fall in love not knowing they are adversaries, there is a conflict when they find out who the other person is, and the stories have a happy ending when the man gives up his plans or they find some clever way of combining their dreams. The movie *When Harry Met Sally* starring Meg Ryan and Tom Hanks portrays a small independent book store owned by Ryan struggling to survive when a mega bookstore chain run by Hanks opens nearby. The story has a happy ending when Hanks integrates Ryan's concept into his bookstore design. In this case, they both won, but in many romantic stories, the happy ending involves the man scrapping his big project to protect the woman's dream.

The Normal Paradox (again)

Some of our subjects had the traits and talents to become successful, but they were held back by friends and family who had lower expectations of them.

> Christina: My daughter, Kate, is getting straight A's and even taking advanced placement subjects. She's going to be valedictorian. I'm proud of her, but she has no good friends. Her girlfriends are all really nerdy and they aren't interested in boys. She doesn't wear make-up, she doesn't get involved in school activities and she has never been asked to a dance. She's pretty and she could be popular. She's missing out on the best years of her life. I'm worried that she is anti-social or depressed.
>
> Kate: I love learning, but I hate high school. If you're not a cheerleader, on dance squad or an athlete, you're a loser. You really don't want me going out with those dirt bag guys in my school, mom. All they think about is their hair, sex, cars, weed, beer, and pranking the geeks. I'm just trying not to get bullied long enough to graduate and get into M.I.T. - where everyone will be like me. Smart.

Christina is high in extroversion and places a high priority on the social need, whereas her daughter, Kate, is high in openness and conscientiousness and places a high need on achievement. Kate probably acquired openness and conscientiousness from her father, which her friends reinforce. It is not uncommon, for non-head-of-household mothers from indulgent parents to be less rational than their minor children.

Along the same lines, some subjects believed bad behavior and poor performance were acceptable when stupid was normal.

> Pete: My son is an average student. I know he can do better. He's very smart, but he's constantly getting in trouble at school for dumb things. He's not taking school seriously.
>
> Cynthia: I'm not worried about our son. I talk to his friends' mothers all the time and they're all in the same grade bracket. He's acting totally normal and having fun. Boys will be boys. Pete needs to stop putting so much pressure on him.

Pete is high in openness and conscientiousness and places a high priority on achievement and financial security. Pete's wife, Cynthia, is high in extroversion and agreeableness and places a high priority on social. She's using the *normal paradox* to justify mediocre performance and bad behavior. I heard this story hundreds of times and the father's response was often, "if his friends all jump off a bridge do you want our son (or daughter) to jump too?" Pete is probably an authoritarian parent, whereas Cynthia is clearly indulgent. She not only shows compassion for bad behavior, she condones it. It's normal. This is a difficult situation for a child. His basic needs are provided for and he takes them for granted, so the pressure from his father to be diligent and responsible appears untimely and superfluous, whereas his mother is promoting fun and harmony, which requires less effort and makes sense for a child. It sounds like Pete is in the minority here and groupthink will trump his rationality.

Another version of the smart-is-uncool case is the belief that success is uncool. Earlier we introduced the idea of collaborative compassion as it applies to health. Just as some groups formed based on a common illness, we also observed that groups can form based on failure. Members with financial problems banded together to support each other against the out-group. The purpose of collaborative compassion in this context was not to help members break the cycle of poverty, but to make members feel good about their attitudes, and the decisions they made that created their situations.

Sometimes, they considered themselves victims of a flawed system or corrupt organization and held very strong opinions against the out-group, i.e. people with jobs or higher incomes.

> Kathy: We weren't born with a fucking silver spoon in our mouths. We hate those corporate yuppie pricks. They are so arrogant with their suits and their gated communities. They aren't human. You don't need all that to be happy. I got my friends. Yeah, life is hard, but we're living it real. Brian. That's right, honey. I was one of them. It's dog eat dog and then you get shit on. We're down to Earth people. If an asteroid hit Earth tomorrow, those wankers wouldn't know what to do. They'd probably all try to drive their Beamers to their mountain cabins, they'd all end up sitting in a traffic jam for days, and everything would burn up. We know how to survive.

Kathy and Brian were an unemployed married couple. They put a high priority on social validation, and a low priority on security. Their statements indicate they are low in conscientiousness and openness, and high in agreeableness and neuroticism. Kathy's and Brian's group did not create bad expectations or set irrational priorities, but it showed affection for people who had a common weakness. The group validated its members' attitudes, decisions and behaviors. Members felt comfortable and became complacent.

Carter: I got my certificate from a training company, and now my parents are putting lots of pressure on me to get a job and move out. The economy sucks and me and my friends are all looking for jobs, but it's not easy. A couple times a week we check the job boards, we send in our resumes and wait. We're all in the same boat. There just aren't any jobs. We got nothing to do and no money, so we just hang out a lot, play video games, drink beer, smoke weed. My parents make me feel like a loser. Why should I wake up at 8:00 am and take a shower? I got nothing to do, nowhere to be, so I may as well have fun while I can, right? They say I need to be getting cleaned up every morning and dropping by these companies to show them I really want the job. That would make me look total desperate. No one does that.

Members of groupthink where collaborative compassion is strong often argue they have no reason to change their priorities or behavior, because "I'm normal" or "I'm getting by just fine and I got my friends." Indeed, they were surviving and they openly recognized their weaknesses, but they claimed they were content, because others shared their misery. If they were indeed happy, why did they attend group therapy? Because they subconsciously knew that something was wrong. Their statements and tone indicated an implied question (in parentheses), because they sought validation.

Stewart: I got fired from two jobs in the last year, but some of my friends also got fired. (It's normal, isn't it?)

Amelie: I can't pay my bills, but my friends are also having trouble. (So, I'm normal, right?)

Ricardo: My house is getting foreclosed, but some of my friends also lost their homes. "It's the economy, right?"

William: I can't find a decent job, but all of my friends are also having problems getting a job today. "I'm normal, right?"

Quitin: I dropped out of school, but I know lots of people who dropped out of school and became successful. "That's ok, right?"

Even if failure was normal, that does not by any means imply that it is good.

Haters

It undermines groupthink to admit a weakness so one tactic is to create their own distorted definition of happiness.

Roger: My finance professor really liked me and after my Junior year he set up me up with a Summer internship in a brokerage firm in Hong Kong. My friends called me a brown-noser and an ass-kisser. It was such an awesome experience. I learned some basic Chinese and learned really fast how to act like a businessman - how to present, how to write, how to dress, how to eat and drink, how to talk. It totally changed my perspective. I facebooked with some of friends when I was there to tell them what I was up to. All they could say was that I was missing out on the best time of my life. They only asked questions like, "How many Asian chicks did you nail?" and "How's the beer?" When I returned for fall semester, I decided to try to continue to conduct myself more professionally. I didn't wear a suit to class, but I made a conscious effort never to wear sandals, jogging pants, hoodies and a baseball cap. I stopped getting shit-faced every weekend, and also stopped swearing and calling everyone "dude." My friends told me to, "Stop acting like a stuck up prude prick."

Roger had a rational view of college and was preparing himself to be self-sufficient. Roger's friends were members of groupthink. Subconsciously, they knew Roger's perspective was right, but, according to Roger's criteria, they were immature losers. To avoid admitting being losers, they used their own distorted sense of achievement, which was a function of beer consumption and hook-up frequency. Using their twisted criteria, Roger was the boring loser, he wasn't normal, so they lashed out against him.

Roger resisted groupthink, but many subjects could not. They made stupid decisions and in order to come to terms with their failure or inferiority, they claimed they had other, more noble priorities.

> Ava: I've interviewed for dozens of entry-level management positions over the past 18 months and I haven't got an offer yet. I'm ok with that, because I tell them that work-life balance is most important for me and if they don't like that then they are not the right employer.

> Briana: The company started to install machines and offered us all paid training to service them, but we knew that most of us would lose our jobs, because there were only a dozen or so positions in maintenance. We all banded together and took a stand against the machines. None of my friends took the training, and we all got laid off, but we still got our human dignity.

> Becky: I come from three generations of farmers. When I was in school, all of the family-owned farms in my county were being taken over by corporate conglomerates. They offered lots of training, agriculture scholarships and job opportunities to us, but no one liked the idea of working for the companies who killed our family businesses. We need to preserve tradition.

In the case of groupthink there is strength in numbers although it is a negative force. This negative force can be so strong, that it can compel rational people to question their own logic and make stupid decisions.

Amy: I won an art contest to attend a program in Paris for three months. All my girlfriends were super excited for me and said I had to go and they would take care of my boyfriend when I was gone. When I was in Paris, we stayed in touch on Facebook. There's a six hour time difference that my friends always forgot to consider and if I didn't reply right away, they would send ten more messages asking if I was mad or why I wasn't responding. They were posting everything about everyone at home. I was up all night chatting and spending hours every day online. After a couple weeks, I started to get really homesick. I was missing everybody and everything. I also started to get jealous, because my boyfriend was in all the pictures with my girlfriends. I was spending so much time online that my host family got concerned because that when they asked me what I did all day, I told them what my friends posted on Facebook. The mother said, "You are here in Paris, but somehow you are not here." They said I needed to take advantage of the opportunity to learn the language and culture. Then the father changed the wifi password and I didn't have internet. That night I couldn't sleep, because I was wondering what was going on at home. I actually got out of bed at midnight and walked around the city looking for an open wifi. I knew I was crazy. I even asked myself, "What the hell is wrong with me? It's midnight and I'm walking around Paris at midnight looking for a hotspot." It was a weekend and it took three days before I was able to get online again. I had hundreds of unread messages. I was missing too much and I told my friends I was thinking about coming home early. They cheered and said they would have a huge welcome home party for me. I know it would have looked good on my resume to complete the program, but friends are more important to me.

Amy barely survived one month without her friends. She desperately needed to learn independence. The program in Paris could have been a valuable edge experience for her. It could have taught her to be diligent, perseverance, and autonomy. But because she was very high in extroversion and placed a very high priority on social acceptance, it was a failure. Unfortunately, she doesn't see it as a failure. In her eyes, her decision to quit was noble. Her friends are complicit in this failure. None of them recognized the value that completing the program would have for her and encouraged her to stick with it for another eight weeks.

> Barb: I did really well in high school in math and science and took advanced placement classes. I didn't know what I would do with math or science, so I took some assessment tests and they showed I'd do well in engineering. I did lots of online research and met with some women engineers to see what they did. It was very interesting. I knew engineers had a stigma as being nerds and women engineers were viewed negatively, but I liked it and the salary and opportunities with an engineering degree were really good. I could work in civil engineering, energy, automotive. I especially liked the idea of going into environmental engineering. When I told my friends my plan, they thought I was nuts. They were all majoring in fluff subjects like social studies, English or art and wanted to become pharmaceutical reps. I showed them the national salary surveys that showed that the starting salary and placement rate for engineers was much higher than for pharma reps. They were constantly riding me about being a nerd, how boring my life would be, that there were no cute engineers, they'd have more opportunities to meet rich doctors. They admitted that their starting salaries were lower, but they would have opportunities to make huge bonuses. I was getting good grades, but I started to doubt myself. Why was I the only one who didn't think being a pharma rep was a good job? I must be missing something, I thought. So I changed my major. I got a job

as a pharma rep straight out of college. I'm happy I got a job right away, but I'm earning much less than I would be if I had my engineering degree. I hate this job. I'm a math major giving scripted medical advice to a doctor. That's not right.

Barb and her friends were high in conscientiousness and they both placed a high priority on obtaining financial security. Their priorities were somewhat aligned. Getting a job and establishing independence was important to them. Barb and her friends also acquired purpose and competence. Their virtues were aligned. Everyone was on the right track, so why did Barb's friends put so much pressure on her to change her major? Rivalry. Her friends were part of a pharma rep in-group and they prioritized social acceptance over income. Barb got drawn into their filter bubble, turned off rational thinking, and shuffled her priorities. Barb's behavior was situational. Today, she has a job and she is self-sufficient. This doesn't sound like a terrible situation. Having a job you don't like and being independent is probably better than not having the job you would love to have. Sometimes it is necessary to settle in order to be self-sufficient. But Barb settled for the wrong reasons and the doubt that triggered her decision was created by her friends. Barb could have had the engineering job she wanted, but now she is unhappy and her growth is stifled, because it's difficult to excel in a job you hate. Barb will likely go back to school or change jobs and experience more stress.

Another mistake Barb's friends made was not understanding her abilities. She did not have the traits to be a pharmaceutical sales rep. This was a common conundrum for subjects. Friends and family made recommendations that influenced their decisions without really knowing the subject's abilities, likes and dislikes.

> Sally: I was working in a gardening center and I was so happy. I loved it. I was working outside in the sun and rain, getting my hands dirty, I had my own little house, I had almost no bills, I had a cute pickup truck, and was spending my spare time in my flower garden or kitchen.

But my neighbors and girlfriends were all in real estate. It started to get really embarrassing for me, because when we got together, they were all dressed business and talked about their listings, showings, and big commissions, and I didn't understand what they were talking about. They'd tease me all the time, 'so Beth, what's new in the plant world?' They somehow drew this link between gardening and real estate and convinced me that I would do better working with them. I took some real estate courses at night and tried real hard to fit in. Bought some business outfits, printed brochures and business cards, bought a laptop, got my first smart phone, and leased a sedan. When I got my license, I quit my job in the gardening center and started working in an agent's office with one of my girlfriends. It sucked. The only time I saw the sun was when I showed houses. I was spending hundreds of dollars a month on gas to show houses. Clients would ask questions about materials and energy ratings, and I didn't know the answers. I hated it. I worked there for six months and only sold two houses. The commissions were big, but when you consider I made nothing for two or three months and then you calculate my hours plus lost weekends and evenings, I was making less than minimum wage and it was totally unreliable. I never lived paycheck to paycheck and now I didn't even know when the next pay check was coming. They kept telling me to hang in there. After working there a year and making less than I was in the gardening center, I asked, 'how do you all make a reliable living doing this?' Their answer was a shock. It was really like getting engulfed by a wave of electricity. They said they didn't need to make a reliable living, because they were all married. I wasn't married. I didn't have a husband who paid the bills so I could chase commissions. I quit on the spot. I was so pissed. It set me back a lot. I spent lots of money on courses, business cards, brochures, clothes, a laptop, I even leased a car. I couldn't get out of the car lease, but I sold everything I could on eBay and now I'm working in the gardening center again. I get a paycheck every two weeks.

Sally was already self-sufficient and happy. She acquired purpose and competence, was high in conscientiousness and agreeableness. Her high level of agreeableness was her vulnerability. She wanted to fit in and was impressionable. Her girlfriends obviously took their basic needs for granted and placed high priorities on esteem. No one considered Sally's traits and her single status when they encouraged her to change careers.

The Exceptional Exceptions

Oddly enough, the opposite situation existed, too. In the cases above, friends and family ignored the subjects' abilities and pressured the subjects to conform and do something they were not psychologically programmed to master. In the following cases, friends and family recognized the subject's likes and dislikes and encouraged the subjects to resist assimilating. The error was neglecting to consider that some professions have high expectations for conformity.

Brandon: I got my first mohawk when I was 13 years old. I've been touting a mohawk ever since. It's my brand. I also got my nose and ears pierced and wear loops. I love music and went to college to become a music teacher. I play in a punk band, but I can play anything from folk to techno. My friends and family told me I would be a great teacher and schools needed more cool teachers that could connect with kids. Although I got top grades, I can't find a teaching position. I got some candid feedback from one interviewer who said that teachers are supposed to be role models and I didn't look like a role model. It wasn't just my mohawk. She said some administrators didn't like my t-shirts, my army boots, my torn jeans. I told her I am a real musician and this is what real musicians look like. She liked me, but she said administrators were more concerned with how parents would perceive me. I really need to start working soon, I have student loans and want to move out of my parents house. I was thinking about toning down my look and being more preppy, but my friends said I need to stay true to myself.

Brandon sounds like he could be an excellent music teacher. He is passionate and competent. He is thinking rationally about toning down his self-expression to get his first job. He could probably plan a punk music day to express his true identity once a month. Over time, he would probably win acceptance from the school administrators for his punker identity and be able to express himself more frequently. But his friends are standing in his way of getting his first job. They prioritize self-actualization *visavis* expression over financial security. Meanwhile, Brandon is jobless, not independent and frustrated.

One of the common arguments used by subjects, their friends and family in such cases is the exceptional exception.

> Dick: I work in an accounting firm and my boss told me I needed to wear a shirt and tie to work. I told my friends this and they said, Mark Zuckerburg is the CEO of Facebook and he wears jeans and a hoody to work, too.

> Zoe: My agent told me that I'll probably get fewer modeling jobs if I continue to get more tattoos. I told her Angelina Jolie and Megan Foxx have lots of tattoos and they are some of the highest paid actresses in Hollywood.

> Kai: My boss knows I smoke pot and he said I should probably smoke less if I wanted to become creative director. I told him Michael Phelps smokes grass, too, and he has more gold medals than anyone else in Olympic history.

Most of us are not billionaire entrepreneurs, A-List actresses or Olympic superstars – yet. Most of us have to fake it until we make it. We have to conform to some extent and earn special status to afford such flexibility.

Using the behavior of exceptional people as some template for the actions of not-yet-exceptional people is tenuous.

At least Zuckerburg, Jolie, Foxx and Phelps are real people. A similar error that subjects made was using fictitious characters as role models. Friends influence the media we consume and the hero in many movies is a reject. This genre is referred by sociologists as *social outcast cinema*. Linda Seger points out, there are universal stories that form the basis fall all stories. "One character who always seems to steal the audience's heart is the one that doesn't fit in or who is different than the others."[201] This character is known as the outcast archetype. The outcast archetype is usually isolated from others due to some oddity, but prevails in the end owing to their uniqueness. Such movies are popular, because viewers recognize themselves in the archetype and the archetype gives them hope that they, too, can succeed despite their flaws. Society will accept them and celebrate them as heroes.

Social outcast cinema validates and perpetuates immature attitudes and behavior. I can't list the numerous movies starring a belligerent cop, scientist, or convict, who some secret organization or government agency firmly believes is the only person who can save the free world or the planet. The outcast is usually found incarcerated in a top security prison or hold up in a shabby inner-city apartment, old camper, or run down farm house – cut off from the world that rejected him. A confrontation ensues where the reclusive archetype denies the opportunity, because he had been unfairly treated and underappreciated. He admits that he didn't get along with co-workers and used unusual methods, but explains that he was driven by passion and he was results-oriented. The recruiter lists the archetype's numerous infractions and character deficiencies and gives a speech about patriotism and liberty. They board a private jet and fly off to a secret base somewhere. When the archetype gets off the plane and meets his team, they are disappointed that they have to work with a dangerous oddball, or they, too, are outcasts and happy to be reunited with their old comrade. Thanks to his bizarre tactics and outstanding talents, the mission is completed and everyone shows him great appreciation. The series *XXXX, Fast and Furious, Rambo,* and *Lethal Weapon* follow a similar script. Other versions of the outcast script involve a young hacker, mathematician, dancer, athlete, or musician who is bullied by the popular kids until the other kids realize they have extraordinary talents. The message of social outcast cinema is, if you don't fit in, it's because you are superior and destined for greatness so embrace your oddness and hang in there.

The message is an ideal, but not completely realistic. Indeed, we all need to recognize and develop our talents and use them for good. Humanist psychologists believe we all have this potential. However, due to different parenting styles, experiences and the friends we have as dependent children, most people do not discover and fully develop their talents or purpose during adolescence. Therefore, self-discovery extends into adulthood for most people. Until we find our purpose, we need to find a way to be self-sufficient adults. This means we need to adapt, but as Moslow noted, mature people adapt to societal norms only enough to survive. Being curious and seeking out diversity is not the same as looking and behaving differently. And adapting does not mean permanently compromising values or identity. It means fitting in if only superficially and just long enough to (a) become self-sufficient and (b) develop your talents.

> Keith: When I started my first job, I hated everything about it, but my dad always said, "Fake it until you make it." I did. I volunteered for every stupid assignment, took every shift, attended every dumb class. I was always a half hour early and I never missed a day of work. I really hated that job, but it was fun making up silly ways to earn recognition. I went to work sick one day, and my boss wanted to send me straight home so I wouldn't infect the others, but I told him I could clean out the stock room by myself. That day, my boss told everyone my initials stood for "Kick Ass." One of my friends whispered, "K.A. stands for Kiss Ass." My boss overheard this and said if he heard any more hater jokes he would "nip it in the butt." Anyway, I moved up the ladder real quick, my friends are pretty much stuck and they have more or less

abandoned me. I still don't love this job, but I have so many opportunities now and I can afford my hobby.

Keith's parents were clearly authoritarian. He acquired hope and competence, he is high in conscientiousness and agreeableness. He is working on finding his purpose and developing competence. Meanwhile, his priority is being self-sufficient. He is doing whatever he needs to do to fit in and survive. His behavior is attributed to personality. Keith is maturing fast, but his friends are not. They are low in openness and conscientiousness. They are jealous player haters.

> Stacey: After school, I had a hard time finding a job and finally got an entry level position in a bank. The bank puts a lot of pressure on us to cross-sell services and we have to memorize these scripts and hit certain numbers every week. I'm not comfortable offering some little old lady some investment vehicle or giving a young person who works part-time at McDonald's a credit card with a $5,000 limit and a 19 percent interest rate. I told my boss I did some research and it's a predatory practice. He said everything was approved by legal and if I continued to be insubordinate and didn't hit my numbers next month, I should probably start looking for a new job. I needed that job, but my friends and family said I should not compromise my values and stick to my guns.

Blood is Thicker Than Water

Another error subjects made was being charitable and risking their financial security and the safety of their families.

> Becky: My husband has a big heart, but his head in is the wrong place. We both have good jobs and I'm great with money. I always manage to put enough of our income aside for a rainy day, but then it disappears. He's always buying stuff for his loser friends. If he went to Walmart

and bought groceries or toiletries for them, I'd understand, but he buys them expensive stuff like flat screen televisions and smart phones. Our air conditioner is always breaking down and we haven't gone on a family vacation in two years, but he just bought his friend a new laptop.

Becky is high in conscientiousness, but her husband is clearly high in agreeableness. It's not clear if he was motivated by helping others, looking good, or social acceptance, i.e. was he focusing on self-actualization, esteem, or social? It actually doesn't matter why he is helping his friends. These are higher needs and he is placing them above his family's financial security. This is irrational. This conflict between Becky and her husband created a low vulnerability for stress, but the situation will likely escalate. Becky is unhappy and she probably sees the signs that her husband will increase his commitment to his friends, one that could have a more negative impact on their financial security and family life. I heard similar stories hundreds of times and I predict her husband will either lease something like a car, a condominium, or a motorcycle for a friend, or invite a friend to move into his home.

In some cases, letting a friend or family member who was "down on their luck," "having a bad year" or "going through a difficult time" move in, worked out for the host and the guest. The friend or family member eventually got back on their feet, some paid rent, which improved the financial situation for the host, and a few even paid back their sponsors. But this situation always triggers a combination of stressful events. In a few cases, the friend or family member conducted illegal activity in the host's home and this jeopardized the generous host's financial security and his family.

> Roger: My younger brother was in an accident and was out of work for a long time. He was on pain killers, unemployed, divorced, depressed, hung out with the wrong people and got involved in drugs. I gave him money all the time, took him to counseling and checked him into a rehab center. He completed the program for the fourth

or fifth time and he moved in with us while he looked for a job. Weeks later, my wife called me at work. She was hysterical. Our teenage daughter had been arrested for dealing drugs on school property. I felt like I was having a heart attack. She was a good girl, an honor roll student, and we never had any problems with her. When we met her at the police station, she was handcuffed, crying and scared. She confessed immediately to the police that my brother had given her the drugs to sell. "I'm so stupid, dad. I thought it would be cool." The police told us she had hard drugs in her possession and asked us if they could search our home. We agreed. They arrived in full force with drug sniffing dogs. It created quite a spectacle in the neighborhood. The police found drugs hidden everywhere in our home. In the air conditioner vents, in the toilet bowls, inside our t.v. My brother was arrested and taken away. We cooperated fully with the police and held a meeting that evening to explain what had happened to the neighbors. I invited a police officer to speak about drug prevention. It cost us thousands of dollars and took two years to get the drug dealing charge expunged from our daughter's record so she could go to college.

Roger did what every good person should do. He was in a position to help someone and he did. The problem is, people who need lots of help are usually in their positions, because they make bad decisions. They possess a calamitous combination of traits and priorities and these cannot be corrected through a six month rehabilitation program. Roger should have anticipated that his brother could pose a threat to his family. He should have isolated his brother from the family and still helped him, but Roger was too focused on doing the right thing and overlooked the possible impact that his brother could have on the security and health of his family. Roger's daughter, like most teenagers, was thinking about winning acceptance. She pushed her boundaries in an attempt to impress her classmates. Fortunately, Roger was high in conscientiousness and prepared to deal with this situation.

Now we see the many different ways our friends and family adversely impact our abilities to provide for ourselves. They set expectations that we can only meet when we compromise our financial stability, encourage unproductive behavior, make recommendations that do not reflect our abilities and ignore market realities.

Social Systems

Realizing our full potential as humans requires a foundation of good health and financial stability. Every human has great untapped potential, but most people have not discovered and developed their real talents, because they have neglected their basic needs to focus on higher needs. This decision is influenced by peer pressure (situation) or by a strong emotional dependence on the group (personality). As a result, they have no energy, resources, or time to dedicate to developing their real potential. Our ability to realize our full potential should not be limited by childhood experiences, which were beyond our control. Self-realization should not be limited to rich people or people with good luck. As a society, we have a vested interest in helping everyone achieve their full potential and there are systems that can facilitate this.

Social democracy is a political and economic ideology that promotes social justice within the framework of a capitalist economy, as well as policies committed to a representative democracy, income equality, and regulation of the economy. Social democracy aims to create the conditions so that capitalism can produce greater democratic and egalitarian outcomes. Modern social democracy is characterized by a commitment to policies aimed at curbing inequality, oppression of underprivileged groups, and poverty, including support for universally accessible public services like child care, education and health care. A focus of social democracy is administrative efficiency and a belief that science and technology are the keys to progress.

Under modern social democracies, basic human needs are guaranteed by government. Healthcare is state-funded and access is guaranteed to all citizens, child care is free to working parents, vocational training and college education are provided based on merit alone. Self-sufficiency is independent of parenting, wealth and luck. As described above, young people are matched to jobs based on the forecasted needs of the business sector. Parenting, tradition and passion are kept in check. Of course, citizens in social democracies face compromises. The system protects them against poverty and unemployment, thus making personal development easier, but they have fewer personal liberties. A person can pursue their dream job, but only if they have real talent, and the number of enrollments in trade programs and universities reflects the number of positions projected in the job market. There will always be some demand for art history and communication majors, but in social democracies, the number of students who can earn liberal arts degrees is strictly limited to prevent young people from making mistakes that result is a dependence on social programs like welfare and unemployment. When these students graduate, they have no education debt and are pretty much ensured employment. With access to free healthcare and education, citizens can focus on learning, exploring, self-discovery and realizing their potential.

1. Norway
2. Denmark
3. Iceland
4. Switzerland
5. Finland
6. Netherlands
7. Canada
8. New Zealand
9. Australia
10. Sweden

Illustration 42: Top 10 Happiest Countries

According to the latest *World Happiness Report*, published by the Sustainable Development Solutions Network for the United Nations, nine of the top ten happiest countries are social democracies. The United States came in 14th place, dropping one place from the previous year. Gross domestic product per capita is one of the measurements, but happiness isn't just about money. Aside from income, other important factors are generosity, life expectancy, having someone to count on, perceived freedom to make life choices and freedom from corruption. The report calls attention to the difference between standard of living and quality of life. Jeffrey Sachs, the report's co-editor and director of the Earth Institute at Columbia University, writes, "As demonstrated by many countries, this report gives evidence that happiness is a result of creating strong social foundations. It's time to build social trust and healthy lives."[202]

Chapter 12

Sad

Once a person has fulfilled his basic needs for health and security, they are ready to focus on social needs, achievement, and self-realization. In the prior sections, we described the stress that results when friends and family influence decisions that affect health and financial stability. In this section, we look at how good health and financial stability impact our relationships and how our definitions of romance and friendship create stress.

The most common attitude expressed by subjects who were dealing with stress at the higher need levels were:

- YOU NEVER STOP LEARNING
- KNOWLEDGE IS POWER
- DIFFERENT IS BETTER
- EXPERIENCE IS THE BEST TEACHER
- PREPARATION PREVENTS POOR PERFORMANCE
- QUALITY IS BETTER THAN QUANTITY
- WITH MONEY YOU CAN CHOOSE YOUR MISERY
- JUST BECAUSE YOU HAVE THE RIGHT TO DO IT, DOESN'T MEAN IT IS THE RIGHT THING TO DO
- WAIT IS A FOUR LETTER WORD
- STRANGER IS A FRIEND YOU HAVEN'T MET YET FORGIVE AND FORGET
- IF YOU DON'T HAVE SOMETHING NICE TO SAY, THEN DON'T SAY ANYTHING

Destructivism

One of the surprisingly common cases reported at the social level was by subjects who experienced stress, because they made rational decisions and were healthier or more financially secure than their friends and family. Friends and family felt inferior, but instead of recognizing their own mistakes and failures, they tried to sabotage the subject's happiness, discount their achievements and block their development. The subjects were sad, because friends did not recognize their achievements.

> Michelle: The economy was bad and when my friends and I graduated, it was very difficult to find jobs. Adding to the problem, the market was flooded with people with degrees from online universities. I took a job working in a fast food restaurant. I know this is a cliché. Everyone says the most important words a college graduate needs to learn are, "Do you want fries with your Big Mac?" but I had loans and bills. I could afford a tiny studio and a used car, and I was independent. My friends rode me hard, which is weird because they never had any money and I had to buy pizza and beer all the time because they were always hanging at my place. They said working at McDonald's was embarrassing and they would never drop so low. I told them it was more embarrassing that they had college degrees and were living with their parents and mooching off me for almost a year. So, strangely I am an embarrassment for my friends, and I'm tired of them mooching off me all the time.

Michelle made a fully rational decision to attempt self-sufficiency. Her friends were more concerned about maintaining their pride than establishing independence. The modern urban phrase for this behavior is *player hater*. Moslow identified this paradox in the 1950's and referred to it as *destructivism*. There are many forms of destructivism ranging from destroying things to violence directed at others. In this context, we use destructivism to refer to emotional aggression. Like all behavior, destructivism is motivated. In this sense, the negative behavior directed at others is rooted in rivalry. Self-reflection does not exist in groupthink and destructivism is a common response to diversity. When members of groupthink discover that they are less efficient, less healthy, less intelligent, or less successful than another person, the impulsive, immature response is to (a) attack that other person's character, (b) establish other criteria for happiness, and/or (c) make excuses.

> Marv: I was working with my friends on the assembly line in an automotive parts factory for seven years. None of us had any sort of training, but it was a good paying job and we all started right after school. I was always mechanically inclined and I noticed that out jobs were pretty mundane. A monkey could be trained to do what we were doing. I knew that we would be replaced by machines someday so, when I saw a company advertisement for a two year technician training program, I applied. I was excited to get accepted into the program. The starting salary was almost double what I was making on the line. When I told my friends I was in the program, they accused me of trying to kill their jobs. I told them the company was growing and there were dozens of new training programs for lots of new positions in materials management, inventory, and shipping. Basically, automation would kill the dumb jobs but everyone had an opportunity to get a better job, they just had to get some training. One of my friends was really keen on getting retrained, but he was pressured not to. He said something like, "We're going to stand our ground." They basically thought their jobs could be saved if no one signed up for the trainings. Sure enough, a year later the company started installing machines and my friends all got laid off one after the other. By the time I got hired on as a service tech, my friends were all unemployed. The company even had to relocate dozens of people from other plants to ours to fill positions that my friends and others in our plant didn't want to train for. They branded me a

"backstabber" and "sell-out" and called the new-comers in town "scabs." I really like my new job, it's physically easier than working on an assembly line and it pays better, but I can't stay here and I'm applying for a transfer. The town is small and there are too many haters. They vandalized my new car the day I got it. One night they saw me coming out of the movie theater with some friends from work and they threw beer bottles at us. One of the scabs yelled back, "Thank you!" Then the guys came back and asked, "Are you being a smart ass?" And the scab said, "No, I'm totally serious. Thank you. I got this job, because you were too fucking stupid to get free training!"

Marv made a mature, rational decision. He leveraged his abilities to improve his self-sufficiency and stability. His friends were entirely irrational and placed a high priority on social acceptance and felt strong as a group of unemployed player haters, or destructivists. If Marv and his friends grew up in the same town, had the same level of education and the same vocation, why did they respond differently to the same situation? Why did Marv seize the opportunity and friends reject it? The answer lies in acquired virtues and traits. Marv had hope, will, and competence, he is high in openness and low in neuroticism, he prioritized financial security over social acceptance. This combination of virtues and traits are acquired by children of authoritative parents and prerequisites for learning and personal development. Marv's friends were low in openness and high in agreeableness and neuroticism, which are the counter-productive results of authoritarian parenting.

Andy: I got to a point in my life when everything seemed like it was on cruise control. I had a good job, a family, a home. I realized I wasn't getting any younger and started to focus more on my diet and fitness. I tried lots of different diets and fitness regimes, and discovered the Atkins diet and cross-fit. I really liked the cross-fit workouts, because they were only 30 minutes long and it's easy to fit in a couple workouts in a busy work week.

I lost more than 20 pounds in just three months and got in shape really fast. My family got really worried, they thought I was getting too skinny, but my BMI was in the ideal range for my age. Summer came around and we went to a friend's house for a BBQ. When I took off my shirt, everyone laughed. Standing next to my friend, it was obvious why. He was probably 30 pounds heavier than me and his gut hung over his waist band. He had man boobs. We looked like Laurel and Hardy. I felt super and thought I would get compliments, but instead they started insulting me. "Why are you so skinny? Are you sick? What's wrong with you?" I told them I was in the best shape of my life. The conversation was really strange. He said, "well, my priority is my family." I said, "Mine, too." He said, "I've been working a lot." I said, "Me, too." My wife supported me and said she was proud that I was fit and sexy again. A week later she told me her girlfriend asked her if it's possible that I'm gay. She asked, "Why would you think Andy is gay?" Her girlfriend said, "He looks too good. All of the straight men I know in their late 40's are fat and bald."

In the eyes of his friends and family, Andy wasn't normal. He was fit and healthy, and they were not. Instead of reflecting on their own fitness, they used classic groupthink us-versus-them tactics. They insulted him and claimed to have other more noble priorities. When that didn't work, they lashed out against Andy. If he's not sick and he has the same priorities, then the only other explanation in their eyes was he must be homosexual.

Rebecca: Right after school I packed my bags and took off for Europe. I had been planning the trip for a long time and it was not surprise to anyone. I thought I travel for a year or so, but I ended up staying a decade. I fell in love, went to college, fell out of love, graduated and got a job. When I went back for my tenth year reunion, I was shocked. My friends hadn't changed. They were living in the same neighborhood, hanging out with the same people. Sure they had careers, husbands, and families, but they were the same. I was actually embarrassed to tell them I was a doctor. They all tried to downplay my achievement. One classmate said, "Well, medical school in Europe is probably a lot easier than in America." What the hell did that supposed to mean? Another classmate said she wanted to go to medical school, but she didn't want to get into debt. I had no college debt. And yet another said starting a family was more important to her than having a fancy career.

Classic immature groupthink. Instead of congratulating Rebecca for her achievement, her classmates insulted her by implying that she wasn't smart enough to earn her degree in America, she was probably in debt, and they had more noble priorities.

Bastian: I loved my fifth grade teacher. She made everything fun. She wrote songs for math, geography and history to make memorizing things easy. Science was my favorite subject. I could recite the periodic table of the elements and I knew all the body organs, muscles, cells and bacteria by their latin names. I remember at parent-teacher conference my teacher told my parents I was going to become a doctor. My dad didn't like that prospect at all. He said he couldn't afford college, I was going to serve my country like he and his father did, and she shouldn't put highfalutin ideas in my head. My teacher and I ignored my dad and she made sure the other teachers in high school knew about my plan. Eventually, my mother somehow got in on the secret. I got straight A's in school, did super on my SATs, and even got a partial scholarship to state university. I didn't know how to tell my father. My mother told him one night at dinner and he got really pissed. He called me a sneaky bastard and said, "I bet you think you're better than everyone now, huh?" Because I was only 17 and had a partial scholarship, I needed his approval. He did everything he could to block me. He wouldn't sign the financial aid application or anything else to do with college. I found ways around everything and I'm in my third year of pre-med, but my father has disowned me. He calls me "unpatriotic" and "the black sheep in the family."

Bastian's father was authoritarian and his mother more authoritative or indulgent. This combination worked in his favor. He acquired conscientiousness and diligence from his father and openness from his mother. He rebelled against his father, but in a positive manner. Bastian's father clearly felt inferior. He was the patriarch of the family and Bastian's career choice would threaten his status.

Micky: I earned a general business degree which I thought would be pretty useless but it has opened a lot of doors for me. I have over 25 years business experience and I'm on my third career. I worked for several years in publishing and saw the trend to online media so I took some classes and switched to digital marketing. I worked in online marketing for almost a decade and saw the trend to environmental technologies. I took some courses, got a sustainability certification and I've been working in environmental tech for the past five years. Every time I changed careers, I made a lateral move and got a huge salary bump. And all of my jobs required lots of travel so I've seen the world. I've had several girlfriends, but I've never settled down. My friends make fun of me. Every time we see each other they ask me what I'm doing now and who I'm dating. As if I changed my job and girlfriend every three months. One of my oldest and best friends told me recently that I needed more relationship stability and job security. Then he gave me this really lame speech. He goes, "Mick, I've been working 30 years in the same company, I put in my time and I'm Senior

Vice-President. SVP. I make $80,000 a year plus. $80,000 plus. My mortgage will be paid off next year and I'll retire in 10 years." As if that was all very impressive. I couldn't help not to grin. He looked confused. I told him I didn't want to have a pissing contest about income, because I stopped using income as a success metric a decade ago. He pushed me, so I said, "Rick, I'm earning almost three times what you make and I have more than $1 million in my retirement account. But none of that matters. I'm retiring in five years and then I'm moving to Asia or Africa to do farming or environmental projects." He accused me of lying. I took out my iPad and showed him my bank balance and my monthly salary deposits. He looked like a ghost. Then he accused me of somehow cheating. I told him the world is constantly changing and I always caught the next wave. He reacted so stupidly. He told the story totally differently to our friends and everyone now thinks I'm mixed up in something illegal. Even my family is asking questions. I recently got back from a trip to the Middle East and my brother asked, "So, what kind of so-called 'charity work' are you doing over there?" It was so obvious he had talked to Rick. My mother asked me when I was going to finally settle down, and my father asked me if environmental tech was a cover. A cover for what?

Micky's friend, Rick, is high in conscientiousness, but higher in conformity and very low in openness. Rick has lived what he thinks is a normal successful life. He is self-sufficient and measures achievement in terms of income, but his development halted at the social level. His approach is conservative. His mistake was believing that there was only one path to success. In his eyes, Rick was aimless and unstable, and needed help. Rick's parents were probably authoritarian. Micky has will, purpose, and competence, he's high in conscientiousness, very high in openness, and low in conformity. Micky's parents were probably authoritative. Micky has developed further. Income and social are no longer priorities for him and he is focusing now on achievement and altruism. Instead of congratulating

Micky and apologizing for under-estimating him, Rick attributed Micky's success to personality, i.e. Micky must be corrupt.

> Daniella: I worked for 18 years in a job I didn't like. It was the only job I ever had and I worked hard, but as soon as my house was paid off, I decided I needed to change something. I couldn't work in that field another 22 years. I started exploring other jobs that always interested me. I took some entry level courses in physical therapy, cooking, human resources, and programming. Not all at once. I admit that I was all over the place, but I was looking for something that I really liked and could picture doing for another 20 years. My friends and family were all worried about me. They kept telling me I had a good job and I should stick with it. I told them I wasn't happy and felt suffocated. I hated going to work. They told me I needed help, because I was burned out or depressed. I found that I really enjoyed cooking and went to a culinary institute for two years. When I finished I got a job offer as a dessert chef in a five star resort and immediately quit my first job. My boss of 18 years was very sad to see me go and she was super supportive. She told me I could come back if my adventure didn't work out and she would find something for me. But my friends and family were really disappointed and especially shocked about hearing that I would make much less. I told them I love cooking and didn't need to make so much anymore because my mortgage was paid off. It's been six months and I no longer enjoy being with my family and friends because they simply won't accept the fact that I am very happy even though I am earning less. My dad actually called me "stupid." Recently, I started working with the chef in the resort to create a collection of dessert recipes for people with celiacs or diabetes. My 18 years as an editor for a woman's magazine are paying off and we published an article last month in a magazine. The resort was super excited for us and offered

me a contract to lock me in. They knew other restaurants and resorts would make me job offers. One of my friends saw the article and asked me, "Did you have to call in some favors? Are you doing that for some extra money?" No, I submitted an article just like everyone else and it got selected. Because I worked as an editor for 18 years, I know how to write to appeal to editors. Now we're talking about me being a regular contributor. I've never been so excited about anything. Why can't my friends and family be happy for me? I am avoiding them now, their always negative. I'm making new friends.

Daniella is the offspring of authoritarian parents. Her father dictated her career choice, and she didn't have the freedom for self-discovery as a child. This wasn't bad, because she achieved financial security and learned some valuable skills. Her rebellious, self-discovery phase started late in her life when she had means and time. It took her a couple years to find her calling and she is now realizing her potential and also applying herself to helping others. It is not normal to throw away a career after 18 years, but normal is not our goal. We want to be exceptional. We should want to be exceptional.

Several subjects had careers that enabled them to achieve financial stability, but they were not happy. They all embarked late in life on self-discovery and eventually compromised their income, although not their stability, in order to apply their talents to helping others. Still, they were sad, because friends and family did not understand and support their decisions.

Frank: I quit my job as a crane operator to become a paramedic. I wasn't unhappy operating a crane. I just wanted to do something to help people. My girlfriend left me, because she didn't approve of my plan to make less money.

Tina: I worked almost ten years as an accountant and quit three months ago to buy an assisted living home. As an accountant, I was impressed with how efficient and stable this facility was run. I had to meet the owners. They were an elderly couple who were looking for someone to take it over. It is a real feel good project. My friends don't understand me and criticize me for throwing away my education. It's a lot of paperwork, but that's my specialty. I'm already thinking about expanding.

There is a good reason mature personalities are called over-achievers. They have accomplished more than the normal person. They have fulfilled basic and social needs, broken out of the normal career-family-retirement paradigm and were focused on personal achievement and self-actualization. They were successful, not always rich, but very efficient and productive. Because they had identified and developed their talent, they were doing something they loved and were starting to apply it for the social good. Nevertheless, they all suffered the same type of stress. They did not need approval from others, but they were lonely. They had learned that when they spoke up, others often felt inferior or stupid and became defensive or insulting. It was easy to avoid a conflict by being silent and modest or outright avoidant.

Liam: I've been divorced for several years, it was an amicable separation, and my kids are grown up, so I have lots of time and money to do what I want. I love my job, I travel a lot, I live in a condo so I don't have to do yard work, and I'm a minimalist so I don't have lots of stuff. I used to make a lot of time for my friends and family. I would help them with their landscaping and remodeling projects, help them write business plans, even run errands for them. Of all my friends, I'm definitely the most positive in all senses of the word. I have no debt, no bills, no big problems, no stress. They're whining all the time and the few times I've asked them for help, like picking me up at the airport, they don't have time or they didn't have any money. They asked my advice a lot and I'd give them my honest opinion, but then they just ignore me and always making the same stupid mistakes. For example, I was at a friend's house last weekend for a BBQ and he started out right away complaining that he was working like a dog and needed a vacation, but he couldn't afford one. Then he says, "Hey, check out my new BBQ." It was one of those monster stainless steel outdoor kitchen islands that cost around $2,000. I was speechless. He wanted me to high-five him, but I just shook my head. Then he said, "What?" I told him I didn't understand him. He starts in right away ranting. A man needs a BBQ, my life isn't as perfect as I think, family is more important. I think that was supposed to be an insult, because I'm divorced. I didn't want to argue and I just let him rant. Apparently, he talked to some other friends and now everyone is trying to convince me that I must be depressed and in denial. Even though it's been seven years, they say, "It's normal to be depressed after a divorce" and because I wasn't depressed something bigger must be wrong with me. These conversations got really annoying so I've been keeping to myself lately. I always wanted to fix up a vintage Italian motorcycle so I bought an old bike and I spent my spare time working on it. I never worked on anything so complex. I read several books and watched how-to videos. I found a couple sites to order original parts and ended up buying a second identical, broken down bike just for parts. I worked with some specialty shops for engine work, chrome plating and paint. It took me several months to complete the first bike. So, the sun was shining last weekend and I took it out on an inaugural ride to Starbucks. When I pulled up, four of my friends were standing outside. One of the ladies said directly, "Why are you riding a motorcycle? Don't you have a car?" I told her I restored it myself. Then we went inside to have a coffee. As we stood in line to order, one of the guys shouted, 'Wow, Zach's bike is worth more than $40,000." He actually googled my bike on his iPhone to see what it was worth and showed everyone the webpage. That was really weird. I didn't mention that I had a second identical bike that I was also going to restore next. Then his wife said, "Looks like someone is having a midlife crisis."

Axel: I don't like stuff. I hate shopping, cleaning things, dusting, fixing things, connecting stuff, throwing things away. So I just don't buy much. I always lease my cars because if something is wrong with it, I don't want to deal with it. Except for my kitchen, which is a full-on stainless steel commercial kitchen, because I love to cook, my place is pretty much empty. I'd rather spend my money on food, entertainment and travel than on stuff. I do have the necessities like a bed and a cappuccino machine, and I only buy top quality. I don't even have a t.v. When I want to watch a movie, I either download something on my iPad or I go to the movie theater. Anyway, my family complained that they're always having me over for dinner, and I'm such a good cook that I had to host a dinner at my house. I agreed. My house echoes because it's mostly glass, steel and concrete and empty. When they arrived, they all started whining right away. "There's no place to sit." "It's not cozy." "It's not child friendly." "Where's the t.v.?" They got really negative when I told them to take a seat for dinner. I don't have a typical American style table with chairs. I have a low Asian table with pillows on the floor. I bought it in Japan. Then my parents dropped the bomb. "If you're doing so well, why don't you have carpet, furniture, a t.v., or chairs?" I told them my minimalist philosophy and they said, "That sounds like an excuse for poor money management."

Micky, Liam, and Axel were very mature and happy. They were healthy, self-sufficient, and focusing on achievement and self-actualization. Friends and family were stuck at lower need levels like financial security, social and esteem. Subconsciously, friends and family felt inferior. Micky earned a higher income and had an adventurous career, Liam had time to explore new interests, and Axel opted for a simpler life so he could spend his time and money on cooking and traveling. These subjects' friends and family were uncomfortable with their nonconformist approaches and success. The only way friends and family could explain these subjects' achievements and happiness was, they must be doing something wrong. Andy must be gay, Bastian is unpatriotic, Marv is a sell-out, Tabatha is objectifying women, Rich is a loser, Micky was doing something illegal, Liam was having a midlife crisis, and Axel must have money problems.

Out of the Box

We should not criticize some people for identifying and leveraging their abilities in ways that do not reflect our expectations when those people are self-sufficient and on the path to achieve their potential. We read about some subjects who couldn't find work that permitted their form of self-expression. Here, we have subjects who chose occupations that reflected their traits and talents and allowed their form of self-expression. They were healthy, self-sufficient and happy, but they were critcized by friends and family, who had different expectations for them. The strongest example of this was shared by subjects who had jobs that friends and family referred to as "loser jobs."

> Tabatha: I'm hot, I love fitness, I love to dance, I really like to be naked, and I like to be the center of attention. It's what I can do better than most women. Besides, I make a good living and I get to travel. I'm doing exactly what I love to do. But so many people disapprove. They say I'm objectifying women. Well, I admit that I'm not very smart. We can't all be nurses, teachers, lawyers or activists. I can't sing, I can't act, I'm not skinny enough to be a runway model and I have no patience for children. I'm not the kind of person who can be someone's stay-at-home or trophy wife and I despise soccer moms. My asset is, I'm young and super sexy so I don't see what's wrong

with me using my assets to earn a legitimate living while I can. I know I can't do this forever, so I'm saving up to open a lingerie shop in a couple years.

Obviously, some feminists think someone like Tabatha perpetuates the view that women are sex objects, that she facilitated the exploitation of women and did not project a modern image of a woman. This is an outdated version of feminism. According to Holt and Cameron, the third wave of feminism, which started in the 1990's, distinguishes itself from the second wave through its celebration of sexuality as a means of female empowerment. Tabatha leveraged her sexuality to become fully independent and happy. From a humanist perspective, it is preferred that Tabatha leverage her assets to become self-sufficient and achieve self-realization than for her to conform, be dependent on others and not realize her potential.

> Rich: Look at me. I'm huge. I'm intimidating. No one fucks with me. I was always a foot taller and a hundred pounds bigger than everybody around me. Everyone said I needed to play football or basketball. I tried out and I was good, but not good enough to get a college scholarship. I didn't do good in school so I enlisted in the army. I loved the brutal workouts and became a full adrenaline junky, but I had constant problems taking orders so I did my four years and got out. Because of my size and military experience, I got job offers working security. During the days, I guard jewelry stores or provide event security, on weekends I am the bouncer in a popular nightclub. It's perfect for me. But my friends and family are always asking, "Why don't you join the police department?" "Why don't you become a fire fighter?" and customers are always asking, "Why don't you play pro basketball?" What's wrong with these people? I love this and I could do this forever. I have time to work out, I have a lot of variety in my life, I get more respect than cops, and I'm making good money. Then they say negative things like,

"How can you be happy, you don't have a real job?" Most of my army buddies are still trying to get into the police department and I already earn more than cops who have been on the force for years.

Rich has will, purpose and competence. He is high in openness, conscientiousness, and extroversion. He can efficiently satisfy his basic needs, he has income stability, and he enjoys respect. But his friends and family prioritize esteem over security and health. They do not respect Rich's career choice, because they are ignoring his traits and personality. Rich is probably the offspring of authoritarian parents and he does not like authority. He knows he would not succeed as a police officer, so he leveraged his talents in other positive ways. We need security guards and a security guard who loves his job is better than a security guard who hates his job and is distracted.

Relationship Priorities

The attitudes that created conflict in relationships were:

- BLOOD IS THICKER THAN WATER
- BROS BEFORE HOES
- ALL I NEED ARE MY FRIENDS
- EVERYONE IS EQUAL

Moslow did not set forth sub-levels of the social need in his hierarchy to show the relative priority of family and friends. In light of the numerous crises involving family and friends, I think it is important to have a framework for making rational decisions at the social level. I assert that your children have the highest social priority, followed by your spouse, your parents, and then your lovers and friends. Accordingly, as with other needs in the hierarchy, you should not sacrifice a lower need for a higher need. The needs of your children must be fulfilled at the expense of a spouse, parent or friend, because children cannot provide for themselves. The needs of your spouse need to be fulfilled before focusing on the needs of your parents and friends. The needs of parents must be satisfied, before helping lovers or friends. Also, I assert that, when evaluating the needs of friends and family, the future higher needs of children and spouse should not be compromised in order to satisfy the immediate lower needs of friends and biological family, unless there is support from children and spouse for the decision.

Friends
Lover
Parents
Spouse
Children

Illustration 43: Social Need Sub-Hierarchies

> Naomi: My husband, Dan, will drop everything to help his family. It's really annoying when he cancels date night with me or even family vacations to help his brother fix something on his house or to drive his sister somewhere because she can't afford a car.

In helping his brother and sister, Dan is not compromising the health and security needs of his spouse and children, but he is compromising their emotional needs. I agree with Naomi. Her and her children's needs have priority over the needs of Dan's family. Dan's brother and sister are adults, they need to be self-sufficient, and his family should not have to make any compromises because they failed in becoming self-sufficient. The analysis changes when the partner making a sacrifice is only a friend and not the spouse.

> Don: My fiancé is from Columbia. We've been saving up for a year for our wedding. She keeps flying home to take care of her mother, we've had to postpone our wedding already twice, and our budget is gone.

Don's girlfriend has rational priorities. She is placing her mother's needs for medical care and emotional support over her fiance's needs.

Naomi: Last year, Dan's mother got ill and she needed a very expensive treatment that her insurance would not cover. I told him he should sell his motorcycle if he wanted to help her, but he plundered the kids college tuition account to pay her medical costs.

Helping his mother was admirable, but Naomi's answer was rational. Dan should have sacrificed his own desires and not compromised the current and future needs of spouse and children to help his mother.

Naomi: Last month, his best friend got married and he wanted to use our vacation budget to pay for their honeymoon, because they couldn't afford one. That was the last straw. I said, "No!"

I agree. Dan is not responsible for satisfying the romantic needs of his friends at the cost of his family.

Tracey: My best friend was going through a tough time and she wanted me to be there for her. She lives on the East Coast and I took time off work unpaid and flew out there. It ended up being for two months. My husband was really stressed. He understood why I wanted to be there, but every night when we talked he told me I needed to come home.

Tracey sacrificed the emotional needs of her spouse and children to address the emotional needs of a friend. That was nice, but not rational. All needs of spouse and children have priority over any needs of family and friends.

Becky: My husband is an over-achiever. He's a multi-talent and self-learner. On the other hand, my girlfriends' husbands are all pretty lame. They have no college education, they're not handy, they're all over-weight, and they're pretty lazy. They are all nice guys, but they're couch potatoes. Every time I'm at their place and their husbands are home, the grass is a foot tall, but they're sitting in front of the t.v. drinking beer and watching sports. When they're at my house, they're always impressed that my husband is building something, painting, pulling weeds, planting flowers, playing with the kids. I am kind of embarrassed for them so to make them feel better, I sometimes show sympathy and complain, too. They're always having money problems and so I tell them that we are also struggling. Their husbands are all blue collar workers and my husband is a chemist, so I asked him not to tell my friends what he does for a living, because I don't want them to be embarrassed for their husbands.

Jerrod: I'm ok with Becky being modest. I don't need to brag. But I don't like it when she lies to her friends and gives them the impression that we're losers, too. She sat on the patio last weekend and her girlfriend started crying because her husband had been laid-off and they had lots of debt. Becky told her she shouldn't feel so bad, because we couldn't afford a vacation this year either, because we needed to pay-off some credit cards and we had to refinance our home because the payment was too high. That was a total lie. We have no credit card debt, we refinanced our mortgage only to get a lower fixed interest rate, and we just booked a long vacation in the Virgin Islands.

Jerrod and Becky are healthy and efficient. Jerrod has will, purpose, and competence and he is high in openness and conscientiousness. Becky is high in extroversion and agreeableness. Jerrod is focused on accomplishing things and he wishes to be appreciated for his efforts. Becky focuses on belonging and compassion and seeks harmony with her friends. She purposely discounts their success to appease her friends. He behavior is situational. She is placing her friend's needs over her husband's needs. This is not rational.

R-E-S-P-E-C-T (again)

Samantha: I married an older, successful business man and was his trophy wife. I knew my role and I loved it. We attend balls, conferences, dinners, charity events. He spoils me with affection. I am his princess. I take care of the house and our social calendar. It is the perfect life I always wanted. But my girlfriends are all resentful. They always knock me for not working and not fulfilling their ideal of a modern, independent woman. I think they are just jealous that I have such a great life. One day, one of my friends said something real mean. I know the others put her up to it. She asked me what I planned to do when I got older and less attractive. I had never thought about it and told my husband what she said. He told me they were just jealous and then joked, "As a business man, I know that owning a classic is always a good investment. I'd never trade a vintage Jaguar in on a new Ford. I'd probably just restore it." He told me I had nothing to worry about, because he had no time for anyone else. He said he needed me. He hated having to attend events and conducting small talk and I was always the center of attention and everyone loved me. I knew he was sincere, but my girlfriends were unrelenting. They told me all these stories about other women like me whose husbands had affairs with younger women and they were suddenly divorced and poor. They said I needed to be more independent. I started to do some really stupid things that put a strain on my marriage. I signed up for classes and got a part-time job in a department store at the mall. I was so focused on having a back-up plan, I started to neglect him. I totally spaced things. I forgot to pick up his suits from the dry cleaner, didn't meet him at the airport, and missed a charity event he asked me to attend for him. Then one of his business partners saw me working in the mall. I didn't tell my husband that I had a part-time job and when he called me an hour later and said we needed to have dinner, I knew he knew.

Samantha is the result of indulgent parenting. She is high in extroversion and agreeableness and has a high priority for affection and feedback. She is not psychologically equipped to be independent and, fortunately, she found a partner who compliments her and, more importantly, respects her. Respect in this case refers to appreciation. Her husband does not expect her to think or act differently than she can. He acquired competence and his priority is achievement. He is probably the product of authoritarian parenting in that he is low in extroversion and high in competence. Samantha and her husband are a perfect complimentary pair. The crisis exists because Samantha's friends are programmed differently, because they are probably the result of authoritarian or authoritarian parents. In their eyes, respect has to be earned. They expect Samantha to think and act like they do.

> Terence: My wife is always complaining that I don't respect her. I totally do. She's very caring, social and creative. I really appreciate that. I'm not expecting her to do anything she can't or doesn't want to do.
> Winney: I want him to respect me as an equal. I can't buy anything without asking him first and he doesn't take me seriously. He laughs when I ask him to do something for me. My girlfriends all think he's a macho jerk.
> Terence: How seriously am I supposed to take you? You don't work, we don't have children, but we have a landscaping and a cleaning service. You hang out with your girlfriends all day. I already work 50 hours a week and when I get home I want to relax, but you always have a long honey-do list for me. I feel like my role in this marriage is just bringing home the bacon and fixing shit. If you want to be the head-of-household, then you need to earn it somehow.

Terence respects Winney by having realistic expectations of her. Terence has competence and will, he has compassion, but he is low in agreeableness. He equates respect with effort and income and is probably the offspring of authoritarian or neglectful parenting. Winney wants to be respected as the head-of-household. She has will, but she did not acquire purpose and competence. Her priority is socializing and she asserts herself as a leader, although she has done nothing to earn this status. Winney is clearly the offspring of indulgent parents. I heard hundreds of versions of this conversation. They have four different endings.

> Wife: I can't earn as much as you, because I'm a woman.
> Husband: You can be the boss at home if you can manage everything so I don't have to.

> Wife: I gave up my career to take care of our children.
> Husband: You didn't have a career.

> Wife: I earn it every Saturday night in about four minutes.
> Husband: So, you want to sex your way to a promotion? I respect you too much to pay you for sex.

> Wife: Then I'm going to stop taking care of the house and get a job.
> Husband: If you want to be equals, then you should think about getting four jobs.

The respect conflict is rotted in attitudes which stem from parenting, activism and media.

To be deserving of respect or love or opportunity in the non-indulgent mind is the outcome of having achieved something or performed something well. When non-indulgent people do a good thing, accomplish a feat, or win at something, they see themselves as being deserving of an award or appreciation. When they work, they see themselves worthy of a salary or promotion. When they help someone, they feel they deserve a "thank you." For non-indulgent people, to deserve something is the result of having done something worthy.

For indulgent people, the concept of deserving is different. They believe they deserve affection, opportunity and respect by virtue of existence. Remember, these children are often referred to "trophy kids," because they were awarded merely for their attendance. This is something that we heard many times – only from women. They often told each other during sessions, "You deserve better" and "You deserve to be happy." No male subject ever said anything to this effect. Why? A study conducted by the Meredith Ashley Stephens at Texas State University showed that parents tend to be more authoritative or authoritarian with boys, and more indulgent with girls. In order to prepare boys to be providers, parents set goals for boys, rewarded them when goals are met, and punished them when goals were not met. The male concept of deserving is congruent with the dictionary definition. Owing to parenting styles, the female concept tends to omit responsibility and accountability. This is statistically supported.

The feminist movement in America started in the 1840's and has undergone three waves. First-wave feminism was focused on suffrage and political equality of middle - or upper-class white women. Second-wave feminism attempted to broaden the fight against social and cultural inequalities. Whereas the first wave involved representing the middle class, the second wave brought in women of color and women form other developing nations that were seeking solidarity. Third-wave feminism is continuing to address the financial, social and cultural inequalities and includes campaigning for greater influence of women in politics, women's reproductive rights, and sexuality.

The objective of feminism in its various waves was to correct inequalities imposed on women by a patriarchal society. It worked. In 1964 Congress passed Public Law 88-352. These provisions of this civil rights act made it unlawful for an employer to "fail or refuse to hire or to discharge any individual, or otherwise to discriminate against any individual with respect to his compensation, terms, conditions or privileges or employment, because of such individual's race, color, religion, sex, or national origin."[203] The courts also addressed affirmative action. It voided arbitrary weight and height requirements (*Dothard v. Rawlinson*), erased mandatory pregnancy leaves (*Cleveland Board of Education v. LaFleur*), and allowed public employers to use carefully constructed affirmative action plans to remedy specific past discrimination that resulted in women and minorities being under-represented in the workplace (*Johnson v. Transportation Agency, Santa Clara County*).

As with any movement that was started to right an injustice, it takes time for measures to take effect. The data proves that progress has been very slow. Decades after creating a level playing field in the courts, women still lag far behind men in most areas of measurement like employment rate, salaries and wages, and executive and management positions. The disappointing results have created frustration among women who believe they are owed something. This is the essence of *feminist entitlement*. A paper titled *From Social Inequality to Personal Entitlement: the Role of Social Comparisons, Legitimacy Appraisals, and Group Membership* by Brenda Major concluded that attribution biases tend to legitimize the perception of being disadvantage and produce an elevated sense of entitlement and correspondingly higher levels of discontent.[204] Accordingly, because women were not and are not the reason for the inequality, and men still earn more and occupy most management positions, men must be the reason that inequality still exists today. As a result, opportunity and respect have become categorical imperatives. Women, and other members of the protected class, ought to be given opportunities and respected, because it is the moral thing to do.

No words stimulate the debate more than *affirmative action*. It refers to both mandatory and voluntary programs intended to uphold the civil rights of designated classes of individuals by taking positive action to protect them from discrimination. The affirmative action process seeks to force diversity in the workplace and ensure that the best qualified candidate is hired regardless of race or gender. There are no quotas nor preferential hiring practices imposed by affirmative action, and hiring people based on gender regardless of qualifications has never been sanctioned. Nevertheless, companies are giving women and other members of the protected class preferential treatment in order to project a more positive image in the marketplace. Most companies' first response was to try to make their hiring processes blind by stripping resumes of names and pictures to eliminate information that might unintentionally bias an interviewer for or against a candidate. This didn't work. When leading technology companies reported their employment numbers in 2015, their diversity hires had only increased a few percentage points since 2013 and, in some cases, the number of diversity hires even dropped.[205] Stripping names and pictures from resumes was not enough, so some companies have set specific hiring goals, set up incentive programs to reward recruiters for diversity hires and linked managers' bonuses to diversity hires. These programs are undermining their initial goals. The existence of diversity incentives puts the qualifications of the women hired in question and when a person's ability is questioned then they will never be really respected.

Finally, media plays a big role in this conflict. Beginning 2000, entertainment companies started producing new shows that blatantly emasculate men to promote female empowerment. In the words of ABC Entertainment's president Paul Lee, the recipe is simple: "women smart and strong, men dumb and weak."[206] Some television shows that follow this recipe are *The Simpsons, Family Guy, King of Queens, George Lopez, Everybody Loves Raymond, Outnumbered, Shameless, Home Improvement, American Dad,* and *Rules of Engagement.* The goal is to attract what the advertising industry calls *aspirational women* as the core audience, by telling stories about women in control and men under emotional subjugation. Advertisers followed the same recipe, especially consumer products companies like Kraft, Proctor & Gamble, and Johnson & Johnson. According to Dan Lattiera, a theologist from Duquesne University in Pittsburgh, these shows and commercials represent "a systematic effort to denigrate men for the sake of exalting women, all in the name of 'equity.'"[207] This sounds like superiority theory, i.e. make the in-group (women) feel superior by degrading the out-group (men). Granted, men have portrayed women negatively in the media for decades, but two wrongs do not make a right. Superiority humor only perpetuates division.

Speaking of division, separation and divorce can have a happy, positive outcome for many people, but none of them were subjects in my study. All of my subjects had relationships issues, they were separated or divorced, sad, angry, confused, frustrated and stressed. Their unhappiness was caused by a conflict between logic and emotions, for example, when the subject separated or divorced for rational reasons, but still had a strong emotional connection to the x-partner. Leaving an abusive spouse, no matter how wealthy or efficient they are, is completely rational, because health and personal safety are more important than financial security.

> Candice: Markus is handsome, very successful and a great lover. When I see him today, I want to jump his bones. But he had really bad anger management issues for years and he refused treatment. He never hit me, but if he had a bad day at work, I was really afraid he would. I had to get away from him to protect myself. I had a very easy life with him. I am doing ok now, but it's very hard.

Candice prioritized her personal safety over financial security. This is logical, yet she experienced stress. Leaving a spouse who is affectionate, but very bad with money or has unhealthy habits, is also fully logical, because health and security are more important than intimacy.

> Jim: I still love Carey. It hurts me to see her here today. She really cared for me and she's so kind. But her addiction was a huge problem. She was constantly getting into legal trouble, causing accidents, going to the hospital. I tried to help her, but she wouldn't change. She was pushing us toward bankruptcy. I couldn't imagine having a family with her.

Jim placed his security over love. This is rational. It sounds romantic to stay loyal to someone through thick and thin, but if it puts your health and security in jeopardy, or compromises the health and security of children, separation is logical.

Another conflict exists when the reason for the separation or divorce was emotional and the subject realized later that their decision was not logical.

Linda: I met Stan at dance class. He was so charming and he adored me. He is a true gentleman and I loved being the center of attention. I left my husband of ten years, because the romance was gone. We worked well together. We had a great system, but we were more like business partners than lovers. Even though Stan puts me on a pedestal, I need to leave him, too, because he's a slacker. He's telling me all the time to take it easy. His answer to every problem is a cheap bottle of red wine, a hot bubble bath, and a foot massage. That worked on me for two years, but we live in a tiny apartment and we never have enough money for anything. He's constantly changing jobs and his credit is really terrible. I'm the only one who could get approved for our apartment. He couldn't even get approved for cable t.v. I feel trapped now. Like a princess in a tower. I've had to put all my dreams and plans on hold. In retrospect, leaving my husband was a huge mistake.

Linda and her husband achieved financial security and had stability, which is the pre-requisite for growth. A conflict was created when she took her basic needs for granted and prioritized intimacy. Linda fell for a *white knight*, a man who pandered to her emotional needs. She is stressed in her second relationship because her new partner focuses on intimacy and fully neglects financial security. In the absence of financial stability, personal development is stifled.

I think I know what you're thinking right now. Relationships are emotional not logical. It really depends on how you define love and romance. Immature love is emotional and physical. In the traditional sense, love is equated with affection and providing. And in the mature sense, love is equated with respect and growth.

Jill: We are very romantic. We spend lots of time together and make love three to four times a week.

Barry: My husband is so loving and a super provider. He is so caring and I am constantly overwhelmed by his generosity.

Logan: We have a very deep relationship characterized by mutual respect and undying support for each other.

The mature person sees the relationship as a mechanism for achieving more together and intimacy plays a minor role in the relationship. That sounds very practical, but humanist psychologists argue that there is no greater sign of love than helping someone to achieve their full potential. It is a uniquely romantic relationship when both partners support each other even when their ideas of self-actualization are completely different. These different ideas of romance and fidelity created a lot of conflict among for our subjects, their friends and family.

Cherie: I suspected my husband was having a fling so when he said he was going on a golf trip with some guys from work, I came up with a plan and packed his clothes for him. When he returned from his so-called golf weekend with the boys, I asked him how he golfed. "Did you get a hole in one?" He said they played four rounds and he finished 15 over par. Then he said, "Honey, you didn't pack my shaving kit." I said, "Oh, I put your shaving kit in your golf club bag." I knew he wasn't going golfing and he wouldn't even use a single club. And now he knew that I knew. I won't say we have an open marriage. I'm not happy that he has his flings and I know those sluts don't mean anything to him, but I tolerate it. He's just being a caveman. I made the mistake of telling my girlfriends what I did. They said I should throw him out. He disrespecting me. Why? His idiot digressions don't affect our relationship. I don't feel any less appreciated or loved. Should I really sacrifice everything we've worked together for, because he's being a total asshole behind my back? I tried to imagine my life without him and it would be miserable. I wouldn't be poor, but we need each other and he's always been there for me. Our commitment to each other is more than our genitals. My mom said I'm doing the right thing by letting him know that I know but not starting a fight. But my girlfriends are getting really nasty. It's the only thing they talk about. I am sure I am making the right decision, but they are threatening to get involved. I don't know how to keep them out of my relationship.

Cherie is being completely rational. She doesn't define respect in terms of sexual fidelity. For her, respect equates to expression and growth. These aspects of her relationship didn't change. Her basic needs were not being compromised for respect. Cherie was capable of rare mature love, because she acquired all virtues – hope, will, purpose, and competence. She was compassionate, conscientious, and high in openness. She was clearly the offspring of authoritative parents. Her friends were low in openness and compassion. Her friends defined respect as sexual fidelity. This is an immature perspective based on an incomplete set of virtues. I suspect her friends do not have purpose and, therefore, are not seeing the big picture. They placed a higher priority on fidelity than on basic needs and think she should sacrifice her basic needs due to her husband's sporadic disrespectful behavior.

Happiness depends on aligning definitions of love and romance. Fulfillment requires a deeper relationship that may or may not include an open arrangement. Mature love is uncommon for heterosexual couples, but quite common in gay relationships. More than half of the homosexual couples we interacted with had open relationships and a study by the Center for Health, Identity, Behavior, and Prevention Studies at New York University in 2015 mirrored our observation. It found that more than 40 percent of gay men had an agreement that sex outside the relationship was permissible, while less than 5 percent of heterosexual and lesbian couples reported the same open arrangement.

Just Fit In

> Wanda: I'm in love with someone who my friends don't like. They say 'he's not cool.' I admit, he's not a hipster dude. He doesn't like clubs and he doesn't drink a lot. He's a total yuppie prepster. I've never seen him in torn jeans or a hoody. He has a nine to five office job and he's totally responsible. My friends are complaining and causing trouble all the time when we go out. The music is bad, the drinks are weak, the waitress is a bitch, the other guests are dressed wrong. He almost never complains. I guess he's just more mature. He's the first guy I've gone out with who never touches his phone when we're together. The other guys were always texting the whole time, but I'm the center of attention for him. He's the kind of guy you want to marry and have a family with, but my friends say it's party time. They want me to get back together with my old boyfriend who is one of those cool, bad boys. They think we would have beautiful kids.

This was a common issue for people in their twenties. Their focus was on not on health and security, but rather on social and esteem. Their goal was to make and impress friends. Wanda was thinking rationally about her future. She clearly had a traditional view of romance. Her boyfriend was less extroverted and agreeable, more open and conscientious than her friends. Her friends placed a high priority on social and esteem. Wanda's vulnerability was, she also placed a high priority on agreeableness and social acceptance.

Other subjects were dealing with similar stress. They were dating or had married people who their friends and family did not approve of because they were of the wrong country, wrong age, wrong city, wrong college, wrong career, wrong color, wrong religion, wrong size, wrong class, and/or wrong attitude.

Greg: My girlfriend is a total hippy. She has red dreadlocks and is into organic, vegan, home grown, homemade natural everything. She has such a free spirit. I know the environment is important, but I'm totally clueless when it comes to that. I think she's good for me. My parents said she's not wife material and my friends joke if we have 'organ-ick' sex and if I gave her a natural pearl necklace? I told them when we get married, they have to come naked, because all of her girlfriends will also be there in the nude.

Sandy: My friends and parents found like ten things wrong with my fiance. He's too short, too poor, too many freckles, too light, etc…I told them he's the first man I met who opens the door for me, knows how to sew on a button, can change the oil on a car, and doesn't live with his mother or in his friend's garage. He gave me a cactus on our first date anniversary. I was confused and asked him why a cactus. He said, 'it won't die.' And he's the first man who told me the truth when I asked him if my butt looked big in my jeans. He said, "The jeans must have shrunk a little, sugar." That was so cute.

Tracey: I'm from Poland and my husband and I met online. I was still at university and we had a long-distance relationship for two years. He learned some Polish for me and we only saw each other twice for a week, before we got married in Poland. His family was really mad that we didn't have a wedding with them. My family loves him. I mean they really worship him. They are kind of rich by Polish standards and they visit us at least once a year and always bring him a luggage full of sausages, veal, venison, and my mother's pickled vegetables. He has a big family and they don't accept me at all. Even though I'm a dentist and we work together, they always call me

306 | *Prof. Dr. Michael J. Capone*

'the immigrant wife' and pretend they can't understand my English. And they hate it when we speak Polish together. They say it's an 'ugly language.' Things got really terrible when he suggested that we should spend Christmas with my family in Poland. It was his idea, but his family says now all the time mean, stupid things like, "The immigrants steal our good jobs and now they are stealing our good men."

Greg, Sandy, and Tracey were healthy, self-sufficient, and in love. They placed a low priority on social approval, they are low in agreeableness and high in openness and conscientiousness. They are primed for achievement and self-realization. Their friends and family were lower in openness and placed a higher priority on acceptance and esteem. They are stuck at the social level and will not grow.

In the case of a divorce or separation, friends and family showed support for the subject by abruptly disliking the x-partner in retrospect.

> Friend: We never liked him (or her), anyway.
> Amber: Why didn't you say anything?
> Friend: We just wanted you to be happy.

Such abrupt disliking is always fake and always triggers a crisis, because it is subject to different negative interpretations, which put everything in question: (a) If friends or family really did not like the partner, but never said anything, then they are bad friends. (b) If friends and family did like the x-partner and are only pretending to dislike him (or her) in order to make the subject feel good about the separation, then the implication is the subject made a bad decision.

(a) Amber: How did expect me to be happy married to someone who you apparently knew was wrong for me? What kind of friend are you?

(b) Amber: So you really do like him and are only pretending to dislike him to make me feel good. Does that mean I am making a mistake?

Part III

Treatment

Misery loves company. If you could relate to any of the subjects in this book and are unhealthy, financially unstable, constantly dealing with stress and problems, you do not have to change. Being normal and mediocre is easy and comfortable.

But if you constantly sense that something is wrong and you frequently have the feeling you could accomplish so much more, it's because you can. We all have enormous potential. We just have to recognize and develop it. Believing this is a tiny first step, but hope is not a strategy. You have to think and behave differently.

In the final section I describe the different therapies available today, an outline for a do-it-yourself approach, and an idea for an aggressive method to help you realize your full potential.

Chapter 13

Treatment Methods

In summary: Stress and depression are a process. Parents instill virtues and traits and produce deficits. Deficits influence needs. Needs dictate priorities and the role friends play. Traits influence the level of attitude assimilation. Attitude assimilation steers behavior. Behavior can have negative or positive outcomes. A negative outcome (results do not match expectations) can cause stress, which can trigger physiological (e.g. over-weight) and/or psychological (e.g. sadness) issues. Depression occurs when the physiological manifestation involves a dysregulation of brain chemicals. Just as there are many variables in this equation, there are many different methods for treating the results.

The following are fictitious dialogues to illustrate the various approaches to dealing with stress and depression.

Medication

Medication can be effective, but only in the most severely depressed, and it can only address the symptoms and not the causes of dysregulation in brain chemicals.

> Patient: Work is shit, my marriage is on the rocks, my mother is driving me crazy, and my son is doing poorly in school. I can't sleep, I can't focus at work, I'm irritable, I sometimes sit in my office and cry.

Physician: Are you eating well and exercising?
Patient: I'm exhausted. I have no energy.
Physician: Then, let me write you a prescription that will help you sleep.

Taking medication may help this patient to sleep, but it will not fix this subject's marriage, work and family issues. The depression will continue and may manifest as something else such as an eating disorder.

Therapy

The root causes of stress and illness can only be resolved through therapy and there are several methods practiced today. They all serve to help an individual to overcome their problems, albeit by focusing on different variables. Illustration 44 shows the focus of the various approaches.

Variables	Therapy Methods	Focus Question
Virtues, Traits, Needs, Deficits	Cognitive Therapy	How does your past make you feel?
	Psychodynamic Therapy	What conflicts or trauma did you experience has a child and how could it affect you today?
Deficits, Priorities, Attitude, Assimilation	Cognitive Analytic Therapy (CAT)	What beliefs do you have that affect your decision making?
	Cognitive Behavioral Therapy (CBT)	How do we acquire new attitudes that promote positive behavior?
Action, Behavior	Behavioral Therapy	How can you correct undesired behavior?
	Interpersonal Psychotherapy (IPT)	How do you communicate your feelings to others?
Outcome, Emotions, Stress	Acceptance and Commitment Therapy (ACT)	How can you better manage problems?
Stress, Depression	Medication	How can you regulate neurotransmitters?

Illustration 44: Therapy Methods

Psychodynamic Therapy

The premise of psychodynamic therapy is that contemporary conflicts are expressions of conflicts experienced during childhood, i.e. parenting is the root of the problem. The goal is to understand the deficits acquired as children.

> Subject: My friends and co-workers complain that I'm not trustworthy.
> Therapist: Tell me about your childhood.
> Subject: My parents were very affectionate.
> Therapist: What did you have to do to earn their affection?
> Subject: Nothing really. They loved me for who I am.
> Therapist: And who are you?
> Subject: I am me. What do you mean?
> Therapist: What values or goals motivate or drive you?
> Subject: Freedom, I guess.
> Therapist: What does freedom mean to you?
> Subject: To do what I want.
> Therapist: Do your friends have plans or expectations from life?
> Subject: Yes, they're telling me all the time I need to be reliable.
> Therapist: So your situation exists because you were allowed to do what you wanted as a child and your friends and co-workers were brought up in more strict environments.

Such an exercise can help someone understand why they chose the friends they have, i.e. to satisfy some deficit, but does not offer a solution to the situation.

Interpersonal Psychotherapy (IPT)

IPT postulates that stress and depression are functions of communication and relationships. The therapy focuses on improving interactions in the presence and future.

> Subject: My boss is being a bitch and I think I could lose my job.
> Therapist: Why do you think she is being a "bitch?"
> Subject: She says I'm rude and insubordinate.
> Therapist: Are you?

Subject: I believe honesty is the best policy.

Therapist: Can you give me an example?

Subject: We got new uniforms and I told her they were super ugly.

Therapist: Why did that make her angry?

Subject: Because she picked them out.

Therapist: Did you know she picked them out?

Subject: Yes.

Therapist: Do you understand her response?

Subject: Everyone's entitled to their opinion.

Therapist: Do you understand her response?

Subject: They're so ugly.

Therapist: Do you understand her response?

Subject: She knows I'm into fashion. Why didn't she ask me for help?

Therapist: Were you disappointed that she didn't recognize your talents?

Subject: Yeah.

Therapist: Now that you hurt her feelings, how likely do you think she will be to consult you the next time?

IPT can help a subject to understand how communication can affect relationships, but it does not address the underlying issues such as attitudes and deficits.

Acceptance and Commitment Therapy (ACT)

The goal of ACT is to help the subject to develop psychological flexibility by learning techniques for dealing with their problems. ACT does not serve as a way for individuals to avoid or prevent negative thoughts and feelings, but as a way of accepting and dealing with problems by changing their function and affect, a technique known as *cognitive defusion*. One of the core exercises used during ACT involves the client selecting values and choosing a life direction in various domains, such as family and career. The final stage involves the establishment of specific goals and commitments that are consistent with an individual's selected values.

The most notable weakness of ACT in the context of achieving one's full potential is that it relies on a client having rational priorities. If the client chooses to live by values that are not conducive to self-sufficiency and self-actualization, then the client will be stuck in an endless cycle of disappointment. ACT does not help break the subject's pattern of setting irrational priorities and making bad decisions, it only helps the client to deal with the endless cycle of sadness.

> Subject: I live by the motto "stick to my guns."
> Therapist: It's good to have guiding principles. How is that working out for you?
> Subject: My wife complains that I am too sensitive and my co-workers say I can't take criticism.
> Therapist: When you experience negativity, just imagine it as a red balloon and pop it with your finger.
> (two weeks later)
> Therapist: How are you doing?
> Subject: I'm popping lots of red balloons.

This trick can help the subject to respond less often to criticism, but it does not address the underlying issues for over-sensitivity. The subject's frustration will likely manifest as something else, for example, substance abuse.

Behavioral Therapy

The premise behind behavioural therapy is that behaviour can be both learned and un-learned. The goal is to help the individual learn new, positive behaviors which will minimise or eliminate the negative emotions. Behavioral therapy considers the subject's past in order to understand where and when the unwanted behavior was learned, but places a stronger emphasis on ways in which present behavior can be corrected. Originally this type of therapy was known as *behavior modification*, but today it is usually referred to as *applied behavior analysis.* There are various methods for modifying behaviour.

Flooding is a process used for those with phobias and involves exposing the individual objects or situations they are afraid of. An example of this would be exposing a person who is afraid of dogs to a friendly dog for an extended period of time. The longer the subject interacts with nothing bad happening, the less fearful the person becomes. The idea is that the person cannot escape the object or situation during the process and therefore must confront their fear head on. Another method called *systematic desensitisation* works on a similar premise to flooding, however it is more gradual. The therapist begins by asking the individual to write a list of fears they have. Once this list is written, the therapist will teach relaxation techniques for the individual to use while thinking about the list of fears. Working their way up from the least fear-inducing item to the most fear-inducing item, the therapist will help the individual confront their fears in a relaxed state. This pairing of the fear-inducing item and newly learned relaxation behaviour aims to eliminate the phobia or anxiety. *Aversion therapy* pairs undesirable behaviour with some form of aversive stimulus with the aim of reducing unwanted behaviour. An example of how this is commonly used is when an alcoholic is prescribed a certain drug that induces nausea, anxiety and headaches when combined with alcohol. This means every time the person drinks, they get negative side effects. *Token economies* relies on positive reinforcement, i.e. rewarding an individual with points for good behaviour, which can be exchanged for privileges or rewards. This is a common tactic used by parents and teachers to correct the behaviour of children. *Extinction* works by removing any type of reinforcement to behavior. An example of this would be a disruptive child who is given a time-out or told to sit in the corner. By removing them from the situation and center of attention, the behaviour should stop. *Modelling* involves learning through observation and imitation of others. Having a positive role model can give individuals something to aim for, allowing them to change their behaviour to match that of their role model.

In the context of self-actualization, some behavioural therapy approaches can be effective. For example, immersing a xenophobe in a foreign culture may help that person to at least appreciate disparate attitudes, provided the subject has no negative experiences during their submersion. A token therapy can modify behaviour, but not the underlying attitudes.

> Subject: Climate change is a huge hoax.
> Therapist: I'll pay you ten cents for every plastic bottle you recycle.
> Subjects: I earned $25.00 last week and gassed up my SUV.

Extinction can work in diverse group sessions, but not always in sessions attended by members of the same in-group where punishment is a status symbol.

> Ron: I got expelled from school for two weeks.
> Ben: Well, I got expelled for three weeks.

Modelling can be very effective, especially when combined with flooding, which is what I propose later.

Cognitive Therapy

Cognitive therapy relies on an empathetic relationship between the client and the therapist. Working as a team, cognitive therapy has two elements - the analytic side and the cognitive side. The analytic side of the therapy involves the exploration of previous events and experiences that could link to current issues being faced. The therapist will aim to help the subject to understand why events from the past could be affecting them now and why things may have gone wrong in the past. After the therapist helps the subject to understand the implications of such experiences, they will look at the ways the subject currently copes with the problem.

> Subject: My boss is being a jerk and I think could lose my job.

Therapist: Have you been fired before?
Subject: Yes, five years ago, and again three years ago.
Therapist: How did it make you feel?
Subject: Afraid.
Therapist: Are you afraid now?
Subject: Yes.
Therapist: Maybe being fearful is affecting your performance.
Subject: What can I do?
Therapist: Let's work on channelling your fear into diligence.

Note that the reason for being dismissed twice is not addressed. Clearly, the subject is behaving in a way that makes them vulnerable to being terminated. There are underlying attitudes that affect this subject's performance.

Cognitive Analytic Therapy (CAT)

CAT focuses on helping develop tools so that one can better deal with any future psychological problems. The therapy works by investigating any learned behaviours or beliefs from your past and whether or not they are contributing to your current difficulties. Cognitive analytic therapy aims to show you how you can change such beliefs and help you to devise ways of coping that will be suitable for you in your life.

Subject: My boss is being a jerk and I think could lose my job.
Therapist: Why is he being a jerk?
Subject: He complains that I don't put in enough hours.
Therapist: How many hours does he expect?
Subject: 40.
Therapist: How many do you put in?
Subject: Maybe 30, 32.
Therapist: How do you explain the difference?
Subject: I believe in a work-life balance.

Therapist: What would you sacrifice if you worked 40 hours a week?
Subject: I wouldn't have three day weekends.
Therapist: What would you have to sacrifice if you lost your job?
Subject: Well, everything.
Therapist: So, it looks like you have to compromise.

Cognitive Behavioural Therapy (CBT)

CBT combines two different approaches for a practical, solution-focused therapy. The idea behind CBT is that our thoughts and behaviours have an effect on each other. That by changing the way we think or behave in a situation, we can change the way we feel about life. The therapy examines learnt behaviours, habits and negative thought patterns with the view of adapting and turning them into a positive. Unlike other therapies, CBT is rooted in the present and looks to the future. While past events and experiences are considered during the sessions, the focus is more on current concerns. During a CBT session, your therapist will help you understand any negative thought patterns you have. You will learn how they affect you and most importantly, what can be done to change them.

Subject: My boss is being a jerk and I think could lose my job.
Therapist: Have you been terminated before?
Subject: Yes, five years ago, and again three years ago.
Therapist: Why were your terminated then?
Subject: I wasn't putting in enough hours.
Therapist: How many hours did your managers expect?
Subject: 40 plus.
Therapist: How many hours did you work typically?
Subject: Maybe 30, 32.
Therapist: Why were you only working 32 hours a week?
Subject: I believe in a work-life balance.
Therapist: Why is your boss being a jerk now?

Subject: The same reason. I believe in a work-life balance.
I like three day weekends.
Therapist: That belief got you fired already twice. How
did you feel about getting fired?
Subject: Terrible. I had to give up everything.
Therapist: Would you like to reassess your priorities?

All of the therapies today address different variables in the stress equation
and some, like CBT, address the most important variables like the
relationship between attitudes and action. But none of the therapy methods
addresses the source of attitudes, i.e. friends and family.

Every human has enormous potential. My subjects sensed, subconsciously,
that they had not achieved their full potential, and some were not
appreciated by others when they had tried. The 6,000 plus subjects in my
study had not been diagnosed as clinically depressed, but they were sad,
mad and frustrated. They knew something was wrong, but none had put
their finger on it. No one recognized that their friends and family were
making them sick, stupid and sad by setting unrealistic expectations,
establishing irrational priorities, espousing negative attitudes, giving bad
advice, and encouraging irrational decisions and behavior. Friends and
family did this instinctively. They were not purposely trying to make others
sick, stupid or sad. They belonged to a group made up of other immature
personalities, they believed in strength in numbers and they needed others
to be like them so they could feel normal about their mediocre, unfulfilled
lives. We must recognize the significant relationship between friends,
attitudes, actions and outcomes. If we want to reduce the effects of social
identity crisis, we need to develop new, mature attitudes and that means
finding new, mature friends. Instead of using friends to cope with a deficit,
we need to seek friends that help us to grow. There are two methods for
accomplishing this.

DIY Transformation Method

You could disrupt yourself. You could make a clean break from the
people who are having a negative influence on your attitudes, actions and

outcomes. You can make new friends and begin to reshape your life. A full disruption is necessary for some people who find themselves in unhealthy or dangerous situations. But disruption it is impractical for most people, because we often live and work with friends and family. Even though they may be negative forces in our lives, we may rely on them for shelter, food, security, and love. A sudden break up can trigger other life changing events. Therefore, a cautious transformation is usually recommended. You don't have to suddenly break up with your friends and family. You can become the silent, efficient, rational person in your existing group and slowly migrate to a new, mature group. I can tell you from dozens of reports from subjects that maintaining two friend groups works, albeit only temporarily. Eventually, one of the groups will have more influence over the subject and the subject will have to make a choice to abandon one group. It's possible, albeit very difficult to belong to more than one group because, as we learned above, group membership has some requirements.

> Nate: I didn't know what my talent is, but what I was doing wasn't working for me. My friends and me rode motocross, we were having fun, but our lives had stalled. I knew I could accomplish more in life and wasn't getting ahead due to my conduct and appearance. I needed a better job so I could become more self-sufficient and work toward fulfilling my potential. I haven't really changed all of my attitudes. I still think punching a clock sucks, but I realize that I have to do this to get ahead. I have adopted some mature attitudes to be self-sufficient. For example, I learned to be a "yes man." My friends and I worked in a factory that makes dirt bike parts. I stopped complaining and don't argue with my boss anymore. I just shut up and do whatever she tells me to do. When I cut my hair and shaved my beard to apply for a job in outside sales, my friends said I looked "pretty." When they saw me wearing a button down company shirt and Dockers to work, they called me an "office dick" and asked, "Are you afraid to get your hands dirty?" They also said I lost my identity. I

told them part of my new identity was being efficient. They teased me. "You're being all responsible. How dull." It's weird how easy my life got just by shutting up. My boss gave me more responsibility and I started earning more. Within months, I could afford to take night classes at the community college. It's been about two years, my life is so much easier and I can afford to invest more in motocross. My old friendships are fizzling away. They had shitty attitudes that held them back, but they criticized me for moving up. I told them all the time, life is like a dirt bike race. You can't win with a shitty bike and if your bike breaks down all the time, you can't blame the guy with the good bike. In my job in outside sales, I've met everyone in the industry and I hang out a lot with the sales reps for the other companies. We trade parts and I've been able to trick out my bike. I'm winning races now and it looks like I will get a sponsorship next year. Maybe motocross is my talent. I know I should do something for the community and I'm thinking about teaching kids how to work on dirt bikes and getting them away from the computer and on the track. I told my boss about my idea and she said she would help me.

There are three steps in a DIY Transformation.

Step 1. Become efficient. You know now what it means to have rational priorities so adjust your life accordingly. Put your health and financial security first. Create a plan so that you can satisfy these basic needs easily. Set a goal such as making your monthly bills less than 50 percent of your take home income. If you have a job then do whatever it takes to keep your job and maintain income stability. If this requires kissing ass, sucking up, and brown-nosing, then do it. If you are having difficulty paying your bills, then lower your expenses, downsize, cancel subscriptions and memberships, cut your entertainment allowance, stop buying luxury items and junk foods. If you don't have a job, swallow your pride and accept any job you can get. Becoming self-sufficient is only the first stage in your personal development. This situation will not be permanent. You just need to get to a point when you have surplus time and resources so you can pursue better positions and focus on fulfilling higher needs like respect, achievement, and self-actualization.

As soon as you are efficient, establish some security. Get health insurance, save enough money to cover six months of expenses and support the next phase of your development. Your next step may involve taking classes, traveling, moving, or buying tools, equipment and new clothes.

This method will cause stress. Your friends will be dismayed when you begin to ignore their advice, when you do not get excited about some stupid idea, and when you begin acting responsibly and do not meet their low expectations for you. They will become disappointed when you stop meeting them for happy hour, when you cancel your gym membership, and change your appearance. They will think that any action you take that is not normal in their eyes is an affront to their values. They will become jealous when your plan starts to take effect.

This is the first stage in your plan to escape mediocrity and become exceptional. Once you are efficient and have money in the bank, be cautious not to revert back to your old ways. Don't tell friends and family about your plan. Their questions will only create more noise and distraction. You are doing this for yourself. When you are efficient, you do not need their help or approval.

> Nate: Less than a year after I accepted my first job I had my total bills below the 50 percent point and over $1,000 a month to spend or invest. A year later, I had $5,000 in my savings account. It was burning a hole in my pocket. I made the mistake of telling my friends I had saved up some money. They convinced me to buy a bass boat. They said it would be an investment because we would catch our own food. Of course, I got stuck paying for storage

and gas. I'm so mad at myself. Now I'm starting all over. I need to sell it and get back on track.

Step 2. Seek out diversity. Once you are efficient, you can embark on self-discovery. Your goal is to uncover your interests and talents. Expose yourself to disparate views and try to understand different attitudes. Take some classes, attend events, go to museums, visit new websites, travel, read different magazines and books, eat different foods, and listen to and read different sources of news. YouTube is a wonderful source of information and has millions of videos about history, politics, technology, medicine, environment, jobs, hobbies, cultures, religions, and food. Challenge yourself to consume content once or twice a week that your friends and family would not approve. If your friends do not like guns, attend a gun show. If your family doesn't believe in global warming, watch a documentary about the environment. Is your group afraid of Muslims? Visit a mosque. Do your friends hate John Oliver or Alex Jones? Watch the shows Last Week Tonight and Infowars.

Get in the habit of fact checking and second screening. When you're reading Facebook posts, watching the news or reading the newspaper, check the facts using other sources online.

Discover alone to avoid being influenced by friends and family. Their criticism may influence your perceptions and ability to absorb new information. Don't debate with your friends. When you start to consume information outside your group's filter bubble, you will learn new views and perspectives. If you try to discuss these with your old friends, they will suffocate your opinion and mob you.

> Roy: When I told my mother what I heard on NPR news about gun laws, she asked me why I was listening to that liberal bullshit. Later that evening, my dad called me to lecture me on the second amendment, and my brother texted me a picture of a sign he has in his front yard, "No Trespassing. I won't call 911. I have a .45."

Step 3. Make new friends. Surround yourself with other mature personalities and experts. If the friendship process is an onion, then the world is a giant onion farm. There are many groups and every group is looking for members. Most groups believe in strength in numbers and such groups need members to fill some emotional deficit. A few groups believe in strength in diversity and these groups seek members to learn from and grow. Now that you know the signs of groupthink, you can quickly determine if the group is made up of mature or immature persons. Illustration 44 shows this process. Each set of circles represents a group of friends and the concentric rings represent the level of assimilation.

When you like the attitudes of your new friends, you will integrate them into your belief system and progress through the levels of assimilation, effectively changing your identity and backing out of your old group. Theoretically, you could manage two identities. As described in previous chapters, you could be a programmer Monday to Friday and a punk rocker on weekends, a dentist by day and a stripper at night.

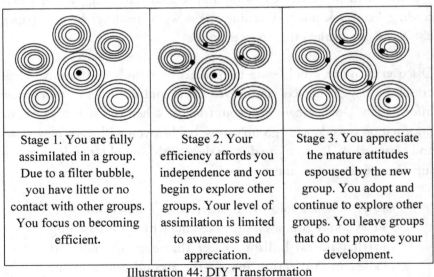

Stage 1. You are fully assimilated in a group. Due to a filter bubble, you have little or no contact with other groups. You focus on becoming efficient.	Stage 2. Your efficiency affords you independence and you begin to explore other groups. Your level of assimilation is limited to awareness and appreciation.	Stage 3. You appreciate the mature attitudes espoused by the new group. You adopt and continue to explore other groups. You leave groups that do not promote your development.

Illustration 44: DIY Transformation

Social Transplant Therapy

In the course of my study, which was conducted over four years, we interacted with hundreds of individuals who belonged to groupthink that was so strong that the subjects constantly struggled with regressing. In some cases, the group was demanding and coercive. It did not tolerate passivity or dissent. Members were required to express themselves and act in a certain way and when they didn't they were punished. In other cases, the subject's affection for the group was so strong that simple things could trigger immature behavior. We observed this dozens of times and created a list of *momentos*, because they were seemingly little things that stimulated a memory and associated behavior. Many things can serve as momentos - a piece of jewelry, a part of a tattoo, a baseball cap, a t-shirt, a photo, a song, an advertisement. We observed the first momento case early in our study and dozens of similar cases thereafter.

Joel was a stereotypical college frat boy. He wasted his college years partying and hooking up. He graduated with a "bullshit" degree, bad grades, and more than $50,000 in college debt. Owing to a string of criminal charges for vandalism and drug possession on campus, he was unemployable. He blamed his predicament on his parents, because they didn't pay his tuition, didn't buy him a new car, and didn't give him a credit card. Joel had a twisted sense of accomplishment. He believed he was owed a job and deserved respect for putting himself through college. He lived with his parents and was so belligerent and lazy, they gave him an ultimatum: get counseling or get out. Working with Joel was difficult. Even though he was a college graduate, it was often impossible to understand him due to his extensive use of jargon. He was disrespectful, impulsive, rude, easily distracted, and defensive. Everything we tried to teach him turned into a debate.

> Coach: When you shake hands, look the other person in the eyes.
> Joel: Why?
> Coach: It's polite.
> Joel: Are you saying I'm rude?

Joel wanted to work in the public sector so we set some clear expectations for him. For example, he had to arrive to session at least 10 minutes early groomed and wearing business casual attire, he couldn't swear, use slang or rapper gestures, he had to sit upright, and he couldn't touch his crotch or pick his nose. Over four weeks, Joel began complying with our expectations and we were somewhat satisfied with his slow development. Then he crashed. We were practicing interviews when another subject entered the office wearing a football jersey. Apparently, it was Joel's favorite team. He leaped from his chair, barked loudly in a deep voice "Go Chargers! Yeah!" and ran over to greet the other subject with a high-five and a chest bump. They immediately slipped into an animated slang conversation about the last game. The immature Joel emerged instantly and in full character. When we resumed our session, Joel slouched in his chair with his legs spread and his hands cupping his crotch. "Dude, that was so fucking cool!" he said. We were all speechless. My assistant reminded Joel to sit up and stop cupping his crotch. He replied, "Yo, it's all cool." What just happened? A football jersey triggered an instant and complete regression.

The second case involved Craig. I can best describe Craig's appearance as a gang banger. He first came to session wearing baggy pants, an over-sized white t-shirt, a bandana on his head, and tattoos everywhere. Craig had excellent grades in school, a certificate as a commercial electrician, and he was very sincere about advancing. He was intelligent. He wanted to be promoted to foreman and knew that impressing the bosses was more important than fitting in with his co-workers. He was eager to tone down his attitude and he adjusted quickly. Craig came to group session on-time, dressed appropriately as a foreman, and behaved courteously. He made rapid progress, but he crashed, too, and in similar fashion. During a break, Craig and I stood at the coffee machine chatting about his job application when another member of the group approached us. The other member reached around us to grab a coffee cup and his shirt sleeve rose exposing his tattooed forearm. Craig was immediately distracted. "Yo, bro, where did you get that inked?" They started comparing tattoos and then Craig lifted his shirt to expose the tattoos on his chest and back. Several other members of the group saw this and started applauding and laughing. Craig instantly realized his mistake and apologized for slipping out of character. In this case, a small part of a tattoo triggered an instant regression, although in this case it was only a brief relapse.

A third case happened a half year later. A subject was nervous about a job interview and asked me to meet her in a Starbucks two hours before her interview to practice. I agreed and told her to be in character for the entire meeting. When I arrived, she was very polished. She stood up and introduced herself professionally and we sat down to conduct a mock interview. Several minutes into the interview, she suddenly said, "Wooo!" she started drumming on the table and dancing in her chair. I asked her, "What are you doing?" She said, "I love this song." The background music in the café distracted her and triggered unprofessional behavior.

Having observed groupthink and momentos in different therapy and coaching environments, we learned that group sessions were more effective than private sessions when the goal was to instill new, mature attitudes and behaviors. In private therapy or coaching sessions, like the ones we conducted with Joel, an in-group/out-group conflict developed. The subject represented the in-group and the mentor, coach or therapist embodied the out-group. The mentor played an expert authoritarian role, which the subject didn't recognize. The subjects in private sessions often questioned the mentor's credentials and advice and the subjects were sometimes confrontational. Statements like this were common: "Of course you think that, you are one of those spoiled rich kids who went to college. You have no idea what it's like." Again, it is classic groupthink to ignore the message and insult the messenger.

Group sessions, on the other hand, were more effective, although only when members had the same issues, but represented different segments. Even though the members were dealing with the same kind of stress, when members had diverse socio-economic and demographic profiles, a democratic environment existed that favored the mentor. When the coach gave a member constructive feedback, the member often looked to other members for confirmation. "Really? Did I come off as rude?" When the other members validated the mentor, the subjects responded positively to the feedback. This happens because diversity promotes intelligence.

Craig was made aware of his mistake and became embarrassed, because the other members in his session were not in his in-group, they found his behavior funny and they laughed. If Craig's session had been attended only by members of his in-group, they would not have found his behavior unacceptable, he would not have realized his mistake, and the wise therapist our coach would have been vilified.

This was exactly the nature of the challenge we experienced when we conducted sessions that were attended by members of the same in-group, for example, when we worked with prisoners and drug addicts. A strong in-group/out-group conflict developed, the mentor was in the minority, and a tyranny of the majority developed making the mentor powerless and ineffective. The members dismissed any advice from the coach that did not match their attitudes and they validated each other. Confining convicted felons in a penitentiary or cohabitating drug addicts in a private facility for weeks fosters collaborative compassion. Two hours a day with a coach or therapist cannot counter 14 hours a day with friends in the in-group. This partially explains why the recidivism rate for federal prisons in the U.S. is over 76 percent[208] and why the relapse rate for substance abuse therapy is 40-60 percent.[209]

The knowledge that diversity works, behavior and attitudes are inter-related, and that momentos exist led us to develop a concept for a new method for helping individuals resolve their social identity disorder. I call it *social transplanting*. It integrates some behavioral therapy approaches like modeling and flooding with CBT and managed diversity ala JGP. Social transplanting entails imposing diversity by stripping or suppressing all forms of group identification and then placing the subject in an entirely different group of mentors, which are intentionally selected or formed with the subject's background, character and interests in mind. Once in this new environment, the subject hears different words and music, reads different books, eats different foods, watches different t.v. shows, and is exposed to a new culture and attitudes. The subject receives new clothes and is enrolled in a training program to learn a new trade. Because the new group has different beliefs, jargon, gestures and forms of identification, the subject has to adapt to be understood and survive.

We tested the idea of social transplanting and arranged a six month internship in Australia for Joel. His host family owned a chain of bakeries and they were selected due to their diversity and a match to Joel's interests. Joel was a foodie. Joel would have free room and board, he would work for the family to learn new skills, he would receive $500 cash every month, and he would attend courses at the community college. We bought Joel a generic outfit from The Gap and put him on a one-way flight to Perth without any luggage. In essence, we yanked Joel out of his negative in-group, stripped him of his identity and momentos, and stuck him in a new positive group. Because external things like music and advertising can serve as momentos, we deemed it important to send Joel to a foreign country, where the likelihood of him hearing his favorite song or seeing an advertisement for his favorite beer or sports team would be low. His host family received some money to take him shopping for new clothes and toiletries, they agreed not to give him internet access and strictly monitor his television viewing, and we scheduled Facetime calls every other evening to track Joel's progress.

Sadly, Joel's progress was terrible. He did not adjust to his new environment at all. The host father said, "He thinks everything is lame ass and stupid." The family said they couldn't understand him and asked him to speak clearly and enunciate his words. He laughed at them for being "uncool." He arrived at work late and he complained about everything. They didn't have his favorite beer, they had stupid accents, their t.v. shows were stupid, they didn't have his favorite hot sauce, they recycled, they drove "faggy cars." Joel didn't feel accepted and became avoidant. He skipped class frequently, avoided interacting with the family and stayed in his bedroom a lot. The host family wanted to send him home after just six weeks. We were desperate for answers. Joel was deep in debt, he had a criminal record, and he was jobless with no prospects. How could someone so vulnerable feel so empowered in a foreign country? We contacted Joel's parents to discuss the next steps. Then the answer fell on us like a bomb. His parents told us they knew he was unhappy and wanted to come home. How did they know this? Because, Joel was online. Somehow he had acquired a smart phone and gotten internet access and was posting to his Facebook account all day, every day. Compounding the problem, Joel's friends supported his negative opinions and encouraged his bad behavior. This knowledge triggered an immediate and serious intervention. We scheduled a Facetime call with Joel, his host family, and his parents, in which we confronted Joel about his online activity. We instructed him to give his smart phone to his host family while we watched. Then his parents made it very clear, that they would not buy his ticket home. He needed to complete the program and save his income to buy his ticket back to the U.S. or he was stuck there.

By the end of his second month, just three weeks later, Joel's behavior was almost exemplary. Not perfect, but much better. Stripped of the empowering effect of his social media in-group, Joel had to adapt to be accepted and survive. After four months, Joel asked if he could use the host family's computer to start looking for jobs in the U.S. His host mother sat with him to make sure he wasn't using social media and told us he was looking for jobs in the food and beverage industry. Joel used her email address for his correspondence, and, weeks later, she began receiving emails inviting him to interviews. Joel used the host family's computer to conduct interviews via Skype and his host father said he did well and even had a slight Aussie accent. In the last month, he got a job offer working for a commercial bakery in Chicago. Joel reached out to me one year after he returned to the U.S. to tell me how he was doing. He told me he had brief very disappointing contact with his old friends. He posted pictures of himself working in the bakery in Chicago and a friend commented, "So, you're a master baker?" This is a pun based on the word "masturbate." Dozens of other friends liked the joke and posted laughing emogis. Joel decided not to reply, saying "They're so immature."

Social transplanting is forced diversity, but not forced adoption. Joel's assimilation was voluntary. He was given an opportunity, a goal, and an environment. Clearly, there were obvious negative consequences for not adopting, but Joel wouldn't be punished by someone for non-compliance. He was motivated to return home and made a conscious decision to behave maturely and become efficient so he could afford to buy his ticket. Fortunately, the program worked in that it helped Joel to develop mature attitudes and priorities, uncover some interests, develop some skills, and become self-sufficient. How long Joel will stay on track to realize his potential is yet to be seen.

When I describe social transplanting to colleagues, they likened it to reprogramming or rebooting a computer. I do not like these terms, because, again, we are not forcing an attitude adjustment, just providing an environment in which attitude and behavioral adjustments are possible. Modern boot camps for youth follow an authoritarian concept with the goal of teaching discipline and obedience. Although diversity can exist in a boot camp, it is suppressed. The participants are drilled to think and behave a certain way and punished when they do not comply. The behavioral transformation is forced, and the attitudinal transformation is neglected. Like all authoritarian concepts, participants rebel. According to studies by the National Institute of Justice, the recidivism rate for boot camps is 50 percent and "the combined results suggest that there is no general reduction in recidivism attributable to juvenile boot camps."

Next Steps

My next step is to use the learnings from this first transplanting pilot to conduct a broader study whereby we will transplant as many as 100 people beginning in 2018. Imagine we have a subject who identifies strongly with a group that promotes violent behavior and attitude assimilation indicates that this person has a high likelihood of taking some action soon against the out-group, how do we not only prevent this person from doing something unhealthy or stupid, but help this person to identify and develop their talents to become a lasting force for good and do so quickly and permanently?

1. For which subjects can social transplanting work?
2. How do we best match a subject to a host?
3. What environmental factors must exist to help such a person achieve self-sufficiency and develop their talents?

4. How long does the transplant experience have to be? Three months? Six months? Twelve months?
5. How long will the effects of social transplanting last?

What are your next steps? Have you identified your talents and are you on a path to achieving your full potential? Will you make a lasting positive impact on your community or on mankind?

If yes, then congratulations. I look forward to meeting you someday and working together to make the world a better place.

If you haven't yet identified your talents, will you continue to explain your state in life as normal and continue to make the same decisions in order to belong? Or will you act autonomously, seek out diversity, open your eyes to new opportunities and realize your full potential?

Thank Yous

To my mother, Kathryn Mary Capone, born Harvieux (1945-2016†)

Throughout my childhood, my mother sat me down hundreds of times to teach me the following lesson.

> Life is like climbing a tree. The *Tree of Life* can have many branches. A tree that doesn't have any branches is hard and boring to climb. Branches make it more interesting and easier to climb to the top. It's ok to climb out on some of the branches, but be careful not to go too far, because the branch can break and you can fall to the ground. You can get to the top faster and safer if you climb near the trunk. Some trees are tall and skinny. When a storm comes, the skinny trees sway and bend with the wind. And if the roots are shallow, the skinny tree can snap and fall down. Other trees are strong and sturdy. They have deep roots. If a storm comes, they stand fast. A wind can't blow them over.

Maximilian Leist, cover illustrator

Born in 1986 in Gifhorn, Germany, Leist is a recorded rapper and film producer. He is the Director of Animation at BrickBeach.

References

(Endnotes)

1 Capone, M. and Teichert, T.: „Prädiktions-Monitoring am PoS "in *Transfer - Werbeforschung & Praxis*, June 2013.

2 Franck, G.: *The Economy of Attention,* Telepolis, 1999.

3 Helmore, E.: "Snapchat shares soar 44% to value loss-making company at $28bn" in *The Guardian*, March 3, 2017.

4 Davenport, T. and Beck, J.: *The Attention Economy: Understanding the New Currency of Business.* Harvard Business Review Press, 2002.

5 Lobe, A.: „Erzwitschere dir deine Wahl!" in the *Frankfurter Allgemeine Zeitung*, September 30, 2016.

6 McGill, A.: "Have Twitter Bots Infiltrated the 2016 Election?" in *The Atlantic*, June 2, 2016.

7 Woolley, S.: "Social bot interference in global politics" in *First Monday*, April 2016.

8 Quattrociocchi, W. et al.: "The spreading of misinformation online" in *Proceedings of the National Academy of Sciences and the United States of America,* September 2015.

9 Zubiaga, A. et al.: *Analysing How People Orient to and Spread Rumours in Social Media by Looking at Conversational Threads*, in February 2016.

10 Cha, M. et al.: "Measuring User Influence in Twitter: The Million Follower Fallacy" in *Proceedings of the Fourth International AAAI Conference on Weblogs and Social Media*, 2010.

11 Ilyas, M. et al.: "A Distributed Algorithm for Identifying Information Hubs in Social Networks" in *IEEE Journal on Selected Areas in Communications*, September 2013.

12 Quercia, D. et al.: "Lightweight Distributed Trust Propagation" in *IEEE International Conference on Data Mining*, 2007.

13 Aiello, L. et al.: "People are Strange when you're a Stranger: Impact and Influence of Bots on Social Networks" in *Proceedings of the 6th International AAAI Conference on Weblogs and Social Media*, 2014.

14 Ferrara, E. et al.: "The Rise of Social Bots" in *Communications of the ACM*, 2016.

15 Del Vicario, M. et al.: "The spreading of misinformation online" in *Proceedings of the National Academy of Sciences of the United States of America*, September 2015.

16 Peter W.: "Reasoning about a rule" *in Quarterly Journal of Experimental Psychology*, 1968.

17 Munro, J.: "The Scientific Impotence Excuse: Discounting Belief-Threatening Scientific Abstracts" in *Journal of Applied Social Psychology*, March 2010.

18 Luther, C.: „The Calamity" in *Zeit Online*, November 6, 2016.

19 *The U.S. Department of Education's National Center for Education Statistics*, 2016.

20 eMarketer: "Worldwide Ad Spending Growth Revised Downward. Annual gains in worldwide ad spending will hover around 6% throughout the forecast period," April 21, 2016.

21 Tomasello, M. and Carpenter, M.: "Shared Intentionality" in *Developmental Science*, 2007.

22 Evans, V.: "Cooperative Intelligence: The Precursor for Language?" in *Psychology Today*, 2015.

23 Salas, E. et al.: *On Teams, Teamwork and Team Performance: Discoveries and Developments*, 2008.

24 Isaacs, W.: *Dialogue: The Art Of Thinking Together*, 1999.

25 Mayr, E.: *Systematics and the Origin of Species*, 1942.

26 Tetlock, P. and Gardner, D.: *Super Forecasting*, 2015.

27 Janis, I.: "Victims of Groupthink" in *International Society of Political Psychology*, June 1991.

28 Del Vicario, M. et al.: "The spreading of misinformation online" in *Proceedings of the National Academy of Science of the Unitde states of America*, September 2015.

29 Hogg, M.: *The Social Psychology of Group Cohesiveness*, 1992.

30 Heider, F.: *The Psychology of Interpersonal Relations*, 1958.

31 Milgram, S.: *Obedience to Authority: An Experimental View*, 1974.

32 Zimbardo, P.: *The Lucifer Effect: Understanding How Good People Turn Evil* 2007.

33 Chaplin, J.: "Adolescents and Cyber Bullying: The Precaution Adoption Process Model" in *Education and Information Technologies*, July 2016.

34 Cyberbullying Research Center: "New Bullying Data and Definition from the National Crime Victimization Survey," January 2017.

35 Kedia, S.: "Approaches to low carbon development in China and India" in *Advances in Climate Change Research*, December 2016.

36 Trump Donald on Twitter,

37 McDonald, D.: *The Golden Passport*, 2017.

38 Pew Research Center: "Internet/Broadband Fact Sheet," January 2017.

39 Flynn, J.: *Are we getting smarter? Rising IQ in the Twenty-First Century*, 2012.

40 Teasdale, T. and Owen, D.: "Secular declines in cognitive test scores: A reversal of the Flynn Effect" in *Science Direct*, March 2006.

41 Dockrill, P.: "'Digital Amnesia' on The Rise as We Outsource Our Memory to The Web" in *Science Alert*, July 2015.

42 Stanovich, K.: *"The cognitive miser: ways to avoid thinking," 2009.*

43 Hanlon, M.: "The golden quarter" in *Aeon*, December 2014.

44 Weisfield, D.: "Peter Thiel at Yale" in *Yale School of Management*, April 2014.

45 Interview with Edmund Phelps: "Amerika hat seinen Unternehmergeist verloren," in *Wirtschafts Woche*, January 27, 2017.

46 https://www.forbes.com/innovative-companies/list/#tab:rank

47 https://www.fastcompany.com/most-innovative-companies/2017

48 Frisvold, G.: „Genetically Modified Crops: International Trade and Trade Policy Effects" in *International Journal of Food and Agricultural Economics*, Vol. 3 No. 2, 2015.

49 Kluemper, W. and Oaim, M.: "A Meta-Analysis of the Impacts of Genetically Modified Crops" in *PLOS One*, November 2014.

50 McArdle, M.: "School Integration Is So Hard" in *The Atlantic*, May 21, 2012.

51 Williams, G.: *Misguided Notions: The Birth, Death, and Resurrection of Publicly Funded Education in America*, 1972.

52 Judge, M.: *Idocracy*, 2007.

53 Friedman, M.: "Director Mike Judge Says It's 'Scary' How *Idiocracy* Has Come True" in *Esquire*, May 19, 2016.

54 Maslow, A.H.: "A Theory of Human Motivation" in *Psychological Review*, 1943.

55 Maslow, A.H.: *Motivation and Personality*, 1954.

56 Klink, D.: „Der ehrbare Kaufmann. Diplomarbeit," at *Humboldt-Universität zu Berlin, Institut für Management Berlin*, 2007.

57 https://www.annenberg.org/who-we-are/WHO-WE-ARE

58 Preel, M.: "How 'merchant of death' Alfred Nobel became a champion of peace" in *AFP/The Local*, October 4, 2010.

59 Wilson, R.: *Don't Get Fooled Again: A Sceptic's Guide to Life*, 2009.

60 Kraut, R.: "Why Bowlers Smiles" in *Association of Psychological Science*, June 2006.

61 Coleman, E.: "Minimum Amount of Calories Needed Per Day to Survive" on *LiveStrong*, April 2015.

62 Kirk, M.: *Efficiency is Everything – In Life*, 2016.

63 Wolff, T.: „Was ist gesünder – Hausmannskost, Fast Food oder mediterranes Essen?" on *WDR*, 2011.

64 Fingar, K. et al.: "All-Cause Readmissions Following Hospital Stays for Patients With Malnutrition" in *Healthcare Cost and Utilization Project Statistical Briefs*, 2013.

65 U.S. Department of Housing and Urban Development: https://portal.hud.gov/hudportal/HUD?src=/program_offices/comm_planning/affordablehousing/.

66 Charette, A. et al.: "Projecting Trends in Severely Cost-Burdened Renters: 2015–2025" in *Joint Center for Housing Studies in Harvard University*, 2015.

67 Kevin, B. et al.: *Measuring Overcrowding in Housing*, 2007.

68 American Psychological Association: *Stress in America. Coping with Change*, February 2017.

69 Institute for Divorce Financial Analysts: *CDFA Professionals Reveal the Leading Causes of Divorce*, 2016.

70 Schneiderman, N. et al.: "Stress and Health: Psychological, Behavioral, and Biological Determinants" in *Annual Review of Clinical Psychology*, April 17, 2005.

71 Greubel, J. and Kecklund G.: "The impact of organizational changes on work stress, sleep, recovery and health" in *Industrial Health*, March 2011.

72 You, D. et al.: "Levels and Trends in Child Mortality" in *UNICEF*, 2015.

73 Future life expectancy in 35 industrialised countries" in *The Lancet*, February 2017.

74 https://nces.ed.gov/fastfacts/display.asp?id=77.

75 Adams, S.: "The College Degrees That Get The Most Job Offers" in *Forbes*, January 2014.

76 Lino, M.: "The Cost of Raising a Child" in *USDA Food and Nutrition*, Jan 13, 2017.

77 Milkie, M.: "Does the Amount of Time Mothers Spend With Children or Adolescents Matter?" in *Journal of Marriage and Family*, March 2015.

78 Opondo, C. et al.: "Father involvement in early child-rearing and behavioural outcomes in their pre-adolescent children: evidence from the ALSPAC UK birth cohort" in *BMJ Open*, Nov 2016.

79 http://www.atag.org/facts-and-figures.html.

80 https://jobs.web.cern.ch/content/people.

81　http://www.skate-aid.org/en/projects/asia/afghanistan-karokh/the-project.

82 Gleeson, B.: "16 Ways To Live A Happier More Fulfilling Life" in *Forbes*, October 12, 2016.

83 Bohl, D.: "12 Techniques to Help You Live a Happy and Fulfilled Life" in *Dumb Little Man*, March 1, 2012

84 Coulson, L.: "10 Choices That Lead to a Happy, Fulfilling Life" in *Tiny Buddha*, undated.

85 Komarraju, M. et al.: "The Big Five personality traits, learning styles, and academic achievement" in *Elsevier*, January 2011.

86 Berings, D. et al.: "Work values and personality traits as predictors of enterprising and social vocational interests" in *Elsevier*, January 2004.

87 Barrick, M. and Mount, M.: "The Big five Personality Dimensions and Job Performance: A Meta-Analysis" in *Personnel Psychology*, March 1991.

88 Holland, A.S. and Roisman, G.I.: "Adult attachment security and young adults' dating relationships over time: self-reported, observational, and physiological evidence" in *Developmental Psychology*, March 2010.

89 Ball, S.: "Personality traits, problems, and disorders: Clinical applications to substance use disorders" in *Elsevier*, February 2005.

90 National Institute for Mental Health: *Depression*, May 2016.

91 Brhlikova, P.: "Global Burden of Disease estimates of depression – how reliable is the epidemiological evidence?" in *Journal of the Royal Society of Medicine*, January 2011.

92 Richards, S. and O'Hara, M.: *The Oxford Handbook of Depression and Comorbidity*, July 2014.

93 Barchas, J. and Altemus, M.: "Monoamine Hypotheses of Mood Disorders" in *Basic Neurochemistry: Molecular, Cellular and Medical Aspects*, 1999.

94 Saisan, Joanna et al.: "Depression Treatment Therapy, Medication, and Lifestyle Changes That Can Help," on HelpGuide.org, April 2017.

95 National Institute of Mental Health: *Depression: What You Need To Know*, 2015.

96 Dalal, P. and Agarwal, M.: "Postmenopausal syndrome" In *Indian Journal of Psychiatry*, July 2015.

97 Lohoff, F.: "Overview of the Genetics of Major Depressive Disorder" in *Current Psychiatric Reports*, December 2011.

98 Kendler, Kenneth et al.: "Causal Relationship Between Stressful Life Events and the Onset of Major Depression" in *The American Journal of Psychiatry*, January 1999.

99 Plomin, R. et al.: *The Genetic Basis of Complex Human Behaviors*, 1994.

100 Pratt, L. and Brody, D.: "Depression in the U.S. Household Population, 2009-2012" in *National Center for Health Statistics*, December 2014.

101 Center for Hearing and Communication: "The impact of noise on a healthy, happy childhood," undated.

102 Tucker-Drob, E. and Bates, T.: "Large Cross-National Differences in Gene × Socioeconomic Status Interaction on Intelligence" in *Psychological Science*, December 15, 2015.

103 Chetty, R. et al.: "Childhood Environment and Gender Gaps in Adulthood" in *National Bureau of Economic Research*, January 2016.

104 Paxson, C. and Waldfogel, J.: "Work, Welfare, and Child Maltreatment" in *Journal of Labor Economics*, January 2002.

105 Kendall-Tackett, K.: "The Long Shadow: Adult Survivors of Childhood Abuse" in *The hidden feelings of motherhood: Coping with mothering stress, depression and burnout*, 2001.

106 Weissman, J. et al.: "Serious Psychological Distress Among Adults: United States, 2009–2013" in *NCHS Data Brief*, May 2015.

107 Holmes, T. and Rahe R.: "The Social Readjustment Rating Scale" in *Journal of Psychosomatic Research*, 1967.

108 Rahe, R. et al.: "Psychosocial predictors of illness behavior and failure in stressful training" in *Journal of Health and Social Behavior*, 1972.

109 Fuller, J. et al.: "A Lengthy Look at the Daily Grind: Time Series Analysis of Events, Mood, Stress, and Satisfaction" in *Journal of Applied Psychology*, Dec 2003.

110 Kessler, R. et al.: "Age of onset of mental disorders: A review of recent literature" in *Current Opinion in Psychiatry*, July 2007.

111 Schlesinger, J.: "Handling an Inheritance: 5 Mistakes That Keep Americans From Building Legacies of Their Own" in *Certified Financial Planner Board*, May 17, 2017.

112 National Endowment for Financial Education: "Financial Psychology and Lifechanging "Events," October, 2016.

113 Murray, T.: "Why do 70 percent of lottery winners end up bankrupt?" in Cleveland.com, January 2016.

114 Blalock, G. et al.: "Hitting the Jackpot or Hitting the Skids: Entertainment, Poverty, and the Demand for State Lotteries" in *The American Journal of Economics and Sociology*, 2007.

115 Frenkel, M. O., et al.: "Sensation seeking and sport-specific stress" at the *14th European Congress of Sport Psychology*, July 2015.

116 Brickman, Philip et al.: "Lottery winners and accident victims: Is happiness relative?" in *Journal of Personality and Social Psychology*, August 1978.

117 Erikson, E.: *Youth: Change and Challenge,* 1963.

118 Bee, H. and Boyd, D.: *The Developing Child,*2013.

119 Baumrind, D.: "Effects of Authoritative Parental Control on Child Behavior" in *Child Development,* 1966.

120 Maccoby, E. and Martin, J.: "Socialization in the context of the family: Parent-child interaction" in *Handbook of Child Psychology*, 1983.

121 Furedi, F.: *Paranoid Parenting*, 2001.

122 not attributed: "Born Rich" *in Los Angeles Times*, October 27, 2003.

123 Cline, F. and Fay, J.: *Parenting with Love and Logic: Teaching Children Responsibility*, 1990.

124 Federal Bureau of Investigation w/ National Crime Information Center and U.S. Justice Dept.: *Vanished Children's Alliance Redbook*, February 1998.

125 Thomas, R.: *Baby Boomer on Board! — a data-based exploration*, October 7, 2013.

126 Springer, K.: "Etan Patz: A Brief History of the 'Missing Child' Milk Carton Campaign" in *Time Magazine*, April 20, 2012.

127 not attributed: "High-Stakes Assessments in Reading" in *International Reading Association*, June 7, 2007.

128 Stephey, M.: "Where's the Beef?" in *Time Magazine*, May 25, 2011.

129 Tsabary, S.: *The Conscious Parent: Transforming Ourselves, Empowering Our Children*, 2010.

130 Interview w/ Shefali Tsabary: "Children Don't Need Fixing" on Oprah, May, 18, 2014.

131 McGraw, P.: *Family First: Your Step-by-Step Plan for Creating a Phenomenal* Family, September 13, 2005

132 SYZYGY: *EGOTECH. How to win the hearts, minds and wallets of adult Millennials with technology that flatters the ego and indulges the cult of the self*, October 2016.

133 Alsop, R.: *The Trophy Kids Grow Up. How the Millennial Generation is Shaking Up the Workplace*, 2008.

134 "PersonicX - Consumer and Household Segmentation" at http://www.personicx.com.

135 "Prizm - Lifestyle Segmentation" at https://segmentationsolutions.nielsen.com.

136 Taylor, C.: *Sources of the Self: The Making of the Modern Identity*, 1989.

137 Fearon, J.: *What is Identity – As we now use the word?* 1999.

138 Turner, J. C., and Tajfel, H.: *The social identity theory of intergroup behavior. Psychology of intergroup relations*, 1986.

139 Mullin, B. and Hogg, M.: "Motivations for group membership: The role of subjective importance and uncertainty reduction" in *Basic and Applied Social Psychology*, 1999.

140 Cialdini, R. and Trost, M.: "Social influence: Social Norms, Conformity and Compliance" in *The Handbook of Social Psychology*, 1998.

141 Center for International Blood and Marrow Transplant Research: *2016 Annual Report*, 2016.

142 Park, A.: "George W. Bush and the Stem Cell Research Funding Ban" in *Time* Magazine, August 20,2012.

143 Ratzinger, J. and Bovone, A.: Pastoral Care of Homosexual Persons, October 1, 1986.

144 Nussbaum, A.: *Attitudes of Educated Orthodox Jews Toward Science*, 2009.

145 Burgess, J.: "Is wearing a Burqua mandatory in Iran and Saudi Arabia?" on *Quora*, November 24, 2014.

146 Sedikides, C. and Skowronski, J.: *Evolution of the Symbolic Self: Issues and Prospects*, 2003.

147 Kelley, H.H.: "Kelley's Covariation Attribution Model," presented at *Nebraska Symposium on Motivation*, 1967, and published in *American Psychologist*, 1973.

148 Rottman, G.: *The Berlin Wall and the Intra-German border 1961–89*, 2008.

149 Bennett, Shea: "4 Out Of 5 Burglars Use Twitter And Facebook To Select Victims" in *AdWeek*, September 27, 2011.

150 Gerbner, G. and Gross, L.: "Living with television: The violence profile" in *Journal of Communication*, 1976.

151 Rosenberry, J. and Vicker, L.: *Applied Mass Communication Theory: A Guide for Media Practitioners*, 2008.

152 Williamson, D.: "Reality TV encourages us to be rude and aggressive" in *WalesOnline*, April 3, 2010.

153 Straubhaar, J. et al.: *Media Now: Understanding Media, Culture, and Technology*, 2012.

154 Appel, M.: *Behavioral Assimilation (and Contrast) as Narrative Impact*, 2011.

155 Cantor, J. et al.: *Children's Understanding of a Televised Narrative: Developmental Differences in Processing Video and Audio Content*, 1988.

156 Adams, T. and Fuller, D.: "Misogynistic Lyrics in Rap Music" in *Annotated Bibliography of Cultural Anthropology*, 2006.

157 Cundiff, G.: "The Influence of Rap/Hip-Hop Music: A Mixed-Method Analysis on Audience Perceptions of Misogynistic Lyrics and the Issue of Domestic Violence" in *Elon Journal*, 2013.

158 Datcu, S.: *A Second Life in Virtual environment: From Simple Socialization to Revealing Sensitive Information*, 2011.

159 Kandell, J.: *Internet Addiction on Campus: The Vulnerability of College Students*, March 1998.

160 Lam, L. et al.: "Factors associated with Internet addiction among adolescents" in *Cyberpsychological Behavior*, October 12, 2009.

161 Gordon, C. et al.: "Internet Use and Well-Being Among College Students: Beyond Frequency of Use" in *Journal of College Student Development*, November/December 2007.

162 Amelia, A. et al.: "Drug exposure opportunities and use patterns among college students: Results of a longitudinal prospective cohort study" in *US National Library of Medicine National Institutes of Health*, January 6, 2009.

163 Wiseman, R.: Quirkology: *The Curious Science Of Everyday Lives*, 2011.

164 Wyer, R. and Collins, J.: "A theory of humor elicitation" in *Psychological Review*, 1992.

165 Wolff, H. et al.: "The psychology of humor: A study of responses to race-disparagement jokes" in *Journal of Abnormal and Social Psychology*, 1934.

166 Maio, J. et al.: „Telling jokes that disparage social groups: Effects of the joke tellers stereotypes" in *Journal of Applied Social Psychology*, 1997.

167 Escher, E. and Rappaport, A.: *The Rapper's Handbook: A Guide to Freestyling, Writing Rhymes, and Battling*, 2006.

168 Hatzenbuehler, M. and Keyees, K.: "Inclusive Anti-Bullying Policies and Reduced Risk of Suicide Attempts in Lesbian and Gay Youth" in *Journal of Adolescent Health*, July 2014.

169 Dr. Phil Show, "Meet The High School Hero Who Jumped In To Defend Legally Blind Teen From Accused Bully," October 13, 2015.

170 http://www.ethicalconsumer.org/boycotts/boycottslist.aspx

171 https://grabyourwallet org/

172 https://www.democraticcoalition.org/boycott

173 Patterson, R.: "Students of Virginity" in *New York Times*, March 30, 2008.

174 Wiseman, R.: *The Luck Factor*, 2003.

175 Lewis, L.: "Stop Snitching: Hip Hop's Influence on Crime

Reporting in the Inner City in *Scholar Works at WMU*, April 2012.

176 Police Executive Research Forum: *The Stop Snitching Phenomenon: Breaking the Code of Silence*, February 2009.

177 Schackman, B.: "HIV Pre-exposure Prophylaxis in the United States: Impact on Lifetime Infection Risk, Clinical Outcomes, and Cost-Effectiveness" in *Clinical Infectious Diseases*, March 2009.

178 Elborne, E.: "When HIV Is Considered A Gift" on *Vice Blog*, June 23, 2014.

179 Mettebo, M. et al.: "Pornography and Sexual Experiences Among High School Students in Sweden" in *Journal of Developmental and Behavioral Pediatrics*, April 2014.

180 Reardon, C. and Creado, S.: "Drug abuse in athletes" in *Substance Abuse and Rehabilitation*, August 14, 2014.

181 unattributed:: "Under Pressure: College Students and the Abuse of Rx Stimulants" in *Partnership for Drug-free Kids*, November 2014.

182 https://www.deadiversion.usdoj.gov/21cfr/21usc/844.htm

183 Allan, E. and Madden, M.: "Hazing in View: College Students at Risk" in

Initial Findings from the National Study of Student Hazing, March 11, 2008

184 Lenhart, A.: "Teens, Technology and Friendships. Social Media and Friendships" in *Pew Research Center*, August 6, 2015.

185 Barnes, P. et al.: "Complementary and alternative medicine use among adults" in *Seminars in Integrative Medicine*, June 2004.

186 Gupta, S.: "Herbal Remedies' Potential Dangers" in *Time Magazine*, Thursday, Jan. 17, 2008.

187 Rehman, J.: "Accuracy of Medical Information on the Internet" in *Scientific America*, August 2, 2012.

188 Lusardi, A.: "The Alarming Facts About Millennials and Debt" in *The Wall Street Journal*, October 5, 2015.

189 El Issa, E.: "2016 American Household Credit Card Debt Study" on *NerdWallet*, 2016.

190 unattributed: "What Is College For?2 in *Chronicles of Higher Education*, April 22, 2013.

191 https://www.destatis.de/DE/ZahlenFakten

192 Bureau of Labor Statistics: "Employment and unemployment of recent high school graduates and dropouts", July 2015.

193 Quast, L.: "Pre-Employment Testing: A Helpful Way For Companies To Screen Applicants" in *Forbes Magazine*, September 13, 2011.

194 Grasz, J: "CareerBuilder Survey Identifies Generational Differences in Work Styles, Communication and Changing Jobs" on *CareerBuilder.com*, September 13, 2013.

195 Gladwell, M.: *Outliers: The Story of Success*, 2011.

196 Macnamara, B. et al.: "Deliberate Practice and Performance in Music, Games, Sports, Education, and Professions" in *Psychological Science*, July 2014.

197 McGee, S.: "Go for gold, wind up broke: why Olympic athletes worry about money," in *The Guardian*, August 7, 2016.

198 unattributed: "Estimated probability of competing in professional athletics" on *NCAA.org*, undated.

199 Lederman, D.: "NCAA Looks Into Academic Fraud" in *Chronicles of Higher Education*, June 29, 1994.

200 unattributed: "Why Student Athletes Continue To Fail" in *Zócalo Public Square*, Apr 20, 2015.

201 Oher, M.: "Movies and the Outcast Archetype" in *Study Mode Research*, April 8, 2013.

202 Sachs, J. et al.: *The World Happiness Report*, 2017.

203 Civil Rights Act of 1964, Public Law 88–352; 78 Statute 241.

204 Major, B.: "From Social Inequality to Personal Entitlement: the Role of Social Comparisons, Legitimacy Appraisals, and Group Membership" in *Advances in Experimental Social Psychology*, Volume 26, 1994.

205 Huet, E.: "Some Tech Companies Are Trying Affirmative Action Hiring—But Don't Call It That" in *Bloomberg Technology*, January 10, 2017.

206 Tucker, K.: "ABC's new fall TV identity: Home of empowered women and weak little sad men" in *Entertainment*, August 7, 2011.

207 Lattier, D.: "Boys Are Stupid; Girls Are Awesome' – Most TV Shows & Movies Today" on *Intellectual Takeout*, October 24, 2016.

208 unattributed: "Recidivism Among Federal Offenders:

A Comprehensive Overview" by *United States Sentencing Commission*, March 2016.

209 Adler, M. et al.: *Principles of Drug Addiction Treatment: A Research-Based Guide*, December 2012.

About the Author

Prof. Dr. Michael J. Capone is an American psychologist and professor. He specializes in early indicators of dissatisfaction and is an innovator and early adopter of new technologies in behavioral research. He has taught at universities in San Diego, Hebron, Ramallah, Hamburg, Rennes, and Paris. He lives in Hamburg, Germany.

Printed in the United States
By Bookmasters